The Student Assessment Handbook

This book is a comprehensive guide to contemporary assessment, particularly for those professionals coming to terms with new pressures on their traditional teaching practices. Increased use of IT, flexible assessment methods and quality assurance all converge on the area of assessment, making new demands of assessors. The need to diversify and adapt traditional assessment practices to suit new modes of learning is clearer than ever.

The Student Assessment Handbook looks at the effectiveness of traditional methods in the present day and provides guidelines on how these methods may be developed to suit contemporary learning outcomes and teaching practices. It is a practical resource, with case studies, reflection boxes and diagnostic tools to help the reader to apply the principles to their own practice.

The book provides advice on a wide range of topics, including:

* assessing to promote particular kinds of learning outcomes;
* using meaningful assessment techniques to assess large groups;
* the implications of flexible learning on timing and pacing of assessment;
* the pros and cons of online assessment;
* tackling Web plagiarism and the authentication of student work;
* maintaining assessment standards;
* assessing generic skills and quality assurance.

This book will be required reading for practicing lecturers and course leaders and will also be of interest to course designers and anyone with involvement in educational and staff development.

Lee Dunn, Chris Morgan, Meg O'Reilly and Sharon Parry are all based at Southern Cross University, Australia. They are part of a research and development team in the teaching and learning centre, which focuses on curriculum development and students' assessment.

The Student Assessment Handbook

Chris Morgan, Lee Dunn, Sharon Parry and
Meg O'Reilly

RoutledgeFalmer
Taylor & Francis Group

LONDON AND NEW YORK

First published 2004
by RoutledgeFalmer
11 New Fetter Lane, London EC4P 4EE

Simultaneously published in the USA and Canada
by RoutledgeFalmer
29 West 35th Street, New York, NY 10001

RoutledgeFalmer is an imprint of the Taylor & Francis Group

Typeset in Bembo by
Saxon Graphics Ltd, Derby
Printed and bound in Great Britain by
TJ International Ltd, Padstow, Cornwall

British Library Cataloguing in Publication Data
A catalogue record for this book is available
from the British Library

Library of Congress Cataloguing in Publication Data
The student assessment handbook : new directions in traditional and online
assessment / Chris Morgan ... [et al.].
        p. cm.
Includes bibliographical references and index.
ISBN 0-415-33530-2
1. College students—Rating of—Handbooks, manuals, etc. 2.
Educational tests and measurements—Handbooks, manuals, etc. I. Morgan,
Chris, 1957–
LB2368.S88 2003
378.1'67--dc21
    2003013321

ISBN 0-415-33530-2 (pbk)

Contents

Part B: Assessing key learning outcomes

About the authors

Chris Morgan, Lee Dunn, Sharon Parry and Meg O'Reilly are educational developers and designers in the Teaching and Learning Centre at Southern Cross University in Australia. They are engaged in research on student learning and higher education policy and they work closely with academic staff to improve curriculum and teaching quality.

Foreword

Whenever I receive the manuscript of a new book on some aspect of learning and teaching in higher education, the question arises, 'Is there really any need for this book? Does it contain anything that hasn't been covered elsewhere? Is this text really necessary?' This is particularly the case with assessment, for which many forests have been sacrificed in recent years.

However, when I read the manuscript of this text, I found myself wishing I had been involved in its production myself! The first part is a highly accessible, yet scholarly introduction to contemporary issues in assessment that sensibly makes reference to the established generic texts on assessment, but puts a new spin on them, with plenty of practical examples to illustrate the underlying theory. The second part focuses on what I regard as a central issue for assessment, which is 'fit for purpose', that is, selecting the right methods for the context, the subject, the students and the level of study. A particularly helpful feature of this section is the extensive use of illustrative case studies. The third part of the book, looking at assessment in practice, usefully explores the way in which assessment is linked to design issues in a way that encourages constructive alignment. The centrality of the student experience to assessment is emphasized here, especially the need for students to understand fully the process and the reasons behind it, which we know can dramatically impact on student retention and achievement if done properly.

This book usefully draws together many strands of thinking about the complex issues of assessment and brings them together in one accessible work, which both educational specialists and grassroots classroom teachers are likely to find invaluable. I certainly will!

Professor Sally Brown
Director of Membership Services
Institute for Learning and Teaching in Higher Education

Preface

Why this book?

Teachers in higher education are experiencing some difficulties in coming to terms with the variety of new pressures on their traditional teaching practices. The landscape of higher education is rapidly changing and nowhere is this more acutely felt than in the area of assessment, where many of the issues of teaching and learning, new technology, flexible delivery and quality assurance converge.

This book is about reconceptualizing and adapting traditional assessment practices to suit contemporary modes of learning and delivery. It seeks to draw together and extend many of the strands of writing about assessment over the past 15 years, including both the theoretical and the applied. There are, of course, many excellent books available on the subject of assessment, which mostly focus on a particular area, such as information and communication technologies, open or distance education, innovative case studies or an 'A to Z' of assessment methods. As useful and timely as these books are, we feel that there is a need for a book that provides a broader, contemporary overview of key issues, strategic use of methods and quality practices. This overview, we feel, is particularly useful for teachers starting out in higher education, or for those who are being presented with new challenges or seeking fresh inspiration for their assessment practices.

We take the view that assessment is integral to, and almost inseparable from, teaching and learning. With this view, assessment is a very large subject indeed, so we must acknowledge our own limitations. The tendrils of assessment reach out into all areas of education, and it would be naive to think we could possibly know or cover everything. We have sought, however, to represent those issues, themes, practices and cases that will be of most interest to teachers, and with sufficient detail for teachers to consider and adapt to their own unique contexts. We have also sought to present issues in a scholarly way, yet in a handbook format that is easily accessed by those who wish to dip in and out as need arises.

What's in this book?

For ease of access, the book is divided into three parts as follows:

- *Part A: Issues and themes in assessment* introduces readers to some of the foundation principles of assessment and explores some current issues and themes of concern. This part does not seek to answer or resolve issues, but rather to explore how they might be impacting upon teachers in higher education. This part also has a diagnostic flavour, to allow readers to reflect upon their existing assessment practice and to help them articulate difficulties and problems more clearly. The issues raised in this part become themes that recur throughout the book.
- *Part B: Assessing key learning outcomes* is about selecting and facilitating methods of assessment with purpose. It is designed to stimulate readers with a variety of assessment ideas and opportunities, which are organized around eight key learning outcomes (Nightingale *et al*, 1996). We stress that, when selecting assessment methods, we need to be mindful of the particular abilities we are wishing to develop, as well as the disciplinary context in which the tasks are undertaken. For each learning outcome, we present a series of cases or 'snapshots' of how assessment methods are designed and facilitated to engender desired learning. We also consider the implications for teaching when assessing particular learning outcomes.
- *Part C: Assessment in practice* focuses upon good assessment practice, building on ideas and examples from the previous two sections. It deals with a range of 'nuts-and-bolts' issues when facilitating assessment, including designing assessment tasks, developing marking schemes, communicating tasks to students, marking and grading, evaluating assessment and dealing with plagiarism.

We hope this structure will prove convenient for readers, although it does create some problems with overlap. We have dealt with this, wherever possible, by cross-referencing between sections, supported by a comprehensive index.

Acknowledgements

Much of the research and development underpinning this book was conducted at Southern Cross University, drawing on a grant from Australia's Committee for University Teaching and Staff Development. We wish to acknowledge gratefully the contribution of a large number of our colleagues in the University to this project and to thank the University for its generous support. We wish also to thank our colleagues in the field of student learning who have advised and guided us in the development of this book. These are: Professor Sally Brown, Dr Peggy Nightingale, Professor Dan Price and Professor Graeme Speedy.

Part A

Issues and themes in assessment

Introduction to Part A

The matter of student assessment is becoming an important topic for tertiary teachers. In these days of quality audits of teaching, course delivery and curricula, teachers and trainers want to know whether their assessment practices are appropriate and whether they are in keeping with those of their colleagues. Nowadays, researchers have placed student assessment at the peak of the learning pyramid as regards its importance in determining students' approaches to learning, so teachers and trainers want to get it right.

Assessment – an exact science?

Getting assessment right has always been an issue because its solutions seem opaque. This is because assessment is a subjective process and not an exact science. But this kind of definition is a contradiction in terms. Science is often perceived as concrete, objective, demonstrable and able to be generalized from a sample (or assessment task) to the broader population. But student assessment is not concrete and not always demonstrable: it involves professional judgement that is not confined to deductive logic or objectivity measures. Because of the element of subjectivity, there has always been a level of uncertainty about student assessment that led to the development of a kind of pseudo-science growing up around the topic of student assessment. This pseudo-science, fortunately, was largely refuted by the work of Derek Rowntree (1987) and others.

Early research on student learning developed out of the field of cognitive psychology, so its early orientation was to science method, as can be seen in the work of well-known researchers such as Bloom and Eysenck. The emphasis in student assessment as a consequence was driven by the need for objective measures, ranking of performance and rigorous testing by survey methods such as multiple choice questions, short answers, essays and reports. More recently, however, a paradigm of student learning focusing on student approaches to learning tasks was established, beginning with the publication of the

Gothenburg and Lancaster studies in a single book in 1984, called simply *The Experience of Learning* (Marton, Hounsell and Entwistle (eds), 1984). This book signalled a sea change in our understanding of student learning and of student assessment, which derived from understanding learning and assessment from the experience of the student. A distinguishing feature of this publication was that it challenged the predominant, quantitative view of student learning and its outcomes (Dahlgren, 1984). In addition, Marton and Säljö (1976, 1984) successfully demonstrated that learning outcomes were a function of the student's perception of the nature of the learning task. Ramsden (1984) pointed to the role of the assessment task in determining how a learning task was perceived. The central questions surrounding student assessment – its appropriateness, its effectiveness, its validity to the learning experience – quickly came to have multiple layers of meaning in a new conception of student learning in which learning outcomes were seen to be qualitatively different.

As assessment tasks become more centred on learners and their learning needs, students want to know how they are performing against set standards for performance. Ranking according to the performance of others in the class is not a good enough indicator of individual performance. Clear standards of expected student performance have increasingly become recognized as the vital ingredient in effective assessment.

This idea seems like a fairly straightforward principle, but in practice it is clouded by a number of developments in the past two decades in the higher education landscape. The profile of students has diversified, our conceptions of students as learners have changed and the resources available for teaching have diminished.

The changing landscape of higher education

Along with the massive expansion of the higher education sector, there have been fundamental changes to the way institutions conduct their core business of undergraduate teaching. Not only has the number of students increased dramatically, but their profile is different: no longer is the vast majority classified as school leavers. Those enrolled in higher education tend to be more vocationally oriented, as borne out in the withering departments of classics and formerly flourishing humanities specialisms. In two decades the professionalization and legitimization of many fields of practice, such as nursing, accountancy and tourism, have led to the development of strong identities for them in the higher education sector. Disciplinary diversification has changed the nature of undergraduate teaching enormously. Developments in information technology have revolutionized undergraduate teaching. The global learning environment for undergraduates, together with increasing pressure for institutions to be more responsible for their own financial survival, has made competition for students intense.

These influences have ushered in a new era of quality assurance and accountability under the corporate imperative whereby students are paying customers.

All of these developments have impacted on the core business of undergraduate teaching and student assessment. For one thing, class sizes have increased, and small-group teaching, which is relatively expensive to maintain, is reduced where possible. University teachers are faced with the practicalities of assessing larger cohorts of students using different technologies.

Changing student profiles

Higher education expanded rapidly from an elitist endeavour to one of open access and vastly increased numbers. During the 1980s, open and distance education providers proliferated as students with work and family responsibilities began to participate in higher education in ways that suited their lifestyles and commitments. Then, from the mid-1980s, the development of information technology, and in particular the World Wide Web, has opened up the range and mix of flexible study options to a remarkable degree.

The higher education student profile has changed enormously and is now more widely differentiated than ever before. Not only do students enrol in higher education across cultural and ethnic boundaries, but many are the first members of their families to have the privilege of accessing higher education. Courses that are taught across locations and to very different cultural, ethnic or age groups need to be inclusive of these differences, and assessment practices must likewise be appropriate.

Today, students are having to pay more for their tertiary education and training. In most countries, the need for part-time employment while enrolled in tertiary courses has led to increasing demand for flexible study options, and these have had a profound influence on our conceptions of and our practices in student assessment.

New learning options and assessment

Fundamental changes to undergraduate teaching have arisen, of course, from new forms of delivery and the mix of information technology. As students want greater flexibility in how and where they study, the range of media and mixed media options has increased dramatically. With these changes come changes in how we assess students who are no longer in the classroom, face to face, but who may well need interaction with other students and new forms of assessment that are different to traditional paper-based essays. The growing popularity of flexible distance study options has given rise to the packaging of course materials in ways that address the needs of busy consumers, but not necessarily those of independent learners. Concerns about students' base levels of information literacy, search and research skills and capacity for honest authorship as distinct from plagiarism and cheating have, not surprisingly, become more strident.

Flexibility for learners is not just about new technologies. It is also about flexible enrolment and pacing of courses, about students in different years doing the same subjects with different levels of assessment tasks, and about choices in assessment and modes of delivery. With these new conceptions of flexible learning come issues in authenticating students' submitted work. These issues have been compounded by the pervasiveness of the Internet, via which plagiarism seems to be all too easy.

How do tertiary teachers maintain standards when there is a tension between giving students greater flexibility and choice in assessment and ensuring that standards of performance do not decline? The new 'customer-oriented' imperative in higher education has come at the same time that globalization has forced institutions to ensure that their standards are equivalent to other similar institutions. Quality assurance imperatives in universities in most developed nations have asserted the need to document and demonstrate that standards are equivalent across institutions. The implications for assessment practice are not yet fully resolved.

Yet another set of concerns derives from the question of what we assess. Two developments are especially important in considerations of good practice in student assessment. The first is that empirical research into student learning and curriculum demonstrates the need for assessment to fit closely to the learning objectives of a subject and also to the activities that are put in place by the teacher to teach students to be able to perform the assessment tasks. This closeness of fit, or alignment, is the link between what we assess, what we teach and ask students to do in their learning and what we have told students to aim for in their learning. In subsequent chapters, this notion of 'alignment' will be discussed more fully, being central to good practice in undergraduate assessment. The second development concerns the rising interest in identifying and assessing generic skills at the undergraduate level, because this is one means by which standards across institutions and within professions at large can effectively be benchmarked. The question of which skills must first be addressed before the question of how to assess them can be tackled.

All of these areas for consideration embody issues, claims and concerns that have qualitatively different solutions in different learning contexts. In Part A, we explore these issues, focusing on the links between student assessment and student learning. The nature and influence of the learning context, including the impact of assessment, both intended and unintended, are also raised. Underpinning the range of issues raised is the question of what kind of learning higher education might be considered to be. Here taxonomies of learning are relevant, and Biggs and Collis's (1982) SOLO taxonomy is drawn on in particular.

Here we have outlined some of the developments and issues leading to the current interest in how we might assess our students effectively and appropriately. While teachers recognize that assessment is probably the most powerful instrument in student learning, they also know that it is problematic; it is often hard to see why one assessment method might be better than another. In Part A we identify the broad range of issues associated with contemporary assessment as a prelude to Part B, where we explain how the issues might be resolved within an organizing framework of eight kinds of learning outcomes, drawing on the work of Nightingale *et al* (1996). Part B showcases examples to show how particular intended learning outcomes can be elicited by specifically designed assessment tasks. Key themes in contemporary assessment, including the main problem areas, are then discussed more fully in Part C. We now move on to explore the main issues in some detail.

1

The link between assessment and learning

In providing a background to the role of assessment in student learning, it is worth while examining the knowledge base on which it is built:

> Theories of teaching and learning focusing on student activity are based on two main theories: phenomenography and constructivism. 'Phenomenography' was a term coined by Marton (1981) to describe the theory that grew out of his original studies with Säljö, and has developed considerably since then (Marton and Booth 1997). Constructivism has a long history in cognitive psychology, Jean Piaget being a crucial figure... And today it takes on several forms: individual, social, cognitive, postmodern (Steffe and Gale 1995).

> (Biggs, 1999a: 12)

Biggs explains that, while there are different traditions, the main concern should be to work out what it is that helps to improve teaching and learning outcomes for students. The fundamental principle in either school of thought is essentially what Shuell (1986) has argued: it is not so much what the teacher does that influences learning outcomes but, rather, what the student does. Biggs (1999a) would argue in this vein that learning involves doing; it is 'performative': 'meaning is not imposed or transmitted by direct instruction, but is created by the students' learning activities, their "approaches to learning"' (Biggs, 1999a: 13).

Approaches to learning

Many researchers have distinguished between the different cognitive levels of engagement with learning tasks. Perhaps most widely referred to is the distinction between a *surface approach*, in which a relatively low level of cognitive engagement occurs, and a *deep approach*, where a relatively high level of cognitive engagement with the task takes place. In a surface approach to a learning task, the student perceives that it is necessary to remember the body of knowledge. Mostly this would involve the need to rote-learn and then recall the facts concerned. Of course there are many situations where this kind of approach to a learning task is appropriate – such as perhaps learning the chemical tables. At the other end of the spectrum is a deep approach to a learning task, where the student perceives that it is necessary to make meaning of the content concerned, to be able to appraise it critically and to be able to apply the knowledge to other contexts or knowledge domains.

The second main theme concerns the student's *perception* of the learning task. The important work of the phenomenographic researchers (see, for example, Marton and Säljö, 1984; Ramsden, 1992) has shown that students approach a learning task with a surface orientation or a deep orientation according to how they *perceive* the learning task. As exemplified in *The Experience of Learning* (1984), phenomenographic researchers have continued to document students' perceptions of their learning tasks since the early 1980s to the present. The most influential factor in shaping those perceptions turns out to be the nature of the assessment task. If the student thinks that the assessment task requires memorizing and recall, then that is exactly the approach adopted to the learning task. If, on the other hand, the student thinks the assessment task requires analysis, extrapolation, application to other knowledge domains or critical appraisal from a particular theoretical framework, then that is the approach adopted to the learning task. The power of assessment to influence the approach adopted towards a learning task is very considerable.

Underpinning the range of issues raised here is the question of what kind of learning is desirable. The idea of different levels of learning is long established and it fits with the idea of learning tasks at one end of the range that appropriately may be simple memorizing or naming tasks – surface learning. At the other end of the range, learning appropriately may be a higher-order activity that involves making meaning – deep learning. Generally, we would expect that lower-order learning activities would, during the course of an undergraduate programme, lead to their use in higher-order activities. The match between learning objectives and assessment tasks becomes essential if we are to assess in a way that is valid. Learning taxonomies such as Bloom's (1976) taxonomy of learning have been very influential in prompting university teachers to consider what level of cognitive activity is required in different kinds of assessment tasks. Another such taxonomy, which fits with Bloom but advances the importance of emphasizing the performability of intended learning outcomes so that they are more likely to match what is taught and what is assessed, is the structures of learning outcomes (SOLO) taxonomy developed by Biggs and Collis (1982).

There are important differences between surface-oriented approaches to learning and deep or 'meaning' approaches to learning. Researchers mostly agree that students will adopt an approach to learning according to how they perceive the learning task. But what influences whether a task is perceived as a surface task requiring memorizing or a deep task requiring meaning to be made and applied to a context? Ramsden (1992) argues that students are influenced by a whole nested system of elements, from their prior learning to the quality of the teaching, but also concedes that the most influential is the impact of assessment.

From the student's point of view, getting through the assessment tasks successfully – whether that means earning a pass or achieving a distinction – is the objective. So problems arise when the assessment task requires performance that has not been taught or that does not match the desired learning outcomes.

Learning aims or objectives for university-level study may require students to develop a base level of knowledge requiring naming and memorizing. An example of this would be to learn the names of different periods of prehistory as a basis for then locating particular characteristics within periods of time and geographical zones. However, much of what is learnt in higher education is exactly that – higher order – and it requires synthesis, critique, application, analysis, theorizing or hypothesizing. So a particular problem for students is where learning objectives and study guides direct the student to one kind of learning approach, say at the lower end of memorizing, naming and describing, but the assessment tasks require the opposite – say, much higher-order skills. Of course it might also be the other way around. In any case, the student receives mixed messages.

Unintended outcomes

Unintended outcomes are likely to arise when assessment tasks don't match the desired learning outcomes. Many different kinds of mismatches are possible but their effect is singular. They result in students trying to guess the agenda of an assessor. Perhaps the most common form of mismatch is where teachers say that they value higher-order thinking skills and that they are trying to promote them in learning activities, but they set assessment tasks that only call for rote-learnt facts in their exam questions. Another frequent mismatch is just the inverse of this: learning activities focus on the teacher telling students lots of facts, reinforcing these with study materials, but then setting assessment tasks that call for higher-order operations than students have learnt to perform. Yet another mismatch that is easy to recognize is where students are up- or down-graded according to criteria that are neither explained nor explicit to students, a very familiar example being the downgrading of students for poor written expression or referencing inconsistencies when these criteria have not been made clear to students prior to the assessment task. In these situations, expectations held by individual examiners are not explicit to students. But from the students' point of view, there is more still to go wrong. Orrell (1996), for example, has shown that examiners' conceptions of criteria evolve over time in assessing the performance of a cohort of students. Selective assessment may be problematic, too, in that students don't know that they should specialize in selected topics rather than cover the entire range.

Unintended outcomes also are likely to occur when what is assessed has not been taught. Where teachers find themselves teaching much larger cohorts of students, where they find there is a great deal of diversity in the student profile, where subjects are heavily content based, such as in anatomy, physiology or chemistry, or where there are several markers who do not normally communicate about their approaches to marking, these kinds of problems can easily arise for students. In these kinds of situations, the mismatch between learning objectives and assessment tasks leads to unintended learning outcomes. From the students' point of view, those unintended outcomes are unfair because they disadvantage the assessment of students' performance. From the teacher's point of view, the assessments are an invalid indicator of their students' performance.

Side effects of assessment

The impact of assessment practices upon student approaches to learning and learning outcomes is easily underestimated. Not only are there unintended outcomes of assessment, but there are also side effects. A valuable overview is provided by Rowntree (1987: 36), who describes eight side effects of assessment, which are summarized here:

1. The prejudicial aspects of assessment, in which students may be stereotyped by university teachers as having certain levels of ability.
2. The effects on students of knowing they are being assessed, and so their performance becomes a self-fulfilling prophecy or limits the naturally inquiring or motivated student to what will be assessed.
3. The extrinsic rewards of assessment, whereby students who are cue-conscious learn to play the system and selectively neglect topics and skills by minimizing risk and maximizing results for effort.
4. The competitive aspects of assessment, in that many grading systems are competitive. If, for example, only 10 per cent will be admitted to honours, then there will not be enough rewards to go around if the cohort is very able. Rowntree (1987: 52) argues: 'Students generally have all been led to believe that they cannot all achieve a worthwhile level of learning.'
5. The bureaucratic aspects of assessment, where assessment is an instrument of policy, designed to preserve a predetermined standard elsewhere and so depersonalizing the process.
6. The nature of specific assessment techniques, in that many are simply not suited to the kinds of assessment performance to which they are applied.
7. The giving of grades, because they synthesize all of what is known about a student's performance across a range of skills and abilities to a simplistic level.

8. The reporting of assessment results, in that they are not always an accurate indicator of performance or ability to the wider community.

Considering the range of side effects of assessment, it is worth while confronting the real challenges for university and college teachers. What do we have to do to look at assessment from the perspective of the learner? So many of the issues associated with assessment are those of fairness and appropriateness. What can we do to ensure that assessment is fair and appropriate? In this book, we argue strongly for assessment that is aligned closely to the teaching and learning activities in a course. If the assessment tasks are not aligned with the desired learning outcomes or with what students do in their learning activities, how can we make adjustments? Making adjustments might be easy if we are responsible for setting assessment tasks. But what if someone else sets the tasks? At the heart of these challenges is the preparedness of university and college teachers to create learning environments that reward meaningful inquiry and eschew surface or reproducing approaches to assessment tasks. The imperative is to have a conception of learning – and assessment – that is shared by the teacher and by the learner.

2

Roles and purposes of assessment

The question of why students are assessed might at first seem to be simple common sense; it is obvious that their performance needs to be measured. Looking a little further into particular instances, it may perhaps be that the assessment of students has followed disciplinary traditions or regulatory requirements wherein teachers have not had the need or luxury of time to wonder too much about why a particular approach was adopted in that instance. But assessment tasks and strategies vary enormously, both across and within different disciplinary settings. In discussing the rationale for one assessment strategy over another, colleagues may well bring to bear a range of different purposes while others may struggle to resolve questions of whether one approach is likely to be more successful than another.

To be able to make informed decisions about how to assess students, teachers have to take into account the roles and purposes of student assessment, for these may be highly differentiated and they shape our conceptions of what is important. When we consider that the assessment of learning is of interest to a range of different stakeholders, we can also see that the processes and outcomes of assessment have the potential to address a number of different needs.

Maintaining standards

For example, our society expects universities and colleges to uphold standards of excellence in learning. In its turn, the institution is interested in assessment of students in order to maintain its standards and its reputation in the global marketplace. Individual institutions must meet the needs of their communities. The apparently successful achievement of its graduates ensures an institution's programmes remain attractive to prospective students and to those whose loyalty has been gained enough to return for study of higher degrees or to gain additional qualifications. Professional groups might be interested in our assessment practices in order to ensure integrity of practice, consistency within the profession and compliance with specific legislative and safety regulations.

Our academic supervisors and colleagues are also interested in our assessment practices as a means of benchmarking both the teaching and the curriculum, and they will take an active interest in cases where students mount an appeal or complaint about issues of equity or justice. Our colleagues might also be working with us to ensure that, throughout the programme as a whole, our collective approaches to assessments are complementary and developmental. Considering all these different expectations of assessment, it is possible to identify a range of stakeholders in the assessment process. But in the end, the student must be the first and most important stakeholder. Students themselves demand a quality learning experience that prepares them for new agendas in life. They want value for money and they expect their award to be recognized in the global marketplace.

Students – the primary stakeholders?

In considering stakeholders in the assessment process, we must consider the main stakeholders – students themselves. The principal aim of assessment, from the students' perspective, is to improve the quality of student learning. According to Biggs (1999b: 68), 'assessment in practice has two functions: to tell us whether or not the learning has been successful, and in conveying to students what we want them to learn'. Unfortunately, when we begin to investigate the experiences of assessment that students remember, more often than not we find a litany of horror stories, of learning by aversion. The assessment tasks that were a struggle for students to handle or that thwarted their efforts to learn are the enduring ones in the minds of students who vow to stay clear of such subject areas or such assessment methods for evermore.

Overall, a range of roles and purposes for assessment includes:

- diagnosing student difficulties;
- measuring improvement over time;
- motivating students to study;
- judging mastery of essential skills and knowledge;
- ranking the students' capabilities in relation to the whole class;
- evaluating the teaching methods;
- evaluating the effectiveness of the course;
- encouraging the tacit learning of disciplinary skills and conventions.

It is possible for assessment to be designed to meet more than one stakeholder's needs. So, how can our assessment practices focus on the needs of both the student and, for example, the institution? Angelo and Cross (1993) argue that classroom assessment can and should be learner-centred, teacher-directed, mutually beneficial to the student and to the faculty, formative and continuous and context specific. More recently, Angelo (1999) argues that assessment can be used to assess performance while at the same time meeting the account-ability needs of faculty and institutions. But, in practice, the emphases in assessment – either towards summative, accountability ends or towards formative improvement – are difficult to marry, so students need to know in advance how their performance will be assessed. This is because students take assessment very seriously, and whether there is an opportunity for improvement or not on the same task will motivate very different behaviours.

Validity and reliability

It is important for all stakeholders in the assessment process that the measurement of performance is valid and reliable. But what do these terms really mean? Throughout this book, these terms are used frequently, so it is important that they are clearly defined. In statistics and measurement generally, validity concerns the extent to which inferences made from test scores are useful and meaningful. When we speak of assessment tasks being *valid*, we are referring to assessment tasks that actually measure the perfor-mance of the intended learning outcomes specified, and so meaningfulness and usefulness are central. It is possible for assessment tasks to have low validity, such as when a subject is taught at one level but the assessment tasks require performance of a higher order. It is also possible to construct assessment tasks that have little relevance to what was intended in either the anticipated learning outcomes or the teaching. Assessment is said to be valid when it measures what it is supposed to measure. Validity is the concept that underpins the notion of 'constructive alignment' of the curriculum, as outlined by Biggs (1999a).

Reliability, however, concerns the extent to which other assessors would reach the same conclusions. This can be ensured in two ways: either by triangu-lating with other kinds of tasks to ensure that it is the same performance of learning that is being measured, or through processes of moderation, to ensure that others would consider the assessment task to be a reasonable measure of performance. When colleagues review our assessment tasks, do they consider them to be fair and reasonable methods of assessing performance? If we change the assessment task in a subject, does it still measure performance on the same intended learning outcomes? If the assessment task is reliable, the answer to these questions will be 'yes'.

Formative assessment

Whether there is an opportunity for improvement or not on the same task is an important consideration. If there is an opportunity for students to improve their performance *on the same task*, then the assessment is essentially *formative*. If, however, the performance on an assessment task indicates the sum of performance on that task, then it is known as *summative*. A summative assessment task cannot be repeated or improved. The trouble is that sometimes teachers confuse formative and summative assessment.

In situations where students know that the assessment task is formative, they understand that they will receive feedback on their performance that will enable them to improve their performance on the same task or on a similar task. For example, students in a creative writing class may be required to write a draft biography as their first task. The teacher and/or the other students provide constructive feedback on the draft, which students then rework as a second task. A second round of constructive feedback is then provided to students so that they can refine their work even further. Each of these three stages is considered formative. There may be a combination of three purposes of formative assessment: 1) diagnosing student difficulties; 2) measuring improvement over time; and 3) providing information to inform students about how to improve their learning. The key here is that students know that the assessment is directed towards providing information about how to improve their performance before the point where a final measurement of achievement is made. This process is known as scaffolding, which can be tightly organized, such as in a problem-based course, or it can be less directed. One way of teaching mathematics, for example, is to set small groups to work on problems together, with a tutor working across the groups in class, supervising progress and providing feedback. When the groups find a solution, they write it up in their workbooks for assessment. Each of the stages of the feedback and improvement cycle is part of formative assessment.

In formative assessment, the main purpose is diagnostic but for formative purposes: to enable students to obtain sufficient information to identify their own strengths and weaknesses in terms of current knowledge and skills. In some cases, formative or diagnostic assessment tasks also help students recognize their own attitudes, biases and preconceptions. It is thus possible for students to learn, by increments and gradual insights, the specific nature of their limitations. When the assessment tasks take place in small increments with associated feedback to students, it may be hard to see the difference between assessment and effective teaching.

Summative assessment

Summative assessment takes place when students undertake a task that measures the sum of their performance. At some point, whether students have had several opportunities to rework and improve their performance or whether they have had no opportunities at all, the performance must be graded. The allocation of a final grade on an assessment task – or an entire course – is known as summative, and sometimes terminal, assessment. Ideally, summative assessment comes at the end of a systematic and incremental series of learning activities that have formative assessment tasks set at key points during the course. The formative assessment tasks are interwoven with the teaching and learning activities and then a summative task is set. When the interweaving of formative assessment tasks towards a summative event is formalized in a course, it may be called scaffolding. In the mathematics example given above, the summative assessment could be a final exam based on the formulae learnt in the formative assessments or it may be based on students' individual workbooks.

Where scaffolding occurs and students know what is expected of them as part of the teaching and learning activities, there is a formative learning process that leads to summative assessment. The challenge for teachers is to understand the limits of formative assessment. Once an assessment task is allocated a final grade, it is summative, regardless of whether students may use what they learn from it on another task. When students are given a final grade on an assignment together with formative comments, they are highly likely to attend only to the grade and not take the formative comments seriously (see, for example, Butler, 1988). In this vein, Newble and Cannon (1995) have also argued that formative assessment, where students aim to learn from their misconceptions or deficiencies, ought to be kept separate from summative assessments, where a final grade is at stake. Other challenges arise when the summative assessment bears no relationship to the formative assessments and therefore to what has been learnt.

Two more challenges concern workload issues – either for the students or for the teachers. When formative assessments are compulsory and too numerous, student workloads soar while at the same time dampening intrinsic enthusiasm for the learning process. Of course this happens when there are too many summative assessments too, and it is also a problem when the assessment tasks are too demanding, whether formative or summative. The challenge for teachers in these days of shrinking funding and increasing class sizes is to create formative assessment tasks that require a realistic amount of teacher input. Formative assessment can take up extensive teaching hours. In creating realistic formative assessments, the further challenge is to weave them into the teaching and learning activities, so that formative feedback to students is not an additional impost on the department but a way of implementing the curriculum. Black and Wiliam (1998: 5) put this succinctly: 'for assessment to function formatively, the results have to be used to adjust teaching and learning – so a significant aspect of any programme will be the ways in which teachers do this'.

Issues related to workloads lead us to ask 'How much formative assessment is enough?' and 'How much is too much?' The answer is not simple. But one yardstick comes from the much-utilized Course Experience Questionnaire (Ramsden, 1992). We know from this and subsequent studies that students appreciate teachers who 'make it clear what I need to do to be successful in this course'. The difficulty for university and college teachers is to lead students to share their conceptions of the learning that is expected of them. For this to happen, formative assessment and teaching generally need to be aligned with the ways in which learning is assessed.

Balancing formative with summative assessment

Some would argue that, when an assessment task is formative, a summative grade should not be given at all. The danger in this situation is that students prioritize their efforts towards achieving an academic award. If an assessment task counts for nothing towards a final grade, why would a student think it necessary to do the work? One way to make formative assessment count is simply to make it compulsory, whether graded or ungraded.

A useful strategy through which teachers have overcome this issue of balance between formative and summative assessment within a course is by designing the curriculum on the concept of *scaffolding* (Biggs, 1990). Scaffolding is designed into the curriculum when formative assessment tasks provide the basis of the teaching and learning activities in a course, and these lead ultimately to summative assessment. Take, for example, a problem-based clinical diagnosis subject in the health sciences where the students are required to follow successive symptoms over a number of cases and provide tentative diagnoses. These are formatively assessed – no grade awarded but just pass or fail. The summative assessment comes when students have to put all their case findings together: over time, symptoms may change and develop, leading to new hypotheses and new directions of inquiry. The overall assessment task comes as a result of the scaffolding of the parts of the problem. The idea of scaffolding is to interweave formative assessment tasks with the teaching activities, so that students have ample opportunities to know how well they are progressing and how they can improve as they work their way through the course. The summative assessment tasks – which are closely aligned with but not the same as formative tasks – form the basis for a final determination of performance.

3

The grading game: norm- and criterion-referenced assessment

Students, teachers, faculty and broad disciplines need ways of indicating levels of attainment that we call grading. But the grading of attainment is very complex because each of the stakeholder groups will attach different values to the process of grading. Does grading serve to indicate levels of performance? Does it serve to demonstrate that fair judgements are being made about individual or group performance? Can we be open and transparent about the values underpinning assessment practices or about the processes used to grade a cohort of students? How do we justify the grades attributed to individuals in a cohort? How do tertiary teachers rationalize their subjective judgements about performance to students? In reality, most students believe that grading is a science that depends upon reliable algorithms and mathematical precision, though of course it isn't.

Many complex issues derive from the assumption that assessment is a scientific process that is rigorous, unbiased and mathematically defensible. Student assessment can be both quantitative and qualitative, which means that it *may* be objectively measured, but student learning research and policy trends reflect a growing understanding that student assessment is largely qualitative and therefore subjective. The early research into student learning, as discussed in the Introduction to Part A, grew out of the field of cognitive psychology and so was strongly rooted in experimental science. Assessment under that paradigm tended to be largely quantitative, and performance was measured in concrete terms. More recently, however, qualitative assessments of performance against explicit standards have become widely accepted because they accommodate more than concrete facts.

In reality, most university and college teachers do not have much control over the way student grades are derived within a department. The problem is that they need to know the implications for their students and – more broadly – of the processes they are involved in implementing. Unless teachers can point to the implications of assessment practice, they cannot instigate change or improvement.

There are two main approaches to assessing student performance. One is a well-established system whereby precision and objectivity are – arguably – inherent because it assumes that precise marks can be allocated to aspects of performance. These marks are then added together to provide an overall grade. When all of the grades of the cohort are awarded, the cohort is then redistributed according to a normal distribution (bell-curve) of grades of performance. This approach is called *norm-referenced assessment*, and its emphasis upon marks may seem to give it a quantitative emphasis, though this idea is quite misleading. In reality, the idea of a predetermined distribution of student performance may always influence our thinking, whether we anticipate that a task is easy so most students will pass (a positively skewed, probably normal distribution) or whether we consider that, in reality, very few students will achieve excellence (a negatively skewed distribution). Whenever we have an overarching conception of how the grades are likely to be distributed, we are, strictly speaking, assessing according to what we consider the norms to be.

However, there is another approach to assessment that also involves subjective judgement, but which specifies what the norms are in advance. This approach depends entirely upon informed professional judgement of performance against articulated standards of performance or criteria. This latter form is called *criterion-referenced assessment* because it requires that preordained, explicit performance criteria be met by students. Because it is difficult, if not impossible, to specify all of the criteria in sufficient detail, assessors may identify standards of performance (called *standards-based assessment*) in which preordained standards or bands of performance are described to students, and exemplars of these bands are made available. Students' performance on the assessment task is categorized according to those standards or bands.

Norm-referenced grading

These two quite fundamentally different approaches to assessing student performance are used across the range of academic disciplines. Norm-referenced assessment is an approach to deriving grades based on the measurement of performance, usually in percentages. In this approach, each individual in a cohort is graded according to a preconceived notion of how the distribution of grades will turn out – that is, normally distributed. Norm referencing suits subjects where the nature of knowledge is concrete *and* where answers are either objectively right or wrong. For example, a student knows the precise equation or formula being tested and is given a numerical grade. From the teacher's point of view, the marks are clearly defensible to students. A mark of 97 per cent means that 97 out of 100 elements of the task were correctly answered, and this should be the case no matter who marked the assessment task. When the grades of all students are derived, they are distributed in a bell-shaped or *normal* pattern of grades.

In the normal distribution of grades shown in Figure 3.1, grading categories are fail, pass, credit, distinction and high distinction. Approximately 10 per cent of students can expect to fail, 10 per cent can expect to achieve a high distinction, 20 per cent can expect to achieve a pass and 20 per cent can expect to achieve a distinction. This leaves a big group in the middle clustered around the mean, which in this case is the credit group, 40 per cent.

However, it is also possible to norm-reference a cohort of essay grades because essentially the process involved is the distribution of grades across a normal distribution. But this kind of distribution really relies upon the awarding of grades being objectively 'right' or 'wrong'. In the case of essays, which are interpretive, the assessor makes a subjective judgement about performance that is backed by professional expertise rather than objectivity. There are dangers in normally distributing grades:

1. If the group of students is exceptionally talented or, conversely, under-achieving, this will not be reflected in their grades because the grades indicate performance relative to the rest of the cohort and are adjusted so that they are normally distributed. In this way, norm referencing, though it looks like a scientific way of deriving grades, disguises absolute performance. While it is possible to use past performance as a yardstick for skewing the distribution upwards or downwards, this rarely takes place.

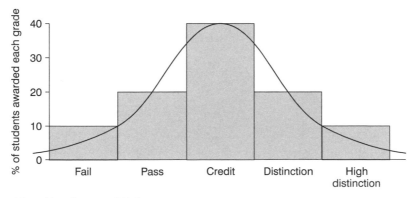

Adapted from Rowntree (1987)

Figure 3.1 *Normal distribution of grades*

2. Norm referencing suits subject areas where the measurement of performance can objectively be considered right or wrong. Biggs (1999a) would argue that, in these cases, knowledge is declarative and tends to be lower-order, performed by verbs such as 'name', 'describe' and the like. In higher-order tasks, an answer might be right or wrong in certain contexts, so that students can apply, interpret and analyse information. In these cases students will achieve better grades if they do more than just declare knowledge. Professional judgement must be applied, but then any normal distribution of the cohort would be artificial. Moreover, this kind of scenario also illustrates how professional judgement can be disguised so that it looks scientific, regardless of whether it is sound.
3. Norm referencing is not appropriate to small cohorts; indeed, the likelihood of a cohort naturally falling into a normal distribution of grades is extremely low unless the cohort is very large indeed – such as in a cohort of more than 300. As a result, the grades that students achieve in a normal distribution are less reliable indicators of performance the smaller the cohort. This is quite disconcerting when we consider a cohort of just 20, for example.
4. There is evidence that normal distributions of grades are manifested differently across academic disciplines. Bridges *et al* (1999), for example, compared the natural degrees of skew in the distributions of grades and found three different clusters in separate disciplinary groupings.

The problem is that, however we award grades, teachers in universities and colleges tend to have a preconception of how the grades usually turn out, on the basis of probabilities. But norm referencing in itself is problematic because it is difficult to differentiate it from cohort referencing, where every student receives a grade in relation to the other grades awarded to the cohort. The question to be asked is 'How rigorous would norm referencing be for my classes?' And, as Nightingale (personal communication) would argue, that depends upon the purpose that norm referencing serves, along with the problem that many universities and colleges require norm referencing according to how they conceive of assessment grades.

Mixed messages

The problem with norm-referenced assessment is that the overall performance of the cohort is moderated to fit a normally distributed set of grades regardless of the real level of performance of the group overall or of the individual performance of individuals within it. Furthermore, while it is measurement oriented, it is still subjective. Long-held notions about the need for assessment practices to be scientific and rigorous are increasingly coming into question. The UK Student Assessment and Classification Working Group (SACWG) (1999: 294) recently pointed to entrenched inequities in assessment practices that derive from discipline-related marking and grading conventions. They showed that 'in most – but not all – disciplines [the problem is] unwarranted precision which percentage marking requires, particularly in subjects in which the assessor's judgement is qualitative'. And of course the issue is compounded when the grading of students' work does not utilize numbers or percentages, and is based on subjective judgement.

Many universities have in recent years moved to change their assessment policies from norm-referenced systems to criterion-referenced systems, even though assessors still tend to conceive of performance across a cohort as being – on the balance of probabilities – reasonably normally distributed. This move has taken place because of concerns about trying to quantify what is essentially a qualitative process. In addition, it makes sense to identify performance criteria or standards to students in advance since assessment is such a powerful learning tool. But these considerations do not detract from the rule of thumb that, in medium to large cohorts, on the balance of probabilities, one would expect a reasonably normal distribution of grades. In some institutions, this conundrum is well understood, so a mere justification of the awarding of grades over a cohort by an assessor is all that is required. But cultural change does not happen overnight, and due consideration to the levels of performance of the cohort, and how they are derived, must be given if assessors are to justify confidently the grades that they award.

Moving towards professional judgements of performance

The idea of standards-based assessment (and also of the more particular criterion-referenced assessment) depends upon the good judgement of the assessor in two key domains. First, assessment tasks are derived from explicit, 'performable' learning outcomes for which specific performance standards are determined in advance of the assessment task being performed. A fundamental assumption in standards-based assessment is that judgement is subjective, even though it should be backed by benchmarking in the field and, sometimes, by psychometrically defensible objective testing. While it is subjective, this does not mean that it is arbitrary. Second, the goals of the teacher, the teaching activities and the assessment methods are coherent. But a teacher may set criteria for assessment that are not appropriate for the goals of the subject. Good practice in assessment depends on constructive alignment, but the concept of standards-based assessment does not necessarily guarantee either good practice or constructive alignment.

To be confident about a professional judgement about performance, the judgement needs to be well informed about the knowledge base, about appropriate and acceptable levels of skill and knowledge and about appropriate analytical, methodological and theoretical frames of reference and their applications. These kinds of professional understandings are not necessarily explicit features of academic professions. There is also a tacit dimension to these professional understandings that is culturally based and learnt from being part of the profession itself, as Becher (1989), Becher and Trowler (2001) and Parry (1998) have shown. Professional judgement, if it is to be good judgement, should reflect knowledge and understanding not only of the knowledge base but also of the professional culture in which it is located – its conventions, traditions and values. So, how do university teachers develop confidence in their own professional judgement?

The answer lies in *benchmarking* assessment practices with those in the field, the department and the profession at large. Although quality imperatives have advanced this agenda for some time, institutions have not been swift to embrace benchmarking practices in relation to teaching, and certainly not in relation to assessment practices.

In much of the assessment literature, the pervasive issue in student assessment remains that, while educators overall acknowledge the value of criteria- or standards-based assessment, institutions are resistant to change. In a government-funded project aimed at advancing the status and practice of university teaching in Australia, James, McInnis and Devlin (2002) noted this issue and recommended frameworks for institutional, faculty and departmental change based on case studies in several institutions.

Part of the difficulty with implementing new assessment policies in line with the global movement towards student-centredness is that the assessment is a value-laden process, whether we like it or not. The value-laden nature of student assessment means that the complexities vary according to the value frames of disciplines and specialisms, faculty and individual assessors. Individuals and groups of tertiary teachers, when faced with challenges to long-held values and assumptions, are not usually quick to act.

Grading categories: standards and criteria

So far we have discussed criterion-referenced assessment and standards-based assessment as though they are similar processes. In practice, these terms refer to very different processes, as we have suggested, because grading categories indicate standards or bands of performance, while criteria refer to specific performance attributes. Levels or standards of performance are premised on the idea that performance and achievement can be qualitatively gauged according to preconceived achievement levels that are able to be described, interpreted and exemplified.

Nulty (1997) argues that, in *standards-based assessment*, the assessor has constructed a view about levels of performance into which students can then be categorized. He cites examples from the literature where the standards are not preordained, but where markers presuppose particular grades or levels of performance. Examiners may have five bands or levels of performance in mind when categorizing performance, or they may grade relative to the performance of others in the cohort, or they may have a notional distribution, such as a normal or skewed normal distribution in mind.

Essentially, the most defensible way to determine grades is through the identification of predetermined levels of performance as standards of achievement. Conceptions of what the standards represent can be articulated to students. In addition, this method reduces the possibility of there being different interpretations of a range of criteria. One of the big questions in setting assessment tasks concerns how many criteria to include when telling students what is expected of them. Expressing everything in concrete terms is likely to lead to conformity, but then leaving criteria out is likely to mean that students overlook them. In setting standards that refer to predetermined levels of performance, an overarching conception of what is expected at different levels of performance can be shared by the teacher and the student.

In *criterion-referenced assessment*, the various interpretations of the criteria themselves by students and various assessors can differ dramatically, depending on what prior knowledge or assumptions the learner brings to the task. The drawback with depending literally upon a range of criteria is that it is just not possible to make explicit all the criteria upon which assessment will be based. In addition, the assessors' understanding of criteria is likely to change as they work their way through a pile of assignments. A notional idea of performance bands is a much neater framework for understanding. While there may be ambiguities in and differing interpretations of performance bands, there is an advantage in that students can be taught what the different bands imply and describe by the use of exemplars, practice and formative feedback, and by benchmarking understandings with others in the class. Standards-based assessment is sometimes referred to as construct-referenced assessment.

Standards-based assessment categories in an ascending scale, such as fail, pass, credit, distinction and high distinction, are frequently used for construct referencing. Here is an example from an undergraduate human rights subject in law:

> In general terms the assignment requires students to investigate and report (in 2,000 words) the extent of human rights protection for a particular interest group and the desirability of a bill of rights from the point of view of the interest group.
>
> *Pass:* The report demonstrates a sound understanding of human rights and of its application in the context of a particular interest group. It reflects an awareness (where appropriate) of gender and cross-cultural issues as they affect human rights in law, and it shows evidence of a capacity to examine critically a range of legal and non-legal issues in human rights. The argument in the report is generally logical and objective, and the report is clearly and concisely written.

Credit: In addition to satisfying the requirements for a pass, the report reflects mastery of a wide range of literature concerning human rights in law. The argument is consistently logical and objective, and the report is very clearly and concisely written.

Distinction/high distinction: The report is exceptionally well researched and argued. In addition to satisfying the requirements for a credit, it demonstrates a high order of critical and argumentative skills appropriate to the discipline and field, and a highly developed ability to write clearly, creatively and concisely.

Constructed standards such as these can have different kinds of labels, such as F, then D, C, B, A. But these labels have no meaning unless there are clear construct descriptors that explain what they refer to. And of course, it is this explanation that is often neglected by assessors, so students haven't a clue what the standards of performance are.

Throughout this book, we assert the value of standards-based assessment, based on the range of challenges associated more broadly with the grading game. In Parts B and C we explore the issues and practices in much more detail, but for now it is worth while to reflect on your own grading practices and what they imply:

- Have I determined in advance of the task what the standards of performance – and therefore conceptions of quality – are in relation to this task?
- How can I be sure that performance standards will be the same no matter who marks the assessment task or whether it is marked first or last?
- How do the various markers of this task know what the performance standards are? How do the students know?
- How clear to students are the standards of performance expected of them? How do they know this?
- Is my cohort likely to fall into a fairly normal distribution? Why?
- Is subjective judgement used in my assessment?

4

Valid assessment

One of the central concerns of teachers is whether they are assessing the right thing when using one assessment method or strategy or another. In this book, we frequently refer to the concept of 'alignment', which we have explained earlier. We also refer to authentic assessment. This latter term derives from a growing body of literature showing how important it is to implement assessment tasks that relate to the real world – to the professions and communities that contextualize them. Another concept that is relevant to valid, authentic assessment concerns assessment having a basis in the core skills and attributes that are desirable in graduates.

The big picture: core skills and attributes

There is a movement – in the UK, Australia and, more recently, the United States – towards institutions developing their own distinctive set of desirable graduate outcomes. In the related literature, these outcomes are generally referred to as *core skills and attributes*. Educators need to be clear about the core skills and attributes they expect students to attain during a programme of study, for these may be regulated or constrained by professional bodies, accrediting agencies or community standards. Today, education systems in many countries are encouraging institutions to articulate core skills and attributes as a way of identifying the *brand* of each institution. Faculties too may identify core skills and attributes that they consider important to their field or profession.

Core skills and attributes need to be articulated if teachers are to be confident that they are 'assessing the right thing'. Explicitly articulated core skills and attributes set the agenda for what is to be taught and assessed in a programme of study. Then, each unit or course of study within the programme makes a systematic and strategic contribution to the assessment of the skills and attributes. The conception of grading standards is then far from arbitrary, but is determined by explicit, strategic learning objectives.

In Figure 4.1, each stage in the development of assessment tasks fits neatly with those preceding it. Alignment between the desired core skills and attributes of graduates and overall programme objectives is equally important. The alignment of learning objectives with articulated levels of skills and knowledge in the discipline or profession at large is essential if, as teachers, we are to be confident that our student assessment practices are not arbitrary. This latter kind of alignment provides a broader base for assessment validity beyond the boundaries of the faculty or the institution. Peer review and feedback, self-reflection and evaluation of assessment methods and outcomes, student feedback, departmental reviews and feedback from employers are all sources of affirmation of the validity of assessment items and processes. Since students are the principal stakeholders in the process, their retrospective views on how effective their assessment has been in a programme of study are vital for formative improvement.

The middle picture: disciplinary differences

The nature of disciplinary learning and professionalism are food for thought. Those who teach in practical or clinical fields will recognize the power of unconscious learning, or tacit learning, in mastery of a field. This notion is raised

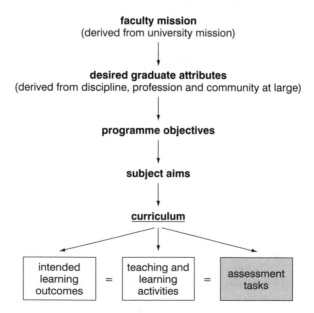

Figure 4.1 *Achieving assessment validity*

several times in this book because it is a part of learning – and assessment – that cannot be ignored, and yet it is difficult to put into concrete terms. When educators give assessment criteria to students, it is assumed that the criteria themselves are indicators of quality. But how do we know that they are? We must look to disciplinary and professional benchmarks for answers to this question. However, in doing so, the diversity and complexity of fields of knowledge in the undergraduate curriculum need to be taken into consideration, for these aspects of disciplinarity and fields of professional practice have implications for authentic assessment.

From the work of Entwistle and Tait (1995: 101) it is clear that, in order to achieve in a particular field, students need to acquire more than just discipline-specific, declarative knowledge. Students are assessed on their functional knowledge, and this means that discipline-specific study and communication skills have to be learnt, because these are essential to being able to express what they know in an assessment task. For instance, the stylistic rules for various genres of writing, such as reports, critiques and essays, vary according to the nature of the field, so students need to be familiar with them and be able to reproduce them. Not surprisingly, the inexplicit conventions for many other aspects of student assessment seem to vary across disciplinary settings. We also know that typical assessment tasks and grading practices vary across academic disciplines (see, for example, Neumann, Parry and Becher, 2002). Not only are there differences in typical assessment tasks across different disciplines, but the typical concerns about assessment vary too. A concern such as how creativity should be assessed would be unusual in science, but not in history. Smart and Etherington (1995: 56) show that the goals of undergraduate education differ across disciplines, especially with respect to knowledge acquisition versus knowledge application and integration. The implications of this finding are that varying goals of undergraduate education are associated with different kinds of complexities in setting standards of performance. In Part B and Part C of this book we discuss these different kinds of complexities in more detail, but we raise them briefly here because we acknowledge that they exist and yet they are seldom addressed in the literature on student assessment.

The little picture: ensuring alignment

We have argued that there are three dimensions of authentic assessment. The first is the 'big picture' in which programme goals direct subject aims, as outlined above. The second dimension concerns the course aims, which should explicitly identify disciplinary knowledge and skills, including field-specific conventions, traditions and values that are expected to be demonstrated. The third concerns the fine detail, in which the curriculum for a subject is coherently – or constructively – aligned, as described by Biggs (1999a).

In Figure 4.1, there is a clear and obvious match between intended learning outcomes, the teaching and learning activities and the assessment tasks. This coherence is what we mean by *valid* assessment, because the assessment task measures what it is supposed to measure. While this kind of match may seem obvious, it is not always evident in practice. Biggs (1999a) shows that the setting of learning objectives for a course is the foundation of the curriculum because it directs the choice of appropriate forms of assessment to measure the achievement of objectives. Biggs's argument is that the learning objectives should be expressed as verbs that relate to levels of thinking skills. Johnstone, Patterson and Rubenstein (1998) crystallize the issue: 'If there is a disjunction between the expressed learning objectives and the chosen form of assessment, students will tend to adopt learning strategies that help them complete the assessment, rather than seeking to achieve the expressed objectives of the subject.'

Unfortunately, where students are misdirected in their learning efforts by inadequate assessment tasks, they are more than likely to achieve inadequate learning outcomes – and it may be through no fault of their own. Students need to be very clear about learning objectives, and performance must be measured against these objectives. When these conditions are not met, a 'de facto curriculum' (Rowntree, 1987) takes over. Appropriate design of assessment indicates to students where to put their focus, energy and time.

There are some key challenges for teachers in making sure that they are assessing 'the right thing'. One danger is where teachers make changes to assessment regimes and individual tasks with only scant reference to their original intentions about the desired learning outcomes for students. Another danger is where teachers make arbitrary changes to assessment because they have personal preferences for other methods. Many factors, such as the desired core skills and attributes, the specific intended learning outcomes, the nature of the discipline, class size and the nature of the teaching and learning activities, all have to be taken into account. Perhaps the most dangerous situation for students and for teachers is where class sizes increase and teachers feel that they must seek out easier or more automated forms of marking and assessment that bear little or no relation to what was originally intended.

What individual assessors can do

Assessing the right thing is dependent on three kinds of benchmarks being applied. The first is to ensure that there is a neatness of fit between the intended core outcomes of the overall programme and the specific learning objectives for a particular course of study. There is then the need to ensure that there is clear alignment between the intended learning outcomes, the teaching and learning activities and the assessment tasks. The second set of benchmarks applies to the requirements of the discipline or profession at large. Here it is relevant to ask the question, 'How would my assessment tasks hold up in another institution or setting, but in the same field of knowledge?' The third benchmark concerns checking that there is a clear and obvious match between learning objectives, the teaching and learning activities and the assessment tasks. Some understanding of taxonomies of learning that depict thinking skills of deepening levels is necessary to determine whether an assessment task is appropriate to the level of thinking skills that are expected.

Assessing the right thing may be hard to do in practice, especially where a teacher is not in charge of the course or unit of study and the assessment tasks are set by a more senior person in the faculty. Unfortunately, the increasing casualization of teachers in tertiary education means that this problem is growing rather than being addressed. In addition, there are three dimensions of validity. We know that, in practice, synthesis may be overlooked in the wish to simplify the marking tasks. Assessment, particularly of large classes, can be governed by what is easy to assess rather than what should be assessed. Legitimate fears of expanding staff workloads can drive the critical decisions of whether or not to set an exam and, if so, what kind of examination this might be. While individual short answer and multiple choice questions can be successfully structured to indicate higher-order thinking, in practice the overall effect of such assessment methods is to dissect knowledge into small pieces and therefore provide the student with little or no opportunity for synthesis, or development of a coherent knowledge base.

Individual teachers can check that their assessment tasks are valid – are they aligned and do they assess what is intended? Teachers can also check that the tasks are authentic – are they appropriate to the real-world knowledge that should be acquired, whether this is from a disciplinary or a professional practice base? Of course, the litmus test is to ask, 'Will the students think the assessment tasks actually measure what the students have been taught?'

5

Assessing in flexible modes

The drive to offer flexible learning experiences is being felt by teachers in most universities and colleges around the world. No longer is flexible or open learning the domain of dedicated institutions such as open universities. Many universities that had previously only catered to school leavers in on-campus undergraduate education are now broadening their horizons to include adults returning to study, international students and distance learners. For some, this has been undertaken in the belief that their programmes are more attractive to students and thus more viable. For other universities, it has been essential for their survival in an environment of reduced funding and declining student numbers from traditional sources.

Thus many teachers are now confronted with a variety of new challenges in delivering their programmes, including multiple learning modes that may include components of print-based and online learning; new teaching periods, flexible enrolment and pacing, mixed cohorts of local and international students, to name but a few of these new options. At its heart, flexible learning is a philosophy and an approach to education that seeks to place students and their needs at the centre of considerations. The range of considerations includes the university's organizational systems, approaches to pedagogy within courses, learning environments and support structures offered to students. For teachers who are moving into these new learning environments, it may require a radical rethink of almost all areas of their operations.

Who are 'flexible learners'? It is not possible to generalize across national systems or even institutions, each of which may well exhibit a different profile. But for the purpose of the discussion here, it might be said that these students will be studying with prepared resources, with perhaps only occasional attendance on-campus; they may be working part or full time to support their study, and many will be dipping in and out of courses to fit in with work or family responsibilities. In some ways, the new flexible learners are not dissimilar to the distance learners of prior times, yet it would be wrong to conflate the two, as much traditional distance education was anything but flexible.

How flexible learners go about their study

As assessment drives and shapes much student learning, it is clearly a key area of attention in flexible education. Yet ironically, there is so much attention and effort placed into the development of flexible learning materials and resources that assessment tends to be an add-on consideration – something to be revisited after the resources are developed. We tend to assume that our carefully crafted resources will guide student learning and that students will work through our materials more or less in the manner directed. However, research into distance learners' use of study materials (Marland et al, 1990) and use of formative activities (Lockwood, 1992, 1995) suggests that there are far more complex behaviours at work. With their materials laid out before them at the commencement of the term or semester, distance learners have greater autonomy than their on-campus counterparts regarding how they go about their study and what they choose to read and do. Not surprisingly, the assessment tasks and what they perceive is expected of them are uppermost in their minds. Unless the assessment tasks are carefully interwoven into the study materials, with formative activities supporting summative assessments, our finely crafted resources may well be bypassed altogether.

It is important to understand how flexible and open learners go about their study, and what they bring to the learning encounter, if we are to design meaningful assessments for them. Since many are adult learners who are returning to study or upgrading their qualifications, they bring with them a wealth of existing knowledge and experience. In addition, they bring a variety of approaches and motivations to study, and a rather haphazard collection of prior learning experiences, both positive and negative, that have impacted in differing ways upon their confidence and self-esteem. Almost always, they struggle during their studies to balance a complex mix of family, work and financial commitments, with perhaps only limited outside support. When study conflicts with work commitments or a family problem, study almost certainly will take a back seat. Our understanding of the realities of flexible learners' lives will need to inform our decision making regarding the type of assessments we set, the degree of choice of assessment we offer, the manner in which we support and prepare learners for assessment, and the policies that guide our decision making about extending submission deadlines and the imposition of penalties for late submission of work.

Notwithstanding the difficulties faced by many, it would be a mistake to conceptualize flexible or distance learners as belonging to a 'deficit' model – on the contrary, they bring with them a wealth of abilities and resources that create dynamic learning encounters. The challenge for teachers is to create learning environments and assessment tasks that focus upon the strengths and opportunities inherent in distance learning, by encouraging learners to engage with their own communities, workplaces and applied projects and problems. In addition, with the advent of computer-mediated communications, many of the 'deficits' of the past in terms of geographical dispersal and inequity of access to resources are less likely to be of issue (Morgan and O'Reilly, 1999).

Some common issues

When it comes to designing and supporting assessment tasks for flexible learning, teachers will commonly grapple with a series of issues, including:

- *Effective early communication of assessment tasks*. Flexible learners often have less opportunity in which to diagnose their own errors or mistaken assumptions before they commit to a formal assessment task. For example, it may not be until midway through a semester or course, when a student's first assignment is returned, that a simple error is discovered, to the detriment of the student's final grade. While face-to-face learners can often rectify these problems long before they submit an assessment, flexible or distance learners do not necessarily have the same kinds of opportunities to check their understanding of an assessment task or compare approaches with other students. Distance learners are more dependent upon effective, early communication of assessment requirements, together with well-designed and cohesive assessment tasks, useful and timely support, and a transparent marking scheme that explains how judgements are to be made (Morgan and O'Reilly, 1999).

- *Interwoven formative and summative tasks*. Assessment tends to be more powerful in flexible learning if the formative and summative components are interwoven so that one assignment builds upon the next, with formative feedback from the first contributing to the next, and so on. Benson (1996) notes that the planning required for flexible learning lends itself to this strategic approach, providing useful structure and feedback on progress, which builds confidence and creates a source of dialogue between teacher and learner. This approach, of course, is dependent upon rapid handling and return of assignments, and appropriate spacing between assignments, so students have the benefit of feedback from one before commencing the next.

- *Tailored, appropriate tasks*. As flexible learning claims to put students at the centre of consideration, assessment tasks should be tailored, at least to some degree, to meet the needs of learners. This includes tasks that provide opportunities for students individually to construct and negotiate meanings and to apply their learning to relevant work-based problems and projects. Students should also be encouraged to develop skills in self-directed learning and self-assessment where they make their own judgements regarding their achievements. Naturally, the nature of these tasks will vary between disciplines, but the principle remains the same. Students have come to expect university and college teachers to meet their learning needs in this way, regardless of the media or mix of media in which a subject is delivered.

Some tensions

Not only do students who want flexible learning options have different needs from those who are full-time and on-campus. Students who choose to learn using more flexible options such as supplementarily or wholly moving to distance mode or online will probably want flexible assessment options as well. In these cases they will be looking for avenues where they can make choices about submission dates or the nature of the assessment task, or choices among assessment tasks.

Teachers often express concerns about flexible approaches to assessment. These concerns often arise from our desire to be open and student-centred in our approach to assessment on the one hand, and the necessity to satisfy institutional policies, schedules and spiralling workloads on the other. Sometimes these tensions are felt more subtly, in the form of learners themselves baulking at the very arrangements that were supposedly designed for their benefit. Tensions may be felt around our roles as facilitators of learning, the additional time required to negotiate and mark individualized assessment tasks, difficulties regarding plagiarism and proof of authorship in the absence of invigilated examinations, and the desire to promote self-directed forms of learning in programmes that are already overburdened with predetermined vocational requirements. Sometimes, too, flexible assessment is criticized by those who consider it to be lacking in rigour. Such claims are likely to be advanced by those who believe that academic standards can only be embodied by time-honoured traditions such as formal lectures and invigilated examinations, and where the process of what is learnt and how it is assessed is tightly controlled (Morgan and O'Reilly, 1999). These issues are all developed and discussed in later chapters of this book, though we recognize that there are no single or simple solutions. Flexible learning challenges us to come to terms with our own beliefs and traditions, and to devise assessment schemes that 'enable us and our students to be genuinely unconstrained by prior expectations of what the syllabus does or should contain, and what the study of a particular [subject] should entail' (Cowan, 1996: 60).

Assessing online

Special consideration should be given here to online learning, as it has changed the face of distance learning over the past five years and has enabled the flexibility agenda to be advanced rapidly. In stark contrast to the restricted ability for communication within older forms of distance education, the online environment opens up greater possibilities for interaction, collaboration and cross-cultural dialogue. Many new forms of assessment have arisen using this medium, and these are given considerable attention in Part B of this book. For now, we simply raise some of the questions confronting teachers when moving to the online environment, such as:

- What kinds of new learning and assessment opportunities can be created through online learning?
- What pedagogies can be employed to support meaningful online assessment?
- What are the losses and gains of this medium for teachers and learners?
- How effectively do old models and forms of assessment translate into the online environment?

Questions such as these have given rise to a burgeoning literature by theorists and practitioners who are exploring assessment forms such as peer and self-assessment, teamwork and collaborative tasks, online dialogue and debate, simulations and role-plays, problem solving, online testing and digital scrapbooks, to name but a few. A key theme in many of these discussions is the online learning community (Palloff and Pratt, 1999, for example), which may extend beyond traditional borders and introduce new challenges for students with respect to intercultural communication and the negotiation of difference. Yet we cannot assume that all learners (and indeed teachers) will comfortably make a smooth transition to online learning and assessment. There are still issues in relation to differences in culture, access, and teaching and learning styles that continue to provide significant barriers to online learning becoming a 'people's' medium for learning or assessment. One of the greatest strengths to date has been the convergence it has created between traditional forms of delivery, such as face-to-face, and packaged distance education. These divisions are now seeming less impermeable and in some cases non-existent, as online learning draws learners together and provides a shared experience, whether on-campus or in far-flung locations, or a combination of both.

Why move to flexible assessment?

Why would teachers wish to upset the well-oiled machinery of their existing arrangements? Underlying the move to flexible learning and assessment is a concern that student profiles have changed and those committed to higher education nowadays have to work to support their studies. There are also far more mature-age students entering higher education than ever before. In addition, there is the realization that traditional teacher-centred methods of delivery are outmoded because they focus on coverage of content and do not engage learners in authentic learning experiences that can be effectively measured. Rather, as Gibbs (1995: 2) starkly describes, it has given rise to 'passive, bored students giving back to teachers what they have been given in a worthless grade-grubbing way irrelevant to their future lives'. At least to some degree we can recognize this as an outcome, albeit unintended, of much under-graduate education.

For students who are dipping in and out of higher education, who are having to earn an income to support themselves or who are not geographically close to their preferred course, the idea of flexible modes of delivery and flexible modes of assessment is very attractive. But institutions that enrol these students need to deliver on these terms.

The principal challenge for teachers when considering flexible learning and assessment is to define what they really mean by 'flexibility', because students need to know what it refers to in their particular institution. Ideally, we would argue that, when we refer to flexible assessment, we refer to assessment practices that take into account the different circumstances and experiences of students, to allow choice in how students are able to demonstrate performance on an assessment task. The difficulty lies in balancing student choice with what is practically possible.

6

Assessing with new technology

The broad picture

The last two decades have seen the rhetoric of lifelong learning become a reality as adults around the globe return to study in order to upgrade or convert their qualifications (Postle *et al*, 1999). Alongside this development is the rapid uptake of the Internet as a relatively cheap and accessible method of information storage, delivery and interaction. The computers of today, with network connections, provide a vast capacity for education, information and communication potentials (Bates, 1995). This convergence of information and communications technology within the educational environment is commonly referred to as ICT-supported or online learning. Information and communications technologies (ICTs) now have the capacity to enhance learning and assessment because they give rise to new opportunities for sharing information, resources and expertise, as well as for networking with student peers and teachers. This latter benefit of ICTs has had the effect of substantially changing the nature of distance education because no longer do these students have to learn in isolation from others in their cohort. Online discussions and interaction through a range of learning and assessment tasks are now much demanded by students in both distance and face-to-face teaching settings.

Assessing students using multiple choice questions (MCQs) is well established using new technologies, and there are some excellent guidelines about doing this effectively (see, for example, Pritchett, 1999). Similarly, the use of optical mark readers and related automated marking systems has made student assessment more efficient when used appropriately. But it is the use of online technologies in student assessment that has vastly changed assessment methods,

the kinds of choices available to students in assessment and the range of skills
that can be assessed as part of a course. Alexander and McKenzie (1998: 6) note
that the most important factor affecting ICT-based learning and assessment is
not the kind of technology that is used but the design of the learning experience that makes use of information technologies. In relation to student
assessment, some of these might include:

- promoting active engagement, such as in simulations;
- making real-life situations relevant;
- including representations from multiple modalities;
- facilitating collaborative activity to solve problems or complete projects;
- working with microworlds and controlled situations;
- presenting interconnections between concepts through hypertext;
- requiring students to collect, analyse and recast their understandings from
  information sources; and
- simulating clinical or laboratory work.

(derived from Alexander and McKenzie, 1998)

All in all, the assessment landscape has changed dramatically with the
widespread implementation of ICTs, and so have the associated issues. There
have been enormous gains in efficiency, but there have been costs too. In this
chapter we have chosen to discuss the broad range of uses of ICTs and the issues
associated with them because of the increasing integration of technology into
teaching. In Part B there are many examples of assessment using ICTs.

ICTs and formative assessment

Perhaps the most significant development for distance students with the advent
of ICTs is the capacity for formative feedback on progress. First, the speed with
which formative assessment tasks can be annotated and returned to students is a
major advantage. In addition, students can receive feedback from each other as
well as from the teacher, so that they are no longer necessarily isolated from the
rest of their cohort. These developments are striking when considered against a
background of typical distance students of the past, who would receive a study
guide in the mail. In all likelihood, the students would find that their only
communication with their teacher was when their assignments were returned
after marking. For students using ICTs in their learning, the design of
coursework can use formative assessment and scaffolding in ways that provide
consistent, timely and constructive advice about progress and how to improve
performance. But it is not only distance students who have gained from ICT-
related developments in formative assessment.

For both distance and face-to-face learners, ICTs have made communication
faster, easier and more enjoyable, and they have made assessment regimes easier

to administer. The function of formative assessment is to encourage reflection and self-assessment, both of which are critical to the adaptive lifelong learner who may have to change careers many times during the course of a working life. In his paper on sustainable assessment, Boud (2000) argued that students today need a great deal more preparation for an uncertain and complex future, and he pointed to the importance of formative assessment in the curriculum. New technologies are advancing the potential for formative assessment and timely feedback at a rapid rate, not only because the new technologies are more expedient, but also because they can support networks of learners and new methods of formative assessment.

In institutions where new technologies have been introduced into the core business of teaching and learning, formative assessment tasks can readily be facilitated using auto-graded quizzes, intelligent object databases (Taylor, 2001), model answers or collective feedback broadcast electronically to the whole class, and discussion forums where students can monitor the developing knowledge base of their group. But there is more to consider than simply the methods of formative assessment. Parry and Dunn (2000) used the notion of benchmarking to describe the formative learning and assessment that takes place in online discussions, through which students can compare their progress, interpretation of a task, use of resources and approach to study. Teachers who are concerned to use the potential of ICTs to support formative assessment may build on these mechanisms and benchmarking processes, but, as we have seen already, it should be on the understanding that formative feedback on assessment tasks must be separated from the allocation of grades.

Formative assessment, especially using ICTs, together with the feedback process is really an intense form of one-to-one teaching. The implications of this are that, while students overall enjoy the feedback, guidance, opportunities for dialogue and benchmarking, one-to-one teaching is extremely demanding of teachers' time. Teachers committed to ICT-based formative assessment find that their workloads increase dramatically, especially when student cohorts increase in size. Not only are development and maintenance costs for systems and programmes costly, but the resources required to provide individualized feedback to students on several formative assessment tasks may come as a surprise. The old rationales for introducing ICTs into teaching, when it comes to saving teachers' time, simply do not ring true. Yet, at the same time, students, whether studying at a distance or in face-to-face settings, are increasingly demanding ICT-supported courses.

There is a wide range of ICT methods or systems available to provide feedback to students about their performance either formatively or summatively. The facility is also now available through ICTs for providing student support of a more motivational and pastoral nature, and it is possible for student peers to engage in online supportive networks that can enhance a formative and reflective focus on learning and assessment (O'Reilly and Newton, 2002). Synchronous (real-time) systems of interaction also provide timely feedback and clarification in support of assessment processes. These are given greater attention in Part B of this book but, for now, we draw attention to the range of feedback options available to students.

At the more impersonal end of the spectrum is a wide array of innovative automated assessment systems, from optical mark readers to auto-graded quizzes, simulations, timed online tests and automated pooled question banks. These kinds of assessment methods are emerging wherever local infrastructure can support them and there is some evidence that their strength is in their formative capacity to enhance learning. Students who are able to access such mechanisms widely report how much they appreciate the immediate feedback about their understanding or misconceptions. Students also appreciate being able to access these systems when it is convenient for them, and they like the rapid availability of test results. The potential difficulties associated with assessment methods such as these arise from several sources. These include situations where the ICT infrastructure is not robust or extensive enough to service all students reliably and equally well. From the faculty perspective, there may also be considerations about how to authenticate students' submitted work or how to check the identity of students sitting an online test.

ICTs and summative assessment

ICTs are also being used in summative assessment. The use of ICTs enables teachers to blend a mixed cohort of on-campus learners with those studying off-campus. At the same time, teachers can gain some efficiencies from broadcasting instructions and tests at the flick of a switch. Students who enrol in a programme of study at a distance or outside their own country are able to complete their awards through the online learning environment, from their place of study. But there are also potential issues to be taken into account. In practice, one summative assessment task is unlikely to meet the needs of diverse cohorts of students from vastly different cultural, ethnic and language backgrounds. But meeting this challenge raises some vital questions about the validity of assessment. Can we design assessment tasks that are valid for all students in all contexts? How difficult would it be to plan and design assessment tasks that are equitable for the whole diverse group? Can we develop a range of assessment options to account for a diverse student group while still maintaining equivalence in assessment weighting, workload and intentions to satisfy the same learning objectives?

ICTs in summative assessment pose a further concern: 'A badly designed summative assessment system can cause widespread adoption of shallow learning approaches. Since the development of any non-trivial computer-based system is time and cost intensive, there is always a pressure to tag a simplistic assessment system onto the learning system' (Patel, Russell and Kinshuk, 1999).

The broader issue of resource investment also needs to be considered. Not only are development time and cost likely to be greater than anticipated, but staff using a summative system of assessment will need to be trained in its use to ensure equity and fairness. In addition, there are educational design matters to resolve. Whereas in the past students could be given a simple assessment task on paper, use of ICTs may well require students to sit examinations on-site so that ID can be checked. In addition, the assessment task itself may need to be designed differently so that it is appropriate for the technology. For example, it has been found that, in content-heavy subjects, students prefer paper-based reading to reading text online (Parry and Dunn, 2000).

Perhaps the most significant concern from both the students' and the teachers' points of view involves the computer literacy and related skills that students need if they are to be assessed using ICTs. The ICT environment has come about at a time when national systems of higher education are concerned to embed newly identified generic skills into the curriculum. Not surprisingly, some generic skills arise *because* of the ICT environment. The demonstration of skills such as online resources management, graphical and hypertextual presentation methods, interaction and collaboration are now expected in courses that are supported by ICT, raising concerns about the entry skills of new students in relation to using new technologies. One of the issues for institutions concerns the extent to which they can mandate prerequisite information literacy skills for entering students and whether they can insist that students demonstrate certain levels of information literacy before undertaking courses in an award. A related issue that is just beginning to be identified by national systems of higher education concerns the extent to which foundation skills in ICT-related information literacy should be embedded in the undergraduate curriculum.

Some gains, some losses

At present, there is evidence that some students feel that, in embarking upon online learning, they are in reality undertaking two courses at the same time: one course in navigating the relevant technology and another in the substantive area. The ease with which ICTs can be implemented by teachers can easily submerge a key consideration: whose responsibility is it to ensure that students are sufficiently technologically literate to be assessed using new technologies? For the most part, institutions have not resolved this question in relation to academic literacy, let alone literacy at the technological level!

One advantage of the ICT environment is that it lends itself readily to a broader range of learning resources such as multimedia, hypertext and network-based assessment. Document links to a vast array of resources, and shared workspace with fellow students and staff, as well as access to specialist subject expertise from anywhere in the world, provide a new set of opportunities for designing meaningful online assessment tasks. But it is important to consider the validity and appropriateness of newly created assessment forms because new technologies are seductive, yet the same roles and purposes of assessment remain regardless of the technology. Teachers are not able to deviate from the need to implement assessment methods that best measure achievement of the desired learning outcomes. And so we need to ask ourselves whether traditional assessment methods are relevant and appropriate to ICTs or whether we need to devise new ways for students to demonstrate what they know using these new technologies. Alexander and McKenzie (1998), based on a large-scale evaluation of ICT projects, noted that teachers should consider revising assessment methods to reflect changes in the content and process of learning that occur when students use new technologies in their courses.

An issue for consideration by those intending to use ICTs in assessment is that, as the technology and the media change, so do the behaviours of the students. Bonk (2000), for example, among others, has demonstrated that learners may need to adopt new roles, such as co-learner, mentor, guide, learning coordinator, model or coach, particularly where formative assessment tasks are concerned. As a result, summative assessment tasks need to reflect those roles and the different kinds of learning experiences of the individual students during the course. Yet another consideration concerns the archival capacity of ICTs. To what extent should students be expected to draw on already developed records, links, presentations, discussion lists and so forth in their assessment tasks?

Finally, our discussion has been confined to the use of ICTs in formative and summative assessment. It is important to remember that our students may be drawn from diverse backgrounds and cultures and they may well vary in their capacity to access new technologies and to develop their skills in using them. These are still relatively early days in the use of ICTs in student learning and assessment, so not only are student needs and profiles important, but staff development needs and institutional supports for their use also need serious consideration.

In assessing using new technologies, it is important to remember that each teaching situation is different. The profile and needs of the students are different; the subject matter, the pace and timing, the kinds of learning activities and the media used will vary. Teachers have to weigh up the gains and losses for themselves of using ICTs. Here are some questions for self-reflection:

- Do all students have equal access to the appropriate hardware and software?
- Are all students suitably information literate to cope with ICT-based assessment tasks?
- Are the assessment items the same as previously or do students now need additional skills, which should be assessed, in order to complete assessment tasks?
- Is the local infrastructure able to support the initiative adequately?
- Have the teaching and learning activities and the assessment tasks been modified to suit the new medium or media?

7

Assessing in diverse contexts

The assessment of diverse groups of students is closely connected with the notion of flexible learning because, as a wider range of flexible learning options have been made available to students, a more diverse group of students can now undertake tertiary study while balancing work and family responsibilities. In addition, online learning creates new, international communities of learners. It's not uncommon to find students in our classes from a variety of age groups, social and educational backgrounds and international locations. In practice, we may find ourselves managing cultural differences, language and communication problems, and widely differing perspectives, motivations and expectations between sexes and generations. In the past, teachers have been able to develop courses that take for granted the entry skills and experiences of students. But nowadays, with a mix of cultures, age groups and socio-economic backgrounds, there can be no simple assumptions about prior learning, access to resources, students' ability to support themselves, academic capabilities and so forth. In reality, the diversity that we commonly experience in our classrooms today renders many of our assumptions incorrect and potentially counter-productive to the overall success of our programmes. Depending on one's point of view, learning either happens *despite* the difficulties that diversity presents or it happens precisely *because of* the richness of interactions that these opportunities offer. Acknowledgement of students' learning in a global marketplace nudges us towards the latter.

As assessment is an area around which many problems tend to coalesce, it's vital that we examine our assessment practices and underlying assumptions through the lens of diversity and equity. Courses are often developed with a concern for issues of gender, ethnicity, disability and so forth. Inclusive language and non-stereotypical representations of people are, by and large, common policy in educational settings. Yet these concerns only scratch the surface of the kinds of complex issues that arise in teaching and assessing diverse groups of students. In his study of the diversity of open and distance learners, Evans (1994) identifies some key themes that provide shape to our understanding of diversity, including money, sex, power, age and motivation.

Inclusive assessment

The notion of inclusive assessment concerns the need to value all students in a cohort as learners. When students find that all the examples used in assessment items refer to cultures, experiences, gender and race that are not their own, they rightly feel alienated and as though their learning relates to a context other than their own. Unfortunately, in devising assessment tasks, it is all too easy to work with overriding assumptions about students' backgrounds and situations. The tendency to become preoccupied with considerations about standards, industry standards, validity and authenticity and matters of sex, ethnicity, disability, religion and so forth can easily override reflection about our assumptions and the extent to which they might not be appropriate. Considering the highly diversified nature of our student populations, inclusive assessment ought to be a primary consideration in the development of assessment strategies. The issue is that each student has different circumstances, and there are no fixed categories of diversity. Instead, it is more a matter of teachers being willing to know who their students are and what kinds of challenges they face in their day-to-day studies.

One inclusive consideration that is increasingly important today is that the majority of students are having to pay for their higher education. This means that many have to work to earn enough money to support themselves while they study. Under these circumstances, the issue of students needing greater flexibility with submission deadlines or with consideration of special circumstances may well be necessary. We have already seen that one reported cause of plagiarism is that students with work responsibilities sometimes resort to cheating in order to meet deadlines.

Another consideration relates to the increasing numbers of students who return to study at different times in their lives. For many of these, there are work and family responsibilities to juggle, so that flexibilities in assessment deadlines, fieldwork and clinical assessment venues and times, choices among assessment tasks and the range of opportunities for formative assessment to develop mastery may all come to be important if study and assessment are to remain manageable. Many of the stresses and strains of returning to study revolve around assessment practices and the lack of flexibility for those who have other responsibilities to attend to.

The changing balance of the sexes in higher education is also important. It is all too easy to make outdated assumptions about particular fields of study – such as that all nurses are women, all sports scientists male and so forth – that can alienate members of a cohort. These outdated assumptions are likely to manifest themselves in assessment tasks because this is where knowledge is applied to particular contexts.

The difficulties for students from different cultural and language backgrounds have been mentioned already. The central question for many teachers is 'Should I assess the students' writing and expression?' Conversely, the central question for students may be 'How can I make my writing or expression sound right?' Better questions for teachers concern whether there is sufficient opportunity for students to express themselves using their existing skills and abilities; whether there are clear standards of writing and expression that are explicitly required in the subject; whether opportunities for formative improvement are available to students; and whether the assessment tasks are relevant to the different backgrounds of the students concerned.

An issue affecting the extent to which assessment is inclusive concerns the power balance between the students and the teacher. In bygone days, teachers held all of the power and students were subjugated by it. Today, students are expected to learn independently and to take responsibility for their own learning as they move in and out of study over the course of their lives. Against this background, it is very much at odds for teachers in interpretive disciplines to impose a particular 'right way' to complete a task simply on the basis of teacher preference. Disciplinary and professional expectations and conventions of course need to be taken into account, but the distinction is an important one. It is insulting to an adult learner to be told what kind of meanings they should be making from their learning. We know that individuals have preferences for particular learning styles and approaches, so assessment tasks must take account of these if our students are to relate well to them.

Some checkpoints for reflecting about the extent to which an assessment strategy may exclude some students would include:

- Are students' different cultural, ethnic and religious backgrounds taken into account?
- Are the assessment challenges reasonable for all of the students?
- Can students negotiate assessment venues, times and tasks that are appropriate to their circumstances and fair and appropriate overall?
- Could students negotiate different levels of achievement or performance in advance?
- Are very able or very dependent students held back by the nature of the assessment?
- Is there an appropriate amount of formative assessment to meet the needs of different levels of achievement?
- Can students bring their own backgrounds and experiences to bear on the assessment task?
- Are students well aware of the writing and expression standards expected of them?

- Are students with better resources advantaged by the assessment tasks set?
- Are students encouraged to engage critically with the learning materials, or is there a 'correct line' that they should adopt?
- Are you willing to learn from the students?

(adapted from Morgan and O'Reilly, 1999: 58–60)

Assessing international students

A useful way to explore the issues for teachers and students when the cohort is diverse is to consider the situation from the point of view of international students. For many of these, learning is difficult and frustrating when teachers do not take account of their difference or of what they potentially have to offer to the learning experiences of the rest of the cohort. Many authors on the subject of teaching and assessing international students (see, for example, Ballard and Clanchy, 1991) recommend providing as many opportunities as possible for formative feedback on assessment tasks, particularly on essays and academic writing, so that students can develop an understanding of what is expected of them. Ryan (2000: 51) highlights an example whereby students submit two versions of one essay – one before it is edited, together with a final version.

For an assessor, it may be difficult to work out whether a student does not know the material or simply cannot express it as is expected. When the cohort is especially diverse, this may be quite a problem. One solution is to provide a range of assessment items – perhaps involving portfolios or presentations, so that student understanding can be gauged in a variety of ways. Of course, opportunities for negotiating from among these options will give the student more freedom while still giving a more comprehensive picture to the assessor.

Benchmarking opportunities

As our cohorts diversify as a result of flexible learning options and the likelihood that some students will be alienated for reasons such as those described above, it becomes more important that students have opportunities to benchmark approaches to learning and assessment tasks, as we have described in earlier chapters. We would argue that benchmarking with student peers is the most obvious way for students to learn the *cues* that are all around them: using resources, approaches to learning and writing, interpretations of assessment tasks and the like. As a result, students from diverse backgrounds will need to feel that they are part of a community of learners, in which they can learn from each other as well as from their teachers. While there is always potential for this to take place in face-to-face situations – and in tutorials in particular – communities of learners may become separated or do not form at all where students learn at a distance or online.

Because communities of learners are less likely to form within diverse cohorts, especially those in distance education, teachers may need to take the initiative in getting them started, by making online discussion forums, group work and peer review part of the assessment regime. We explore these ideas further in Part B, but for now we raise them because they form the basis for changing our attitudes about diverse cohorts of students. When there is a wide range of backgrounds and experiences to draw upon, the benchmarking outcomes are more likely to reflect that richness. In their study of the effects of assessment on online benchmarking practices and learning outcomes, Parry and Dunn (2000) found that the rich but diverse backgrounds of the students were an important factor in successful benchmarking, which itself led to deep approaches to learning and assessment tasks. We have pointed to benchmarking opportunities as a way of setting up a culture of embracing difference within a cohort of students in teaching and assessment practices. But benchmarking is only a part of the process. Assessment items must also take account of difference in a way that encourages students to build on what they already know from their own prior learning experiences.

Considering the importance to successful learning outcomes of students having exemplars and formative feedback, it is curious that more institutions do not take into account the difficulties faced by their students, particularly in the first year. There is little empirical research into the typical mistakes made by different ethnic, cultural and gender groups, and there is a need for empirical investigations of diverse student groups and the various supports and handicaps to success. However, we do know that a vital ingredient lies with the opportunities provided for formative feedback on performance. But formative assessment and feedback are resource-heavy endeavours, so it is important to maximize efforts that do not add substantially to the teacher's workload.

Many students feel that they are not listened to and that their differences are not acknowledged. In reality, they have a lot to offer their learning communities, but their capacity to contribute successfully depends upon whether the assessment tasks encourage them to do so. As assessors, we can reflect on our own assessment tasks:

- Are students able to use different critical approaches to the task?
- Does the assessment task accommodate different language styles?
- Does the assessment task utilize reference points that fit with the various cultures in the cohort?
- Can students negotiate their assessment task and/or learning outcomes?
- Will the students be able to access appropriate resources to do well?
- Are exemplars of good work with annotated explanations provided to students so that they can see what successful outcomes are like?
- Are there subtleties of language in the assessment task that students will need to interpret properly?
- How do my individual students know how to improve their performance?

8

Assessing larger cohorts

As the number of people entering higher education expands and as in most countries the available funding for the higher education sector relatively diminishes, there are pressures on teaching in which more is expected from fewer resources. The higher education systems of many countries have faced the dwindling resource issue, while at the same time having to rise to accountability imperatives, especially in relation to teaching quality. Altbach (2000: 18) provides a good overview of the main developments, highlighting the consequential 'growing focus on the process of teaching, learning and assessment in higher education'.

One outcome of steadily increasing workloads for teaching staff, as described by Langtry (2000: 87), has been increasing class sizes and class cohorts. Teachers often feel compromised by their workloads, looking for quick and easy solutions to the problem of assessing more and more students with fewer resources. Methods frequently employed to reduce workloads in marking and assessment include:

- implementing automated systems with multiple choice marking sheets;
- resorting to examinations instead of project or assignment work;
- using quizzes either online or in classes;
- introducing peer assessment regimes.

There are advantages and potential disadvantages of utilizing 'quick-fix' assessment strategies, and these will be discussed in Part C. In the meantime, however, it is important to remember that assessment is the central driver in students' approaches to learning. Ramsden (1992: 70) demonstrated that 'inappropriate assessment methods may push students towards learning in ineffective and dispiriting ways. Students will study what they think will be assessed; but no student enjoys learning counterfeit subjects.' A useful way to bring forward the range of issues in assessing larger cohorts or classes is to consider the experience from the student's point of view.

Assessing more students

As students progress through a teaching term or semester, practical assessment issues are often at the forefront of their minds. Will I have to do all my assessment tasks at the same time? Will I have too many exams to prepare well for? How will I know how well I am doing? Is this assessment task measuring what I have learnt? What can I do if I think the assessment task isn't fair or appropriate? What can I do if I think my assessment grade isn't fair? In larger classes and cohorts, there are added questions, some of which may be justified and some of which may not. Will all the markers assess student work in the same way? How can I know this? Will my teacher be available to give me advice about my progress? If I am off the track, how will I get advice about how to improve on an assessment task? Will my grades be checked or moderated? Will my grades reflect my performance or will they be norm-referenced against the performance of the class or cohort? If I have assessment tasks marked by different people, will the different markers have different ideas about good work?

Valid assessment with more students

The range of issues falls into several categories. The first concerns the appropriateness of the assessment task – is the assessment task meaningful and appropriate to what is taught? In much of the literature on student assessment, this notion is referred to as *authentic assessment*. An assessment task is considered to be valid if it permits a student's performance, on what has actually been taught, to be measured: a task would be valid if it measures what the teacher intended it to measure. But when it comes to assessing larger numbers of students, it may be more difficult to achieve because the resources required may be considerable. While this might seem like a simple idea, it is one that is hard to get right, because assessors often suffer the burden of heavy assessment loads. How much is too much assessment?

Valid assessment may be difficult to achieve when class sizes are increased and teachers face the need to assess more students with no increase in resources; they have to be creative and come up with effective alternative assessment and marking practices. The introduction of multiple choice tests, for example, is unlikely to measure the performance of higher-order skills; the introduction of peer assessment regimes is unlikely to produce better learning outcomes unless the students are well trained in the process and the values underpinning the grading criteria. In fact, while peer assessment has been shown to have many advantages in student learning outcomes, it is usually very resource-heavy, at least at first. The timetable has to include a considerable number of training sessions where students learn about assessment criteria and how to mark against them. They have to learn to negotiate their judgements in a group setting and they have to learn to take responsibility for the grades they award. While learning may be very much increased, so is the time and effort of the teacher, who has to play an adjudicative role in the process in any case.

Sampling

Selective assessment of content is another option, though this too is unlikely to be truly authentic unless students can choose among topics on assessment tasks. We know from student evaluations of teaching that they resent being assessed on a small selection of the topics for which they have studied. For selective assessment to be fair, students need to be apprised of topic choices in assessment tasks. On the other hand, it is possible to design assessment tasks that involve a broad-ranging understanding of the entire syllabus, but it is difficult to contain all the learning objectives for a subject in one assessment task. The central issue here is that reducing the marking load may lead to a trade-off on validity. Of course, it doesn't have to, and suggestions for handling this dilemma will be addressed in later chapters.

Moderation in marking

Increases in class size provide a setting in which multiple markers must be employed, and in today's higher education sector these are frequently employed on a casual or short-term-contract basis. Hence the coordination of marking becomes difficult at best. However, from the students' point of view, consistency is of the utmost importance. Nobody wants to feel that they get 'pot luck' in being assessed but, when we fail to ensure that markers have clear and consistent marking criteria or when we fail to ensure that standards are consistent across markers, this is the impression, if not the reality, that we convey to our students.

In this vein, it seems that assessing in science-based disciplines, where knowledge is concrete and, for many assessment tasks, answers are objectively right or wrong, marking and grading consistency is less open to contest. Students in humanities and social science disciplines are more likely to contest their grades than those in science, probably because those disciplines are more discursive and debate is encouraged (Neumann, Parry and Becher, 2002). There is therefore more need in these latter settings to ensure that marking criteria and grading standards are clear and explicit to all those marking common assessment items. In addition, there needs to be a moderating process whereby markers can compare their grading practices and identify their implicit values in assessing students. By now, it should be growing clearer that the organizational base for assessment consistency across different markers requires interventions at the organizational level that will head off grading disputes and appeals later on.

New assessment forms

A third notion concerns the appropriateness of assessment forms, and includes the scheduling of assessment, both of which are necessary if student assessment is to be fair and equitable. If the path of least resistance lies in multiple choice tests, then the essay has become the reliable workhorse. Regardless of the form of delivery, essays have become the mainstay of assessment because many believe the genre transcends disciplines, year levels and cultures. However, its implementation over a wide range of settings and knowledge bases is not always the best fit for authentic assessment. There is evidence that conceptions of good essays are so diverse that they cannot apply generically across the disciplines, as Chambers and Northedge (1999: 163) argue. In addition, essays may not be well suited to professional or creative fields of study where portfolios or self-reflective diaries may be better indicators of performance.

One method of reducing the assessment load for students and for staff has been to increase the incidence of final exams. Many argue that exams are the only truly 'reliable' form of student assessment because examinations are invigilated. However, examinations force the teacher to select from the curriculum the skills and content of performance to be measured and also to constrain strongly the circumstances in which performance can be expressed. Whether this approach can provide an accurate picture of student performance is debatable, though it may well consume fewer staff resources, especially if the examination relies on short answers or multiple choice questions. The introduction of open-book exams is a method of offsetting the limitations of examinations, but there is still the need to ensure that the assessment tasks are authentic, fair and reasonable.

Formative and summative assessment of more students

One of the issues with examinations as an efficient method of assessing more students with fewer resources is that examinations run counter to the idea of assessment as a mechanism for providing formative information about how performance might be improved. Of course, final examinations are final, so there is generally little point in expending valuable resources providing feedback that is inconsequential to the student. There are other ways to use exams though. For some teachers of large classes or cohorts, the introduction of online or printed quizzes, when thoughtfully and effectively implemented, provides a useful way for students to assess their own performance and identify areas for improvement.

Some teachers believe that, with assessing larger classes and cohorts, their efforts in formative assessment can really only be a labour of love, bringing extra effort and resources to that which is essential. But this idea is really a misconception. Formative assessment can be very effective because it can replace other forms of teaching, such as giving lectures with activities on which students receive formative feedback. We can, for example, provide students in a subject with the opportunity to get formative feedback from each other, and to have one or more chances to resubmit a major piece of work. Here the teacher needs to weigh up the balance of tasks especially designed for formative assessment and how these fit into the overall teaching and learning regime. In addition, the potential learning value of formative assessment tasks needs to be carefully considered. There are options but they require a little bit of lateral thinking, especially when it comes to keeping students informed about how they are progressing with their learning. For some teachers, formative assessment is a different activity from teaching!

9

Academic fraud and plagiarism

About academic fraud

There is some evidence in the related literature that academic fraud on assessment tasks, which includes plagiarism and cheating in examinations, is considered quite acceptable by students. There is speculation, too, that there is more cheating and plagiarism than ever before, although the evidence on this is yet to come in. Noah and Eckstein (2001), for example, argue that in some countries plagiarism and cheating are considered the norm. Alarmingly, in many surveys of undergraduate students, a considerable proportion admits to having plagiarized or cheated at some time during their studies. Overall, cheating may include such behaviours as writing answers on erasers, rulers or other writing implements, or on the inside of a cap, or on parts of the body such as the arms or legs; programming calculators; organizing seating arrangements for cheating purposes; and ghosting either in examinations or for assignments. It may include paying for exemplary essays and assignments to be ghost-written, using the work of another and passing it off as one's own or failing properly to acknowledge the contribution of other authors to an argument.

Plagiarism and collusion have always been matters of concern in the process of student assessment. With the advent of the Internet and the World Wide Web, both plagiarism and collusion are now technically easier than ever. Today Web sites containing directories of ready-to-use assignments proliferate, for example http://www.revise.it and http://www.essayfinder.com/, and any of a range of search engines can find a wealth of information on any topic. Students can readily download and insert academically relevant material into their own work without citation from the many sources found on the Web, most of which, it must be said, are not actually in the business of flaunting academic integrity. Collusion between students is also as easy as transferring electronic files – use of the word processor means no handwriting analysis and no laborious copying of worked solutions.

It may be tempting to think that, since this age-old problem has recently been brought more into focus through the availability of communication technologies, the solution might also be found through technical means (Carroll and Appleton, 2001). However, research in the United States seems to indicate that such technological approaches to detecting cheating are ultimately 'self-defeating' (Cole and Kiss, 2000), because they result in a large investment in technical solutions while, in parallel, students develop increasingly sophisticated methods of cheating. Practical strategies for minimizing the problems of authenticating students' work as their own depend on a balance of preventative measures that we outline in some detail in Part C.

What is plagiarism?

Plagiarism involves submitting work for assessment that is not the student's own. Plagiarized work, such as writing, computer programs, plans and recordings, is appropriated, stolen or purchased from another source and submitted as original work. In much of the related literature, the terms 'plagiarism' and 'cheating' are used interchangeably and, indeed, plagiarism is a form of cheating. But cheating can be different from plagiarism when it concerns cheating in examinations.

Today, with the ease of access to information provided by the World Wide Web, together with the flexible range of study options that include online assessment, the capacity for plagiarism is greater than ever before. Morgan and O'Reilly (1999: 79) note that increased reports of it have caused stern responses from educators around the world. One response of faculty is to institute invigilated examinations to ensure that students' work is their own; but even then, academic honesty is not guaranteed. In online settings the task of authentication becomes especially difficult, prompting educators to extreme measures such as requiring iris scanning or photographic recognition of the keyboard operator. The difficulty for educators is that the online submission of assessment tasks provides an easy avenue for students to submit work that is not their own for summative assessment. But before we become overwhelmed with concern, it is worth remembering that sophisticated forms of cheating and plagiarism have been around for as long as assessment tasks have been set!

At the heart of the issue is the long-held belief in higher education that academic honesty is central to the pursuit of knowledge. Professors who are found guilty of plagiarism in their published work can expect to throw in their careers if they are found out, because plagiarism is considered to be the lowest form of professional dishonesty. Claiming as one's own the work of another has sometimes cost the positions of very senior academics, so the scorn with which plagiarism is met applies to all – including students.

Generally speaking, institutions mandate policies and processes specifying how acts of plagiarism – or academic dishonesty – will be dealt with. In addition, the faculty may set procedures in place that are consistent with institutional ones. Usually, the severity of the punishment increases with the magnitude of the act, and also with successive acts. Central to the idea of punishment is the level of dishonesty detected, from automatic expulsion from the institution to resubmission of the assessment item. Why do punishments vary so much?

It is generally understood that, if students reproduce part of their source material but do not acknowledge the source appropriately, there may be many different underlying reasons for it. Perhaps the most obvious – and also the most contentious – is that students have misunderstood what was expected of them. Where students don't understand exactly what is expected, they may make minor errors or they may make more substantial ones that are harder to defend. Students from overseas backgrounds may fit easily into this category, but in addition are all those students – especially those in their first year of study – who do not know the disciplinary conventions of the field. The seriousness of the act may range in terms of the amount of the plagiarized material, but it may also vary for other reasons. For example, students may be required to work collaboratively but to submit independent assessment tasks, so that there is a risk of submitted work being similar or substantially the same. Yet another situation might involve open-book exams, where students bring along annotated texts and reproduce them. In cases such as these, the plagiarism may well be unintentional. At the other extreme is the student who continues to plagiarize even when identified and punished. And then there is the case of the academic who is found guilty of misappropriating passages in a major work; the institution would have no choice but to demand resignation. And so it goes with students who clearly understand what academic dishonesty is but still endeavour to carry it off successfully. The issue is one of intentionality, so there is a very clear, lawful distinction between the two though, of course, intentionality may be very difficult to prove.

Who plagiarizes?

In a recent Australian study, Marsden, Carroll and Neill (in press) found that 81 per cent out of almost 1,000 undergraduates admitted to plagiarism at some time during their studies, and that 41 per cent admitted to cheating on at least one occasion in an exam situation. Although these findings imply that a majority of students are *willing* to plagiarize, they say nothing about the degree of dishonesty most students would be prepared to initiate. There is a distinction between intentionality and unintentionality that may not always be clear; a student may only plagiarize a few terms or a string of words. Consequently, both the intention to plagiarize and the extent of the plagiarism contribute to the seriousness of the act. Culwin and Naylor (1995) developed a continuum from collaboration through collusion to copying to illustrate the degrees of intention to plagiarize. The range of reasons varies, but two scales of seriousness are the intention to plagiarize or cheat on the one hand and the extent of the offence on the other.

One view of plagiarism is that students who do not understand exactly what is expected of them are sometimes driven to plagiarism. When we take into consideration the various academic cultures with which undergraduates have to become familiar, and the different, frequently inexplicit expectations of academic staff, this view makes sense. For this reason, much of the related literature recommends that plagiarism be actively discouraged by the nature of assessment tasks, which should be as individualized and appropriate to the individual learner as possible. However, plagiarism may be unintentional for a range of reasons, among them that the student misunderstands the task, that assessment requirements are ambiguous or misleading, that students have not been taught how to communicate effectively in the subject, and so on.

It has been argued that intentionality may be blurred, for example when the distinction between group work and plagiarism is not made very clear to students. Zobel and Hamilton (2002: 25) asked students who had plagiarized why they had done so, and they found that motivations varied in intentionality and severity:

> students who have worked together a little too closely, and submit work that is not sufficiently independent; students who form cooperative groups to share around the work; and students who purchase solutions from outside sources. A major cause of plagiarism is students over committing to other activities (such as socializing, sports, earning income, or in some cases, additional study) and cheating in desperation when the workload becomes unmanageable. In addition, we... uncovered other issues such as deliberate entrapment as part of an attempt at coercion. Perhaps most seriously, a small number of students have completed subjects without undertaking any work or even attending the exam.

Institutions and faculties vary in their approaches to how plagiarists should be dealt with. In some institutions, identified plagiarists fail the subject concerned if the plagiarized material is substantial and intention is evident. Repeat offenders would be dealt with more severely, perhaps by being excluded from the institution. Zobel and Hamilton (2002) recommend that repeat offenders be dealt with more severely while first-time offenders should be given counselling and support so that they do not make the same mistake again. In making this recommendation, they recognize that it is possible that, in many first-offence cases, plagiarism is a desperate measure undertaken by students who either do not know how to perform what is expected of them or who cannot perform it because of other commitments or constraints.

Some studies identify the problem of plagiarism as being greater among international students, but it is worth noting that the evidence is equivocal on this point. Where there is evidence of higher rates of plagiarism among international students, they are also more likely to be affected by a range of mitigating circumstances, such as poverty, isolation and financial pressure requiring longer paid working hours and/or embarrassment at not knowing how to do the task. Marsden, Carroll and Neill (in press) found that younger full-time students were the most likely to plagiarize, that males plagiarized more than females and that plagiarism is more prevalent in some disciplines than in others. Perhaps most interesting is the finding that plagiarism was *more prevalent* in assessment tasks requiring *surface* approaches to learning (such as in fields where concrete knowledge has to be memorized), whereas *lower levels* of plagiarism were associated with assessment tasks requiring higher-order thinking skills and therefore *deep approaches* to learning tasks.

A range of considerations seems to underpin students' decisions to plagiarize. International students, who are often subject to all of the pressures identified above, could be called 'high-risk' simply because of their personal circumstances and the pressure upon them to achieve academically. In addition, Xueqin (2002) argues that copyright has little value in some cultures and that this is reflected in the willingness of some students to copy verbatim. Furthermore, for students in settings where group work is encouraged, the distinction between working together and handing in work essentially produced by others in the group may not be at all clear. These elements may contribute to various understandings of what is required from individuals in assessment tasks.

Attitudes to authentication

Perhaps the most complex group of plagiarists is the first-time offenders, because their intentionality is not always apparent. Recidivists probably should be dealt with more firmly because, whatever their circumstances, they are indisputably intending to cheat after getting away with it in the past – and being rewarded for it in their grades. For this reason, academic departments should keep detailed records of plagiarism and cheating in assessment. Zobel and Hamilton (2002: 25) recommend that these records of the offence and the ensuing punishment be widely publicized within faculties as a deterrent, though we wouldn't recommend identifying individual students, of course.

The related literature clearly identifies two different attitudes towards plagiarists. On the one hand there are those who see plagiarism and cheating, as well as falsification of any kind, as a serious violation of ethical standards. On the other, there are those who see it as a desperate measure undertaken by those who either do not understand how to use the work of other people in support of their own arguments or who are pressed to copy the work of others in order to avoid failure. Whether an educator holds one view or the other is likely to guide the commitment to detection, but there is a much more important issue to consider.

The environment in which students study and develop ethical sensibilities within particular fields of knowledge is largely sketched by educators, principally through assessment. Where educators set up competitive learning environments or heavy workloads, they are providing fertile ground for students to cut corners. Additionally, Noah and Eckstein (2001) argue that the 'vogue' associated with group work has encouraged collaboration but at the same time made it difficult for lecturers to identify ownership of submitted work. The problem is that conflicting messages are given to students when they are encouraged to piggyback and collaborate in some situations but not in others; and the distinction is difficult both for students and for assessors. The challenge for educators becomes one of teaching ethical standards and ensuring that students know what is expected of them – or not expected of them – in assessment tasks.

There may be faculty reluctance to reporting plagiarism. The reasons for this may be that faculties do not want the matter dealt with in the larger institution, or that teachers feel they are in the business of teaching subject matter and not moral values. Fain and Bates (2001), for example, note several reasons for these attitudes: the pressure upon faculties to increase retention; students being increasingly litigious; students threatening physical harm; teachers' fears about being the subject of prosecution; or teachers feeling that administrators will cast off their claims as being insignificant. They question why administrators don't do more to combat the problem of plagiarism.

In reality, detecting plagiarism is laborious and time-consuming. Many teachers are reluctant to adopt a view of students as probable cheats to be constantly checked and monitored. But, for some teachers, it is felt that it is inequitable to ignore plagiarism because it means that some students may achieve grades or awards for which they have done none of the work at all. The easy access to 'paper mills', or sites for purchasing completed essays and assignments, has exacerbated this concern, and reports of large proportions of cohorts caught plagiarizing from a few sources are not uncommon.

Whether a teacher adopts a suspicious perspective on student plagiarism should depend on there being a basis in evidence that triggers action, simply because we should accept that students are innocent until proven guilty. It is certainly the case that students – especially those from overseas – do make mistakes, and so do teachers when they encourage piggybacking in some situations but not in others. As we have noted, an important factor in punishment should be the intention and extent of the plagiarism but, when students become repeat offenders, it is difficult, if not impossible, to give them the benefit of the doubt.

Teaching students academic writing and correct attribution

Exhortations to academic departments to introduce and implement approved referencing style guides may work in some settings but, in others, academics claim that the standards are different in the various specialisms represented within the faculty. Is such an argument fair or reasonable? Parry (1998) outlines three dimensions of academic writing that vary across disciplines and which constrain the ways in which knowledge is expressed. These are the structure of argument, including the ways in which paragraphs are connected and logic is built; the conventions for citation and acknowledgement; and the ways in which the tacit or common knowledge of the field is expressed. Considering the depth and complexity of these dimensions, how prescriptive can a departmental style guide be, especially if the department is fairly mixed and/or transdisciplinary? Of course, when there are no guidelines for writing style at all, the likelihood of students working them out for themselves may well be very slim.

A confusing aspect of academic writing for students is that different genres of writing require various approaches to referencing. For example, writing for an exam, a thesis or a report each requires different levels of acknowledgement and, in addition, each field of study has its own conventions. The difference between collaboration and collusion also requires definition because students need to know where collaboration stops and individual assessment begins.

These issues are most clearly seen among international students and transdisciplinary students, who often do not receive adequate help to understand the cultural and academic expectations of correct citation and attribution in a particular field. In the case of the former, the problem is cross-cultural misunderstanding. In the case of the latter, the problem is also cross-cultural, but disciplinary rather than ethnically based.

Checklist for countering academic fraud and plagiarism

- What kind of institutional policies are in place to ensure that students clearly understand what is honest and what is less than honest in the performance of an assessment task?
- At the level of the faculty, is there a systematic way of integrating the teaching of correct writing and attribution methods?
- At the lecturer and teacher level, what practical strategies have been put in place to ensure that the curriculum design does not encourage plagiarism?
- Do the types of assessment tasks provide for formative opportunities so that students can learn by practice and feedback how to report what they know with honesty?
- Do the assessment tasks encourage cohort competition for grades or do they encourage personal improvement and ownership of ideas?

- Is there a staff member responsible for answering students' queries about plagiarism without prejudice?
- Is there pressure on international students or different social groups to conform to values with which they may not be familiar in assessment tasks?

10

Maintaining standards in a consumer market

Stories and myths about standards

In a landmark case in Australia, an academic reported to the press that 'soft' marking had taken place in his department to ensure that full-fee-paying students did not fail. The vice-chancellor sacked the staff member for misconduct immediately. After a lengthy legal battle, the university concerned was forced to reinstate the staff member even though no evidence of 'soft' marking was produced. The integrity of the university was at stake because the maintenance of academic standards is the foundation upon which an institution's reputation is built.

For many who have been teaching for some time, stories about soft marking and lowering standards come as no surprise. Is it because of recent trends towards the 'commodification' of higher education? Is it because of the trends of open entry and wider participation in higher education? Is it because the idea of a 'standard of performance' is not concrete – the assessment of performance is subjective? Or is it that assessment is not an exact science and so academics must remain vigilant about maintaining standards over time? Perhaps each of these contributes a little to the cynicism, and so it is worth exploring the underlying issues. However, it must be said that concern about the maintenance or decline of academic standards is not new. It certainly is not confined to the new, consumer-oriented focus of universities.

There are several key issues underlying the concept of 'standards of performance', just as there are several key assumptions that are commonly made about marking and grading. One concerns the mooted 'pressure' on academics to ensure that students are successful because they are paying high prices for their higher education. When students are construed as customers, the imperative has to be to sell them a good educational ticket for their investment. The *NTEIU* v *University of Wollongong* case (2001) reported above is one such example of how this pressure might work. However, evidence that this pressure exists or is growing is equivocal. At a broader level, there is some concern that, with the huge increases in student numbers, many students who would not have been admitted to higher education two decades ago now have access to do so. Much of the concern about the maintenance of standards derives from this development: if the same proportion of students is passing and being awarded degrees, either the universities are providing far greater supplementary support to get students through their awards or standards have slipped to enable the students to earn their awards.

The kind of argument presented above ignores the kinds of professional safeguards that academe has always set in place to ensure that standards are maintained. In relation to research, those safeguards are obvious. Research achievements are open to scholarly critique and appraisal. Professional networks actively maintain a watching brief on the development of the knowledge base and its derivative professional and academic cultures. In this way, the nature of the knowledge base constrains and is constrained by the ways in which new knowledge is made and reported, as Becher (1987) and Becher and Trowler (2001) have shown.

In teaching, which as many observers have reported is ostensibly a more private activity than research, there tends to be less scholarly critique and fewer opportunities for professional networks to assert particular values and conventions. While there is a strong body of research on student learning, as we discussed in Chapter 1, it is largely limited to generic observations of students' conceptions of learning and the influences upon those conceptions, and also of teachers' conceptions of teaching and the influences upon those conceptions. Less accessible are studies of teaching in particular disciplinary settings, including standards and values, and learning cultures, although these do exist (see, for example, Hativa and Marincovic, 1995). The issue here is clear. University teachers need to be professionally well informed if they are to be confident about the standards of performance they set. But how do they do this?

The tension between maintaining standards and teaching for success

There has been a cultural shift in universities towards corporate values and client-centredness, where students are treated as paying customers. Higher education students are having to pay higher prices for their tuition in their own countries of origin. In addition, the market for international students has grown enormously, in particular the market for Asian students to study abroad. These students are full fee paying and they come with expectations of earning their university awards in minimum time. Furthermore, more students are returning to higher education at different times in their lives as they embrace lifelong learning.

The increasingly diverse and heterogeneous composition of students provides a dilemma for university teachers. To which level of ability should teaching be pitched? To which performance standards should assessment tasks be geared? One way of addressing this fundamental question is to move towards identifying performance standards and making these clear and explicit to students ahead of their undertaking the assessment task. But this remedy is complicated by the nature of knowledge in academe: the knowledge bases of academic disciplines including teaching and learning are not static. They are dynamic and constantly under redevelopment, so that standards can be articulated, and they need to be reviewed and updated from time to time. And so, of course, university teachers are still faced with the problem of performance standards. How do we know what they should be? How do we ensure that assessment tasks reflect them?

Another way of addressing the problem of setting standards is to benchmark standards and assessment tasks – with colleagues in the department or in the discipline, or externally, with those in similar institutions. While this kind of approach takes more time and resources, it is also potentially more rewarding, in terms of affirming existing practices, in terms of contributing to the knowledge base and in terms of formative development.

As we have discussed, there is a long history of comment in academe about the declining standards of undergraduate student performance but the empirical evidence for the decline is yet to come in. Whether or not academic standards have risen or fallen over time is not really the primary concern of the university teacher. Far more relevant to the student, the profession, the teacher and the institution is whether assessment standards are appropriate and well informed by the profession. The primary concern should be whether standards compare favourably with those in similar institutions or against appropriate benchmarks. Because teaching may still be considered a relatively private activity – even given the recent importance attributed to it through quality agencies and audits – benchmarking has to be pursued by individual teachers because the parameters for well-informed teaching are not explicit in the professions in the way that parameters for research achievements are.

Making assessment standards explicit

The answer lies in the scholarship of teaching because it depends upon teachers keeping up to date with their subject matter and benchmarking standards with other institutions and within academic departments. The determination of standards of performance is subjective, but it is informed by a working knowledge of the field, its theoretical underpinnings and antecedents, its methods and its applications. When the standards are determined and then clearly articulated to students ahead of their performing an assessment task, it may be described as standards–based assessment.

However, the determination of standards is complex and requires qualitative descriptions of performance against identified learning aims.

Do assessment tasks reflect standards?

To reflect identified performance standards properly, assessment items should be closely aligned, as Biggs (1999a) has argued. In norm-referenced assessment, standards are based on the expected performance of the cohort, on the basis of probability, being distributed a certain way. Performance is assessed subjectively against standards that may not be explicit or that may be assumed by the assessor. When the performance of the entire cohort is ranked, relative performance by default sets the performance standard, which could not have been anticipated in advance by the students.

Not only does norm referencing seem to be unfair, it is also unreasonable if a cohort is not very large because the probability of achieving a normally distributed set of grades is low for small to medium numbers. But norm referencing does have its advantages. If class sizes are large, it permits the coordinator to develop an overall profile of performance by performance categories. It also has the advantage that it can be justified in relative terms: 'You achieved a "C" because that was the quality of your performance relative to the others in the group.'

One concern sometimes put forward by university teachers about making standards explicit is that students will only work to the standard that is set. When standards are explicit, they are then fixed and may have the effect of discouraging innovation, creativity and performance that are outside the norm. Another concern is that, if standards are explicit enough, then every student who completes all the learning and teaching tasks should pass the subject. Performance standards should always be worded so that there are qualitative differences in performance that distinguish between unsatisfactory or fail and satisfactory or pass. From pass there should be qualitatively different stages reaching to excellence or high distinction. In Part C advice is provided about how to develop descriptors for performance standards in this vein, and which do not constrain performance above and beyond the stages described.

In this chapter the complex web of issues concerning setting and maintaining performance standards for assessment have been explored. The main theme concerns the need to be well informed as a teacher about professional standards and ways of measuring them. What are the principal issues for you? Do they concern teaching to diverse cohorts? Is benchmarking or being well informed about standards a concern?

11

Accountability and the quality agenda: evaluative purposes of assessment

The 'quality agenda' sweeping higher education has brought with it a new focus on the quality of teaching and learning, so that assessment strategies and the learning outcomes they measure have been brought under scrutiny in many institutions. The main concern for teachers is that they need to be able to demonstrate the quality of processes and outcomes of assessment. To do this, they need to be confident about the validity of their assessment practices. On what basis will they be able to do this?

Earlier in Part A, we identified the importance of assessment tasks being aligned to the teaching and learning activities and to the desired learning outcomes. Of course this is important, but how do we know that we have chosen the right learning outcomes for a programme? The answer seems to lie in the identification of core skills and attributes that provide an overarching framework for the desired learning outcomes for every subject making up a programme.

Core skills and attributes

We have discussed the notion of core skills and attributes in the context of valid assessment. Now we pick them up once more to take into account the extent to which they may derive from employer groups, professional groups, academic disciplines, the community, the institution, the department and even graduates themselves. Essentially, the identification of core skills and attributes is important because, without them, teachers have no way of determining whether they are teaching 'the right thing'. Indeed, unless assessment regimes are based upon identified core skills and attributes, teachers cannot be confident that they are assessing what their students should be learning.

Whether or not our intentions with student assessment are arbitrary depends largely upon whether we are working strategically towards an identifiable set of core skills and attributes (sometimes known as generic skills) that students should be able to demonstrate when they complete their award. For example, medical doctors will have to comply with national registration requirements, professional expectations and community demands that can only be learnt and assessed during their professional studies. All of these demands, when taken together, may be met by identifying an appropriate set of skills and attributes. Similarly, a set of core skills and attributes may be identified for all of the professions and it is also the case as far as academic disciplines are concerned. Becher (1989) has outlined these for the academic professions in considerable detail.

It is important for individual institutions to articulate desirable skills and attributes that will be engendered in their graduates, too. Within higher education systems, institutions seek prestige so that their courses will be competitive. To do this, they need to have a special 'brand' that is recognizable in the marketplace. Students like to shop around and enrol in courses that they believe will give them value and a quality award. As a result, institutions need to specify what it is that their institution offers that is unique. The identification of core skills and attributes at the level of the institution is also essential to having all those working in the institution aiming towards the same kind of educational outcomes.

At the level of the academic department, the idea of a brand becomes much more complex. While fitting in with the institution's overall mission, individual programmes must seek to achieve educational outcomes that fit with the profession at large, the discipline and the community. A law faculty might seek to engender very different kinds of educational outcomes to those of a marine science faculty. But many of the values and attributes they seek to develop in their students will be generically the same. While they can be expressed in the same kind of language, they are manifested differently in different settings. The development of critical thinking and reflective practice is a good example. In principle, the meaning we construct might vary across different settings, but many values and attributes remain generically the same.

If programme and course objectives are good, then they have merit in terms of what the professions and educators – and institutions – are trying to achieve. It is in this way that assessment is connected to the idea of students developing core skills during the course of their programmes of study. The identification of core skills to be achieved in an educational award leads to the identification of overall objectives for a programme and of particular objectives for a course that fits into a programme. If we take a grading scale such as fail, pass, credit, distinction, high distinction, the scales represent levels of achievement that have been constructed. But these *constructs* have no meaning unless they are derived from course objectives that in turn fit into programme objectives, all of which are consistent with clear core skills and attributes that are articulated and understood by the staff. In Part B we discuss eight constructs that represent the range of core skills and attributes embedded in university studies.

Documenting the quality of assessment practices

While institutions might have policies and practices as well as checkpoints in place to show that their assessment practices are internally consistent and appropriate, the documentation of these processes is not always what it should be. Insofar as assessment practices are concerned, we have laid a trail by which assessment may be checked. From the articulation of core skills and attributes to the assessment practices within a course topic, there will need to be a coherence that is obvious. For example, the assessment tasks in a law course will need to be consistent with the desired learning outcomes for that topic. These in turn need to fit into the overall objectives for the course and for the broader programme. Overarching these will be an articulated set of core skills and attributes that fit with the institution's mission and goals. In addition, there will be checks and balances at the subject, programme and award levels to ensure that assessment is fair, internally consistent and appropriate. Thus there will be a document trail through policy and process. But how do we know that these document quality outcomes?

This is where the systematic review from the profession, employers, the discipline and the community should be provided for, and their feedback taken into account so that assessment practices indeed reflect the demands and expectations of these groups. Institutions of course need to enforce policy to ensure that critical review takes place periodically and that this is organized through the usual institutional administration. Without going into detailed quality assurance processes and procedures, which will of course vary across institutions and national systems, we can see that, in a nutshell, student assessment is not arbitrary. What is assessed and how it is carried out are very much the concern of a broad range of stakeholders, all of whom must be taken into consideration.

Evaluative uses of student assessment

One aspect of student assessment that is worth mentioning briefly concerns how student assessment may be used as an indicator of teaching performance for teachers and in their broader faculty contexts. While respecting the needs of students to learn and gain certification, assessment can also be used as an indicator of whether or not the teaching methods and strategies have been effective. In completing the assessment tasks, students are communicating to reflective teachers. The power of individual assessment items should be reviewed regularly in order to determine how well the assessment task reflects student performance. If there is a mismatch, the reflective teacher can identify it. For example, in a multiple choice test, items that are disproportionately correct or incorrect can indicate either a weakness in the assessment question or an issue with what students have learnt. Ideally, this information can then be used to inform changes in teaching approaches that help students in their understanding, skills and knowledge development or to inform changes in the appropriateness of the assessment item. In distance education, the effective evaluation of assessment tasks is especially important because assignments may be the only form of communication between students and teaching staff (or subject coordinators).

The role of assessment in maintaining standards is also very important. Assessment may be seen as defining the curriculum (Rowntree, 1987; Ramsden, 1992), because in effect it provides instructions to students about how and what they should study. For example, the assessment task may require students to work as individuals or in study groups. It may also specify the learning activities to be undertaken, such as self-assessment quizzes or reflective journals etc. However, when assessment tasks do not require certain approaches and specify tasks clearly, students will have to guess at what is required of them. Where we find students' performance on assessment is at odds with what we are aiming for as teachers, there is a case for examining our approach to the objectives of the subject and the overall objectives of the course.

Whose interests are served? How to balance conflicting needs?

Perhaps the most difficult question about assessment concerns its stakeholders; whose interests does assessment serve? Increasingly, in the related literature, a student-centred perspective is being adopted, even in the United States, where this view has been slow to overtake a long-term emphasis on institutional accountability (Angelo, 1999). We have looked at the inherent difficulties in attempting to unify formative and summative assessment; formative assessment is a very powerful teaching tool that loses its strength once it becomes a measurement tool. It is clear that formative assessment provides strong building blocks for learning that is experiential, authentic, encouraging and progressively developing. But formative assessment must at some point — or points — give rise to a summative assessment of achievement at a predetermined stage of the learning process. Eventually formative assessment, which forms the platform for teaching in a course, must give rise to measurement of desired learning outcomes. This balance is exemplified in the effective distance education package, in which formative assessments are set that build upon one another so that skills and knowledge can be accretively developed and constructive advice about how to improve performance is provided at given intervals. Formative assessment is woven into the teaching and learning activities of the course so that at one or maybe two points a summative judgement can be made about achievement. In this case, the interests of the student and the faculty can equally be met.

To strike a balance in developing an assessment regime, it is useful to start with the points at which summative assessment is necessary. This may be at the end of the course, or it could be at intervals during the course, to ease the stress placed upon students when a final grade is yielded from one assessment task such as an examination. Sometimes teachers ask their students how they would like to be summatively assessed. Once the summative assessments have been determined, teachers can work backwards from there, devising learning tasks on which they will receive formative feedback. The checkpoint for the teacher is 'Whose interests does this assessment task serve?' If it isn't absolutely clear, then there are plenty of unintended outcomes that can crop up.

Part B

Assessing key learning outcomes

Introduction to Part B

In Part A, we looked at some of the broad foundation principles of assessment and explored some contemporary issues and themes confronting teachers. Having established this framework, we now focus on an area of key concern in assessment – choosing the right methods to assess students' achievements.

There is no shortage of books on assessment methods and tasks. What's different about this book? Our concern with the traditional focus on methods is that it tends to overlook the vital importance of the disciplinary context and the overall learning outcomes that teachers want to achieve. Using a traditional 'A to Z of assessment methods' text, newcomers to higher education are likely to shop around for methods that they 'like' or those that they are most familiar with from their own undergraduate days. They may tend to view assessment as an add-on event, something additional, rather than integral, to teaching and learning.

In this part, we argue that, when selecting methods for assessment, it is vital for teachers to be clear about the disciplinary and generic skills and attributes that they are developing, the overall aims of the programme, and the particular aims and desired learning outcomes in their subject. If assessment tasks are not congruent with these broader goals, if they are not tailored most explicitly to draw from students the desired outcomes, then, at best, it is an opportunity lost. At worst, it can prompt counter-productive learning and may confuse and frustrate students.

For example, an essay can be chosen as a method of assessment for a variety of reasons. It may be used to develop and assess students' analytical and evaluative abilities, or it may be shaped primarily to test students' written communication skills and ability to order information coherently. Similarly a journal may require students to evaluate and synthesize experience, or perhaps simply to observe and document phenomena. Group work may be facilitated to develop and assess problem-solving skills or to develop students' ability to negotiate difference. Often it is not so much the assessment *method* that counts, but the particular *emphasis* that it is given, which prompts the appropriate responses from students. This emphasis particularly includes the rationale and marking criteria that convey to students what is really wanted in an assessment task and why.

For this reason, we have steered away from 'methods' as the primary focus of this part. Rather we have looked at methods through the lens of *learning outcomes*. In this respect, we are greatly indebted to the efforts of Nightingale, TeWiata, Toohey, Ryan, Hughes and Magin in their 1996 publication, *Assessing Learning in Universities*. Their project entailed collaborative research and consultation to determine the kinds of broad learning outcomes considered desirable across programmes of higher education in Australia, and devised an excellent organizing principle for assessment based on clusters of abilities as follows:

- thinking critically and making judgements;
- solving problems and developing plans;
- performing procedures and demonstrating techniques;
- managing and developing oneself;
- accessing and managing information;
- demonstrating knowledge and understanding;
- designing, creating, performing;
- communicating.

In addition to our debt to Nightingale *et al*, we also draw on the work of Becher (1989), whose contribution to our understanding of the nature of knowledge across disciplinary settings is infused into each of the eight learning outcomes. We acknowledge that each learning outcome will be expressed differently in the different disciplinary settings of the sciences, the humanities, the social sciences and the applied professions, and that transdisciplinary fields of study are even more complex with respect to intended learning outcomes.

We have drawn heavily on the organizing principle of Nightingale *et al* (1996) throughout Part B, applying our own internal structure as follows:

1. *Introduction* – a broad overview of the particular ability or learning outcome. What is it and why is it valued?
2. *Learning outcome in the disciplines* – an exploration of the different forms that the learning outcomes might take in the disciplines. The aim of this section is to reinforce the vital role of context and disciplinary convention in relation to the forms that assessment takes.
3. *Assessment methods* – an overview of the range of assessment methods commonly employed to assess this learning outcome, and how they are facilitated. We do not assume a face-to-face teaching context. Where relevant, we refer to distance and online variations of methods.
4. *Cases* – the cases provide windows into how particular methods have been applied across disciplines. They are not fully worked case studies with all details of the assessment schemes. Instead they are brief snapshots intended

to illustrate a particular method with sufficient detail for teachers to adapt it to their own context. The cases are written by the authors as a synthesis of our practice and that of our colleagues. Where they represent someone else's work in large measure, then appropriate citations have been made.

5. *Implications for teaching* – this is the final piece that completes the picture. It is difficult to separate assessment and teaching – they are natural allies. We take the view that assessment tasks are only purposeful to the degree that they are supported by congruent teaching. By the time students undertake a task, they should be clear about what's expected of them and have had the opportunity to discuss and practise the task with developmental feedback.

The only significant difficulty with the organizing principles adopted here is one of overlap. The same assessment method may apply to a number of learning outcomes although, as discussed, the emphasis is often very different. As this is a handbook that is really designed for dipping in and out of as needs be, we feel it is better to have some overlap and minor repetition rather than complex cross-referencing systems.

12

Communicating

Introduction

Every assessment task is an exercise in communication. Teacher judgement is, to a large extent, based on how well students communicate their responses to a task, and, from the students' point of view, success partly depends on whether they understand how to approach their assessment tasks. Undergraduates are expected to learn academic conventions of communication, particularly those in their disciplinary fields, in order to express knowledge and demonstrate the achievement of desired learning outcomes in any of the domains of learning.

To say that communication in one form or another is all-pervasive in higher education, as in every sphere of life, is to state the obvious. Communication conventions are continuously assessed all the way through undergraduate and postgraduate education, and grades have been shown to reflect whether there is a match of structure and style between teacher expectations and student responses to assessment tasks. A study of engineering students' oral presentations (Dannels, 2002) found that grades depended partly on how well students used a particular results-oriented structure to organize their oral presentations. Students can stand or fall on how they express their knowledge and ideas, but learning outcomes and marking criteria may not always specify expectations about how they should use academic communication styles to improve their results.

Many of the conventions governing how students should communicate orally or in writing are not explicit, although disciplinary conventions for writing and speaking are understood and used by academics and experienced students (Parry, 1998). A study by James (2000: 354) showed that some transferable communication skills, for example the way language is used in a 'good' essay, or the structure of a 'good' oral presentation, are a matter of 'collective received wisdom' and might not appear in the marking criteria given to students before they attempt the task.

The characteristics and transferable features of, for example, a good essay or an effective oral presentation can be difficult to articulate (James, 2000). Such conventions are sometimes considered to be generic, but many studies have shown that disciplinarity has a huge influence on how knowledge is expressed in higher education (Neumann, 2001). Students also want to know what their particular lecturers and tutors are looking for in relation to how they should communicate in their assignments and examinations because there are individual differences of emphasis among academics as well as between disciplines.

What is communicating?

Human communication is about imparting or exchanging thoughts, opinions or information by speech or writing, in visual form or by some other means. Effective communication evokes understanding of what the originator has attempted to impart (Moore, 1993). In higher education, it is also about how knowledge is conveyed to a listener or a reader, in a variety of ways using different media (Nightingale, 1996a). Communication also occurs through works of art, performance and drama to communicate aesthetic values, ideas or emotion. Academics and students communicate their ideas in a great many ways, including:

- *oral communication*: tutorial or client presentation, viva voce, debate, argument, advocacy, moot court, interview, clinical interaction;
- *written communication*: essay, report, diary, journal, creative writing, written accompaniment to an oral presentation, presentation of scientific results;
- *visual communication*: posters, graphics, PowerPoint slides, overhead transparencies, technical drawings, diagrams, charts or other illustrations in hard copy or online;
- *online communication*: synchronous and asynchronous communication through e-mail, discussion groups, student intranet activities.

These methods of communication are complex and need to be situated in their context and the academic purpose that derives from curriculum objectives and assessment tasks. Also, the ways in which students can demonstrate communication skills vary according to the mode of educational delivery. Teachers have to design ways to assess oral communication (if learning outcomes require it) for distance and online students as well as those who can attend classes on-campus. For instance, telephone conferencing can be used for oral examinations when students cannot attend face to face.

Online communication has reduced the isolation felt by distance students, especially when small groups work as project or study groups. Distance students can be part of intellectual and learning communities in a way that was not possible when their communication was paper based (Parry and Dunn, 2000). Yeoman (1996) has argued that students will communicate online whether it is assessed or not, because the process can be so stimulating for them. Her findings suggest that not only is assessment a powerful tool for indicating to students what they should learn but, in online courses, such communication can also be used to direct how they should learn. To be effective, though, online communication and group collaboration in this medium should be task based, and this requires teacher organization and the allocation of roles to students (Pincas, 1997).

Communicating in the disciplines

Induction and socialization into a discipline is mostly conducted through its ways of communicating and using its language. Most frequently, for students, their learning is focused on writing in a way that is acceptable in the field. Language is of immense importance to disciplinary groups of academics, because their individual and collective knowledge, values and traditions are interpreted and expressed through language (Becher, 1989).

Communication in disciplinary contexts might not be taught overtly, but is learnt by students in several ways: through trial and error when appropriate style is rewarded, with feedback on how to improve, by emulating the type of communication that is valued by their academic teachers or by becoming familiar with scholarly journals in their field. Learning how to communicate in higher education is not about developing skills in isolation, but about acquiring knowledge about how and why particular communication is valued and also about the application of that knowledge to practical situations (Burton and Dimbleby, 1990).

Academic writing is mysterious to many undergraduates until they discover the overarching principles that they must follow. Their teachers often cannot articulate the rules and principles, but 'know them when they see them'. According to Parry (1998), the three most obvious domains of writing style are:

- the way the argument is structured and styled;
- the conventions for citation and acknowledgement; and
- the type of terminology used.

In science, undergraduates spend a lot of time learning the rules of academic communication through the precise structure of laboratory reports and by seeing, from the beginning of their course, models of the way arguments should be constructed. In the other disciplinary groupings the structures are not so clear cut and can be more individualistic. In the social sciences it is a matter of finding out whether an argument tends more towards the humanities (built on theoretical or conceptual perspectives) or more towards science (built on concrete research findings) and then choosing which model to follow. How knowledge is reported changes with the nature of the knowledge base and disciplinary paradigms. The following are some examples from groupings of disciplines derived from Parry's (1998) analysis of ways to articulate knowledge orally and in writing:

Science

In the sciences, written reports are information based and argument is developed by building new knowledge from what is previously known. Students learn to communicate within the shared theoretical paradigm of experimental science. Scientific writing is technical and concrete, and knowledge is expressed by reporting and explaining what has been found. Students learn from the beginning of their studies how to structure writing tasks in the proper way.

Social science

In the social sciences students have a more complex task in learning disciplinary ways of communicating because there is not one single paradigm as in the sciences. Social science students have to deal with coexisting but competing theoretical frameworks, some more like the sciences and some more like the humanities. Students learn to construct an argument that is designed to persuade the reader to a point of view by presenting evidence from readings and research. They often learn written communication by trial and error.

Applied professions

In the applied professions, as in the social sciences, there are different theoretical frameworks. Students learn to communicate through reporting knowledge and asserting what is important to take the reader forward. Again, they often learn communication skills through trial and error.

Arts and humanities

In the arts and the humanities knowledge is expressed in an individualistic, personal style. Students learn to communicate through constructing an argument that is designed to persuade the reader that their topic and its consequences are of interest and that the writer's insights will generate parallel insights in the reader. In some branches of the humanities (for example, creative writing or journalism) students have some freedom to develop their own style of written or oral communication.

Assessment methods

'The problem with trying to separate assessment of content from assessment of communication skills is that it fails to recognize just how deeply intertwined are the effectiveness of communication and a student's understanding of the content' (Nightingale, 1996a: 207). Oral and written communication skills are integral to the demonstration of effective learning in higher education, as we have seen. Students who communicate well and in a way that is congruent with their discipline's language and style will probably gain higher grades than those who do not possess these skills. Teacher perceptions of student confidence in communicating can affect grades, as McCroskey, McCroskey and Richmond (2002) assert; students who are apprehensive about the communication demands of education are inhibited in their learning. The process of struggling with how to express difficult concepts can also affect the quality of communication, especially in writing (Nightingale, 1996a: 209). These are factors to consider when preparing to assess students on their communication skills.

Communication is always present in student assessment, but the emphasis is different depending on the purpose of the assessment task. If the purpose is to communicate knowledge and ideas, appropriate communication style will probably be included in the grading. Often communication is the main purpose of the assessment task (for example, a task to assess practical counselling skills). As with the assessment of other learning outcomes, the alignment of assessment tasks with desired learning outcomes is a key element of integrating assessment and directing student learning approaches.

One problem is that when students cannot express what they know it seems as if they do not know it. Essay writing, for example, involves skills without which students cannot demonstrate their understanding (Gibbs, 1995). When does the teacher give them the benefit of the doubt? Some would say that international students whose first language is not English or adults returning to study should be given some leeway in the early stages of their studies, but this has enormous implications for the reliability of academic results.

Oral presentations

In face-to-face environments assessment regimes can include oral presentations to large classes or smaller tutorial groups, and, in subjects that are primarily about communication, oral assessments such as simulations of professional situations are standard. The quality of the delivery of a presentation and its content can be assessed holistically or piecemeal, or the assessment may be through a written reflection of the presentation. In many situations class participation is assessed sometimes by attendance only because of the difficulty of agreeing about assessment criteria, but there are techniques of measuring the quality of participation through self-, peer and teacher evaluation, some of which are discussed in Part C.

There are several issues concerning the assessment of oral communication that need to be considered. Among these are that:

- Some students can become over-anxious when giving oral presentations and suffer performance anxiety of such severity that it can affect their results.
- Students can dominate in discussion or become highly competitive when class participation is assessed.

- The reliability of marking of oral communication is often questioned because the criteria are considered to be subjective.

(from Nightingale, 1996a: 239–40)

These concerns need to be examined when tasks to assess oral communication are designed. Rehearsal and practice can help reduce student anxiety in the 'real' assessment task (see Cases 12.1 and 12.2 below); ground rules can be developed to ensure that students have equal opportunities to participate (see Case 12.3); and reliability can be increased when marking criteria and standards are negotiated with students or clearly explained to them (again see Case 12.3).

Case 12.1: Oral presentation in engineering

Engineering students in their final year gave an oral presentation in the form of a simulation: they had to 'sell' an engineering idea to a 'client'.

Students had worked in teams to design, construct, test and implement a design product for industry. There was an explicit learning outcome about communication: 'Students will have the skills, material and background to effectively communicate about design.' The culmination of the project was the oral presentation. Students made the presentation in their teams. Each team planned their presentation together, negotiated who would lead each section, designed their visuals (including a PowerPoint presentation) and decided how to present the prototype of their product.

Before the actual presentation, students were required to rehearse it in front of their lecturers to gain feedback. Some of the points lecturers made at the rehearsal were:

- *Keep it simple*. Prepare the presentation with straightforward language that will be easily understood by your audience. Translate your engineer jargon into simple words.
- *Give the results first*. Engineering is results oriented. Present the results at the beginning of the presentation because members of the audience are not interested in lengthy discussions about why a particular design was chosen.
- *The visuals speak for themselves*. Make the visuals sophisticated. They are the critical illustration of design claims, ideas and the products described. Include effective graphics in the PowerPoint display. Use physical examples if this will help your presentation.

Those who finally gained high grades for the oral presentation organized their presentation in a particular way to show they could 'speak like an engineer' (from Dannels, 2002). They had followed the advice gained in the rehearsal.

Simulated professional practice

In some fields, especially the applied professions, students need to develop interpersonal communication skills as well as other communication skills, in order to interact successfully with clients. It has long been recognized that written assessment tasks are inadequate for assessing these skills, although written tasks are effective in allowing students to demonstrate their knowledge and understanding of theoretical frameworks, and their analytical and problem-solving skills. The assessment task of simulated professional activity outlined in Case 12.2 is in the health field, but could be adapted for a number of other areas where interpersonal communication is an important element of the profession.

The goal of tasks that assess interpersonal communication skills through performance-based assignments is to 'enhance students' professional communication skills in order to prepare them for their work with clients or patients' (Smit and van der Molen, 1996). Students are placed in a simulated professional situation with a person who takes the part of patient or client, to test their communication skills under as near to professional conditions as possible.

Case 12.2: Simulated counselling interview

This type of assessment differs from role-play in that the 'patient' or 'client' is very thoroughly prepared for the role. In this particular instance a script for the 'client' (another student) was standardized and rehearsed, including non-verbal communication and intonation. The event was a counselling interview and it took place in a room as near as possible to a clinical setting. Students practised under assessment conditions prior to the examination, and were able to view and gain tutor feedback from a videotape of the practice session.

The actual examination mirrored the rehearsal except that students had a different 'client' with a different history, who exhibited different non-verbal and interpersonal behaviour. A rating form, based on accepted qualities of effective counselling interviews, was completed by the student, the 'patient' and the tutor.

The value of oral assessments such as this simulation is that students are able to put the interpersonal communication skills they have learnt into practice in a professional setting. They learn to manage the kinds of interpersonal issues that actually confront professionals in their field, and through rehearsals can learn to handle the anxieties that naturally exist not only in examination conditions but in real life.

(adapted from Smit and van der Molen, 1996)

Assessment of class participation

As we noted earlier, when class participation is assessed it is often simply the students' attendance that is measured, but high-quality student contributions through discussion and debate can play a large part in their own learning and that of their fellow students. In the following example from law (Case 12.3), students were assessed on attendance and also on the quality of their contributions to class discussions on a number of specific criteria.

Case 12.3: Class participation in law

One of the learning outcomes for a law subject was that students should show that they 'comprehend the law and represent it accurately, analyse legislation and cases, apply the law to complex factual situations, discern the principles and policies which underlie legal rules, subject the present law to critical review, and develop innovative answers to hard cases'.

An assessment task to assess class participation in relation to this outcome was designed. Lecturers developed descriptions of 'typical' standards of performance (lowest to highest level), published them to students before classes commenced and used them for grading purposes:

1. Unacceptable level of absence from seminars. Participation virtually non-existent. Little, if any, preparation apparent. Unable to answer questions or to clarify vague or ambiguous answers. Obvious lack of commitment to the course.
2. Irregular attendance without explanation. Inconsistent preparation. Misses the point of questions. Answers are unclear, disjointed, illogical. No apparent attempt to relate issues together.
3. Regular attendance, with reasonable level of preparation. Generally successful in answering questions, but in a patchy way, eg principles and concepts may not be fully grasped or clearly explained. When prompted, can usually explain the point with greater clarity.
4. Regular attendance and preparation. Either a lot of participation of variable quality or less participation but good quality. Demonstrates reasonable comprehension of issues. Able to clarify responses if requested.
5. Regular attendance. Consistent high-quality participation based upon thorough preparation. Evidence of a clear understanding of issues. High analytical skills. Able to cross-relate issues where necessary. Evidence of capacity to develop innovative answers.

(from Teaching and Learning Unit, 1998)

Essays

Much academic communication is in writing and there is constant debate, not only across disciplinary fields but within faculties, about the proportion of marks to be allocated to written communication in assessment tasks. Often the criteria for assessment of written communication in essays are not made explicit to students who learn appropriate essay style through trial and error.

Essays are probably used more often than other assessment tasks in coursework and examinations. They are used to provide a vehicle for students to demonstrate their understanding, knowledge, critical thinking and problem solving. They are also used to assess students' levels of development in communicating using the writing conventions and stylistic norms of their disciplines including the structure of the argument, citation and acknowledgement and the ways in which evidence and theory are used.

Case 12.4: Communication through a sociology essay

An essay was chosen in the first year subject 'The sociology of work' to allow new undergraduate students to demonstrate their level of academic writing skills as much as to demonstrate knowledge and critical analysis.

Many of the students in this subject were studying at a distance and, although it was allocated a small percentage of the marks for the subject, this assessment task's main purpose was to allow tutors to judge the students' level of academic writing skills. By making the essay an element (albeit a small element) of the summative assessment regime, teachers were confident that it would be submitted by the distance students. It was timed to come about one-third of the way through a semester so that students would have time to reflect on their teacher's feedback before submitting a second assignment in the subject. The essay topic asked students to 'critically examine different ways of approaching the social nature of work'.

On-campus students were prepared for the task by a face-to-face session with an academic skills adviser who specialized in social science writing, while distance students participated in an online question-and-answer forum with the same adviser that took place during the course of one week. They were all given an annotated essay by a past student as an exemplar for the kind of academic writing that was expected.

This assessment task had both summative and formative purposes. It was allocated a proportion of marks for the subject (summative) while it was set early in the semester to allow the teacher to provide detailed feedback (formative assessment) to help students to improve their performance in future assessment tasks for the subject.

Laboratory reports

Scientists spend a significant proportion of their time writing reports, memoranda and grant applications. The importance of this writing skill is therefore not underestimated by the scientific community, and numerous guides to writing laboratory reports are available in print and on the Internet, as well as those provided by academic departments. The main principles to consider in writing laboratory reports are in the areas of structure, format and style. Within this framework students will need to understand the function of each of the sections of the report and how and why they cohere together. The structure of a laboratory report differs from the structure of clinical reports or financial reports, and the same applies to the style of language and conventions for citation. It is important for students to be guided from early on in their study to understand the appropriate conventions and begin to develop their mastery of the writing skills that they will rely upon in their future careers.

Bibliographic software such as EndNote™ lists over 600 referencing styles, illustrating how many differences are possible in scholarly journals. Students need to be alerted to this diversity of styles because it is possible they will mix them up when they come to write references themselves. It is a good idea for an academic unit to decide upon a single style guide, so students and teachers can adhere to one style and expectations can be made explicit. However, it is surprisingly difficult to get academics, who may be drawn from a wide range of specializations, to agree to conform to one style, even though it is helpful to students.

In addition to the overall format and style of scientific reports, the specific form, length, content and emphasis in a report are determined by its purpose and the target audience for which it is being written. However, having highlighted the variations in disciplinary styles and bibliographic styles, it is also important to stress that the structure of most scientific reports is similar, each containing sections that describe the nature of the problem, methods, procedures, results and discussion of a project or investigation. This relative standardization of reports goes some way to facilitating a broad readership of reports across the sciences, as well as making the writing of reports more efficient.

Case 12.5: Laboratory reports in exercise science

Students in an exercise science programme were required to write a report about their laboratory work during four weeks in the middle of the semester. During these weeks an experiment was undertaken to see what effects the intake of oxygen has upon the energy levels of sufferers of chronic hay fever. Staff and student volunteers for the study were found through the university's intranet, and students were each allocated one or two volunteer clients. They were provided with exemplars and comprehensive guides to writing up this kind of report. Small groups received their formative feedback from tutors about how to improve on draft reports. In order to obtain sufficient data to inform a report, all students combined their data into one file and were required to use this compilation of information in order to prepare their report.

The report was to be written as follows:

- *Title* – a succinct statement of the question being investigated.
- *Abstract* – summary of the whole report that is clear even without the rest of the report.
- *Table of contents* – a list of headings, tables, figures and plans that have been used in the report. Place each item on a page of its own and include a page number.

- *Introduction* – includes aims and objectives of the study, its scope and limits, and any relevant background information including contemporary theory on the topic.
- *Methods* – description of the experimental set-up, list of equipment used, step-by-step details of procedures carried out, explanation of how data were recorded and any other factual information regarding methods used in the study.
- *Results* – shows results obtained from data collected, and includes relevant raw data and any relevant graphs, tables or plans together with captions for each.
- *Discussion* – this section describes in words how the data were treated or analysed, and any statements about the accuracy of the data can be made here. You need to interpret your results so that you can answer the question 'What do the data tell us?' and also report on any unexpected results, relate the results to any other relevant studies and describe any logical projections from the results, eg the need for follow-up research.
- *Conclusion* – base all conclusions on actual results, explain the meaning of the experiment and implications of results, and provide an answer to the question 'So what?' Make any recommendations on the basis of your findings.
- *References* – list all the published sources that you have cited in your report. If a source is cited in the reference list, it must also appear in the relevant place within the report. Use the style guide provided on the School Web site.
- *Appendix* – details of data analysis should be provided in the appendix. If there is to be more than one appendix, then label each with a letter (Appendix A, Appendix B etc). Further information (eg policies, equipment specifications etc) can also be provided in appendices to ensure that the flow of the report is not interrupted.

(adapted from Southern Cross University Learning Assistance
Web site, 2003)

The most effective communication is achieved through laboratory reports that are written in a language and style most suited to the readership. This example makes clear to students that they may expect the report to be published outside the university in a newsletter format, but not in a refereed scientific journal. One would therefore expect the reports to be less formal and easier to read than they might be if submitted to a journal.

Creative writing

Written communication is always about something, but in some subjects, for example creative writing or journalism, the structure, flow and creative expression of the piece are as important as or more important than the content. Again, the assessment methods and marking criteria should reflect the purpose of the task and the balance of style and content that is embodied in the subject's learning outcomes.

Case 12.6: Assessing narrative writing using a familiar topic

One of the learning outcomes in the early stages of a creative writing course was that students should be able to construct and sustain narrative in a story. The lecturers decided upon an assessment task entitled 'My mother's story'. Students were encouraged to be innovative in their treatment of this topic, chosen because it was likely to be a familiar one. Students were freed from the constraints of constructing an original story to concentrate on the purpose of the assessment task, which was to demonstrate that they could use specific narrative forms.

Clinical practice journal

In the case of clinical areas of practice, the range of communication skills relates both to the interpersonal aspects of communication and to the skills of honest self-reflection. Through a process of critical personal inquiry, students can learn to move beyond basic self-awareness to the synthesis of new knowledge. This approach is most appropriate in professional programmes where there is a like-lihood that students have contact with an actual practice (either their own or that of their workplace supervisor).

For example, by maintaining a reflective practice journal, students in health-related disciplines can note the details of clinical events, cases and experiences. For reasons of confidentiality, these are kept only for their own record as a basis for reflection on practice. By asking (and answering) questions such as 'How did this situation affect me and how did I affect the situation?' students can interpret events in greater detail and begin to explain them from a number of personal and professional perspectives.

In order to explore assumptions further and reflect upon the relevance of knowledge and models of practice, students' examination of their chosen area should also include reference to findings published in contemporary literature. They need to report on and critique the relevant literature in relation to their own clinical approaches. Finally the development of strategies for incorporating contemporary perspectives into their own clinical practice must be made explicit for the benefit of their professional development. The journal should link to professional criteria and standards, while preserving the privacy associated with any details of clinical events.

Case 12.7: Communicating through a clinical practice journal in nursing

Students in a nursing programme were required to keep a journal during practical hospital clinical experience during each year of their programme. The journal was not necessarily written in a formal style, but needed to be detailed enough for students to be able to recall events in their clinical practice and to be able to describe the environment and the experience that was involved. Part of the journal was an informal annotated bibliography of literature they had consulted, models of medical practice they had encountered or issues they considered relevant. The journal also included reflections and insights into their own professional practice that arose out of the experiences and notes detailed there.

The assessable communication tasks included:

- identification of a critical incident for examination;
- explanation of identified areas of practice for improvement, arising from the critical incident;
- examination of literature to support a new approach to practice; and
- an explicit proposal to improve practice, eg to incorporate critical reflection or to amend a clinical approach based on contemporary reports in the literature.

The assessment tasks formed the basis of a series of reflective papers written at the end of each year of the programme. When each paper was considered with its predecessors as the student progressed through the programme, tutors were able to judge development of clinical practice.

Preparing for workplace communication

As they come closer to graduation, students need to master some important communication skills. As we have seen, communication required of graduates entering the workforce may vary from profession to profession. However, the basic process of preparing a job application and the associated documentation, and performing well at interview are skills that, without a doubt, all job applicants need.

Case 12.8: Written and oral communication in a job application

The goal of this assessment task was to prepare students for effective communication when applying for a job. In preparation for a job interview that took place before a panel of assessors (including an industry expert or practitioner from the local area), students prepared a portfolio of their work and a CV for inclusion with their application.

The job description was provided in details that coincided with the desired learning outcomes of the subject. So, for example, students in an environmental science programme studying the process of developing water management plans were given a duty statement that read: 'Provide assistance to the council water management officer with development of a local water management plan. Liaise with Department of Land and Water Conservation and Streamwatch officers and others, as necessary, regarding the conservation of water and protection of waterways.'

Students produced a portfolio illustrating recent relevant activities in which they had been engaged, and which clearly showed the standard of their work. They drafted a personal CV, and prepared to attend an interview. At interview students were asked to provide examples that supported their portfolio so that they could be assessed on their:

- demonstrated knowledge of water catchments and factors impacting upon local sites;
- sound knowledge of the principles of water management planning for prevention and mitigation purposes;
- understanding of the principles of water management planning;
- high level of self-motivation and capacity to work with limited supervision;
- ability to surmount challenges, set objectives and meet deadlines;
- demonstrated oral and written communications skills, appropriate to the planning and advisory tasks of the position.

The performance of interviewees against each of the selection criteria was discussed during the interview in the interests of providing feedback. Assessment was based upon their level of performance in relation to the set standards of performance and presentation (ie fail, pass, credit, distinction, high distinction). The portfolio was assessed according to pre-negotiated standards relating to the criteria as listed (see Chapters 21 and 23).

(adapted from Trevitt *et al*, 1997)

Mentoring

The process of mentoring is based on a partnership between two individuals within a context where the mentor shares his or her professional and personal expertise with another for mutual benefit. Mentoring relationships are characterized by a degree of uniqueness, not only across disciplines but also on a case-by-case basis. In some settings, assessment of mentoring as a form of communication is appropriate.

Case 12.9: Communication in mentoring

In a subject called 'Mentoring in the organization', third-year students actually became the mentors of beginning first-year students who were adjusting to the culture and expectations of a university. The purpose of the subject was to allow the third-year students to practise a range of human resource development skills. All the assessment tasks for this subject were around the effectiveness of the communication between the mentor and the mentee including:

- negotiation, rapport, listening and interpersonal skills;
- assertiveness, respect, effective expression of thoughts and feelings;

- honesty in coaching and feedback;
- self-discipline and balance in terms of study- versus non-study-related commitments.

Students (mentors) kept a reflective journal on the mentoring experience. After each session between mentor and mentee, reflective notes kept by the mentor formed the basis for constructive feedback to the mentee. The learning process for the student (mentor) was supported by communication in the mentoring relationship.

Evidence of successful communication in mentoring was provided in several ways. Extracts from the journal were provided by the student in conjunction with a written reflection on the experience of mentoring and observed links with theories of mentoring. Verbal feedback from the mentee was incorporated into the ongoing journal, and final assessment included an evaluation by the mentee of the effectiveness of the mentor.

Debate

These days the rules for debating are many and varied but it is essentially a very adaptable form of assessing communication skills. In the classroom situation, students can be formed into teams according to the overall number that can be divided into opposing sides. Where the debate format is in itself an important learning activity, teams of six, with three members on each side, are the ideal. Each member would thus have one of the more traditional roles of affirming or rebutting the question, with the final summing up conducted by the first speaker on each side.

Where the formal debate structure is not so critical, classroom debates can be structured such that opposing teams take their turn at arguing their case, alternating in this way until all have had their say. Online, this can take place over an extended period of time (often following a period of team-based preparation in an environment secure from the prying eyes of the opposing team). A very sophisticated form may be found in law faculties with the idea of 'moot courts' where students practise legal advocacy (Gygar and Cassimatis, 1997) (see Case 12.10).

The nature of the issue for debate needs to be one where both sides of the argument have merit or are seen to have constituent representation in the real world. In many contexts where debates are used, students are encouraged – and indeed sometimes compelled – to argue the point of view that is contrary to their own beliefs. This is done in the spirit of examining one's own preconceptions and pushing the limits to one's current understanding.

Grading of debates can be done along the lines of the strength and thoroughness of the argument; clarity and persuasiveness of the presentation; effectiveness of the counter-arguments presented. Where the whole class has observed the debates, students will often nominate a 'winning team', though this may or may not be taken into account in the final grade.

Moot court

A moot court is designed to prepare later-year law students for legal advocacy. Students work in groups of two or three to prepare and present an argument for either the appellant or respondent in a case that is presented to a 'judge', who listens, asks questions and makes a judgement. The moot court is often held in a realistic courtroom and the mooters dress and behave as in a real court (Gygar and Cassimatis, 1997).

One of the benefits of moot courts is that, although they are simulations of real courts, mooting can be seen as a competitive 'game'. The fact that they are not real, that 'no lives are ruined or fortunes lost', means that students are able to practise the skills of legal advocacy in a relatively less emotionally charged setting (Snape and Watt, 1997: 4).

Moot courts are used for summative and formative assessment purposes. The following example is designed for formative assessment. The summative possibilities include:

- Students gain feedback from a formative moot court, and then research and argue a different problem, which is summatively assessed.
- The moot court as presented below could be graded.
- Marking criteria could include those noted under 'judge's feedback' below.

Case 12.10: Moot court

In this example of mooting, assessment was formative (not graded) although it was compulsory for second-year law students to take part in a moot. The proceedings were videotaped and reviewed immediately after all the presentations had been made. The judge then gave each of the mooters verbal feedback on their advocacy.

The judge's feedback covered:

- preparation for the moot (research, reading, knowledge of case documentation, preparation of argument);
- the written summary of argument (handed up to the court before the presentations);
- the case file (its organization, how quickly the mooter found relevant sections, quotations and phrases);
- ability to develop a dialogue with the judge;
- knowledge of the rules of the moot and of the tribunal relating to this moot problem;
- court etiquette and ethics, modes of address, correct forms of speech, dress requirements, organization of the bar table.

Posters

Visual communication assessments such as posters can stand alone for presentation or illustrations within written, oral or online assessment tasks. These tasks assess the ability of students to encapsulate their ideas and to express knowledge, understanding and ideas in creative or succinct ways.

The preparation of posters can also play a part in preparing students for participation in professional conferences. When students confine their ideas to one sheet of paper they are forced to think deeply about the important information they wish to communicate to a professional audience. Posters convey ideas in words and visually in a way that is not an essay, but which conveys the key theoretical frameworks, research findings, project outcomes or other academic outcomes visually (Jenkins, 1994). The product should be elegant, simple, comprehensive and engaging.

When posters are designed as assessment tasks, they may be accompanied by or illustrate an oral presentation.

Case 12.11: Posters in education

Bachelor of Education students were required to make a poster to demonstrate how they would teach a group of secondary school students the fundamentals of designing and building a Web site. The poster was to include graphics, photographs or flowcharts and had a limit of 400 words of text.

This assessment task was chosen for two reasons: 1) the students, who would upon graduation become classroom teachers, needed to develop the skills to design and develop posters; and 2) a poster was an appropriate task to allow students to demonstrate broad curriculum development.

The posters were presented in a tutorial session. Students were allocated a space in the tutorial room to display their poster and they were asked to prepare a short oral presentation to accompany the poster. Marking criteria included:

- the overall 'look' of the poster (design, placement of graphics, placement of text, visual impact);
- whether the poster was self-explanatory;
- how effectively the student encapsulated concepts in the poster's text;
- whether the poster suggested a useful teaching strategy;
- choice of content (text and graphics);
- how effectively the poster accompanied the oral presentation.

Online communication

Students are increasingly taking up opportunities to be assessed by electronic means. Many activities across all modes of educational delivery involve communicating online. This is a kind of hybrid of oral and written communication with its own set of conventions. Some students come to higher education with strong skills in online communication through e-mail and chat groups that they have used in school or in their personal lives. Others, perhaps adults returning to education, are less confident in taking part in either synchronous (students all taking part at the same time) or asynchronous discussions (students contributing at different points within a given time-frame, eg a day or a week). Debates or group collaboration online with the incentive of an assessable activity can encourage some who would be 'lurkers' (observers but non-contributors to the discussion) to participate. Although 'lurkers' can and do learn by following the online discussions and debates of their co-learners, as one student put it 'online people need other online people', that is, as Pincas (1997) has noted, group members are only truly 'present' online when they are actually contributing a response.

Continuous assessment using an online forum for troubleshooting

In areas such as engineering and other pragmatic technical fields, students may be asked to solve a series of problems. In more authentic versions of this assessment approach, such problems are based on unfolding scenarios represen-tative of real-world contexts. These scenarios may be presented as an ongoing series of problem-solving activities throughout the semester (see Chapter 18).

In order to support their learning, students commonly receive formative feedback for their progress through the problem case or scenario. They may be provided with diagnostic information concerning where they are making mistakes or pursuing flawed logic. Alternatively they may be graded on each and every step of the continuous assessment such that all components are worth a small mark towards the final grade with later tasks counting for a greater proportion of overall marks.

In this example where students are involved in continuous problem solving, their ability to understand their own learning process and to communicate their learning needs is vital for the successful completion of such assessment tasks. Parry and Dunn (2000) call this process benchmarking, because students compare their own approaches to learning tasks, interpretations of assessment tasks, theoretical perspectives and use of sources with other students.

Finding roles and becoming critical in an online forum

Social interaction is possibly the most powerful tool for learning, as Lave and Wenger (1991) have shown. In online settings, the processes are similar but the medium is different. In the online environment, where discussion topics may be set for student attention over the span of a week or fortnight, the pace and continuity of such critical exchanges can often be uncomfortably protracted. It is usually important for sustaining a preferred and manageable pace of discussion to allocate students one of several roles in the discussion period so that each knows what and how to contribute. In face-to-face settings, students would work this out, but in online settings they are unlikely to know where to begin.

Bonk and Dennen's (1999) extensive list of roles includes the 'starter', 'commentator', 'editor', 'synthesizer', 'mediator', 'evaluator', 'mentor', 'advisor', 'leader' and 'wrapper', to name just a few. These kinds of roles can be allocated to each group member so that, at any given time in the study period, students will be clear about what they as individuals are required to carry out in the group discussion context.

Initial time allocated for introductions and exchanges of a more personal nature is essential for establishing a basis for mutual understanding of each other's personal assumptions and the diversity of cultural perspectives among the group. The provision of a timetable or agenda for discussion events will further help students to stay on task and on time with their participation online.

Case 12.12: Problem solving and finding roles in groups online

This assessment task was based on an ongoing learning activity that ultimately accrued towards a final grade. The large group of students, who were studying at a distance, was divided into small groups of three or four. Each small group was allocated a private forum on the student intranet so they could 'meet' for problem-solving sessions. An open forum was also set up for whole-group work. The task was clearly defined and, in this case, while a certain number of contributions to the small-group sessions were compulsory and tracked by the lecturer, the quality of the contributions was not assessable. Students negotiated roles within groups, and rotated the role of 'reporter'. Reporters synthesized the week's progress in solving the problem in a report to the large group. The weekly reports were summatively assessed. It was in the interests of each group member to contribute to the weekly discussions because the grading was in the form of group marks. The lecturer's workload was minimized by assessing one weekly report for three or four students, rather than one for each.

The development of an accessible archive of the weekly reports along with questions and answers was held in a communication area. It was valuable both for the students and for the staff, who no longer found the need repeatedly to address the same queries.

Using real-time communication technology

'Real-time chat' is a term used to denote informal conversation between two or more people at the same time online. Real-time chat is also known as 'synchronous' communication.

Students learning to develop their communication skills nowadays need to gain experience in a broad range of text-based communication through the genres of e-mail, bulletin boards and discussion forums. The typical conventions expected from contributors in each of these settings need to be understood by students. However, synchronous chat is not, as yet, very commonly used for assessment tasks, as it precludes any students with insufficient network infrastructure and those with limited keyboard skills who may not be able to complete the required task within the time-frame specified. On the other hand, in cases where the synchronous online features can be equitably built into an assessment scheme, several options might be structured for its use.

For example, a reflective and progressive dialogue can be structured between the student in a workplace placement and the online tutor, such that these reflective pieces can form the basis for a synthesis of learning to be submitted later for grading. Virtual consultancies can be set up where the students' log of interactions and 'meetings' is kept in the chat archives for grading or for evidence to be integrated in the form of extracts into later submissions.

Case 12.13: Cross-cultural perspectives in a gender studies subject

A gender studies subject had a number of international students who studied online from their home countries. The assessment task required students to analyse cultural perspectives gained from their online discussions. Students from a number of countries gathered for real-time chat to share cultural perspectives. Lived experience provided students in all the locations with high-quality information that was immediately useful in the appreciation of multiple perspectives on important global and cultural issues.

If time zones are too restrictive students could contribute to the discussions over the course of a week or two weeks, but the immediacy of the real-time chat would be lost.

Case 12.14: Simultaneous viewing online: visual artefacts in a fine arts examination

Fine arts students had an assessment task that required them to identify and critically discuss visual artefacts (such as those found in online galleries) presented to them in an unseen examination. The lecturers used real-time technology to allow distance students to view the visual artefacts simultaneously. With the students in a variety of geographical locations that were negotiated beforehand,★ the examination proceeded. Students each had the item for discussion present in their view at the same time. They prepared and submitted their response to examination questions online within a time-frame.

★This assessment task was held under examination conditions, that is, each negotiated venue – usually a computer laboratory in a university, school, college or local library – was supervised by an accredited examiner.

A major benefit of using real-time chat in the process of assessment is that archives of the full event are available and academic staff can specify how much, if any, of these need to be provided as evidence of participation.

Implications for teaching

It is part of an academic teacher's responsibility overtly to provide students with opportunities to learn and understand new concepts, knowledge and forms of expression. Although we are concentrating here on how communication skills are assessed, it is worth saying that students have better opportunities for success when assessment tasks are communicated to them clearly and fully. Those students who are less confident in communicating what they have learnt can be encouraged when they have opportunities for rehearsal and practice as they develop communication techniques that are appropriate for their particular contexts. The development of communication skills is well suited to a range of formative assessment methods, especially early in the undergraduate experience. These can be designed for self-, peer or group marking and thus free teachers from the oppression of constant marking of summative tests (see, for example, Gibbs, 1995.)

Cultural and other diversity within cohorts of students is a common element of higher education today and has to be considered when planning assessment of the ability to communicate. The policy shift in recent decades towards equitable access to higher education has enabled many adults to return to study after lengthy periods of time away from formal education. Students with disabilities are more likely than ever before to consider further study, and international and local students with a diverse range of cultural, ethnic, language and other backgrounds are increasing in numbers. There will be a wide a range of past experiences of formal education and different kinds of perceptions about what academic teachers expect from assessment tasks.

If the expectations about style, format, resources, content and critique are not explicitly taught, students can only second-guess what their teachers want.

13

Accessing and managing information

Introduction

The acquisition of a wide range of skills that include information literacy and discipline-specific search skills is valued highly. They are the building blocks of scholarship and are transferable to the world of work where graduates may be hired on the strength of their demonstrated ability to locate and manage a diverse range of information by using a variety of print and electronic media. Everyone needs to be 'information literate', and that means being able to recognize when information is required and being able to find, sort and use the information needed for a particular research project, decision or problem-solving exercise (American Library Association, 1998). The range of meanings associated with the term 'information literacy' will be discussed once we have explored the broad topic of accessing and managing information.

Learning outcomes for accessing and managing information represent the development of a fundamental set of skills that are needed by students in higher education, almost from the beginning of their studies. Although these skills are developed over the course of an undergraduate degree, they are usually overtly assessed only during the early stages. By the later stages of their course it is expected that students are independently skilled in finding and managing the information they need.

What is 'accessing and managing information'?

There are two strands of the skills needed to access and manage information in higher education. One strand is about academic skills and the ability to use the 'tools for the job of being a learner' (the ability to undertake literature searches, for example) and the other is about knowing how to evaluate information for its content, relevance and usefulness according to an academic purpose. The second strand includes 'awareness and understanding of how information is produced in the modern world'. Because the production and transmission of knowledge is so complex and varied students need to become 'critical consumers of information' (SCONUL, 2003).

A familiar way these skills are assessed is through tasks that require students to 'research a topic' (Nightingale, 1996b: 115). Such tasks may be used to ensure that new students learn where to find and how to manage core information in their disciplinary field. Integrated into these early research tasks is the development of both academic skills and the ability to use whatever technology is available.

Much of students' preparation for such tasks as 'research a topic' will be about becoming familiar with particular sources of information, learning how to use these sources to gain access to the right kind of information to research their topic, and sifting through what may amount to mountains of material to classify, categorize and manage the information in a meaningful and timely way. Students learn to appreciate what is possible, appropriate and relevant in their disciplinary field and to develop an understanding of the depth and breadth of particular bodies of knowledge.

One of the challenges of scholarship once students gain a level of critical awareness of the scope of their field is to be able to focus on a particular topic area while remaining open to those interesting pieces of information that appear tangential but can be important to an understanding of the field and which might represent new and cutting-edge information. An element of this skill is that students should be able to demonstrate that they can make the distinction between relevant and irrelevant sources of information. This skill may be examined through a variety of assessment tasks.

Such discrimination is not an easy task for many students, especially those who do not pick up their lecturers' cues about what kinds of information, combinations or categories of it are more important and which are less so. These are the students who demand to be 'told' what to do and how to do it because they cannot make the essential distinction for themselves, often to the despair of their lecturers.

Miller and Parlett (1976: 144–46) found that students generally fall into one of three categories in their approaches to finding out what is required of them, particularly in their examinations. Members of the first group are 'cue-seekers' who actively search out clues to help them decide what kinds of information will help them to be successful. The second group is made up of 'cue-conscious' students who notice cues that are dropped by lecturers and who know how to pick them up and act upon them. The third group is 'cue-deaf'. They are the ones who want to be 'told' because they take everything at face value without realizing that not everything in the learning environment is explicit or that many cues are available to them.

There are often overlaps between the different kinds of learning outcomes discussed in this book, including those that deal with finding and managing information, particularly using ICTs. If students are to conduct online searches effectively without missing or overlooking important information, they have to use their critical faculties and higher-order thinking skills, such as critical thinking and problem solving. Their academic skills should include an understanding of how knowledge is constructed and what constitutes evidence and argument in their discipline. Brem and Boyes (2000) assert that the quality of the outcomes of online searching by students has not increased to match the rise in the number of online databases and other resources. They argue that students should be asking questions like 'What do I know? What do I not know? Will I ever find an answer?' These kinds of questions bring us to the issue of information literacy in that the quality of outcomes of searching for information by whatever means is central to it. As we explore various interpretations of the term, the overlapping nature of the eight kinds of learning outcomes we discuss in Part B of this book will become more obvious.

Information literacy

While the term 'information literacy' was coined in 1974 by a US businessman and thus is relatively new (Bramley-Moore and Stewart, 2000: 4), the concept is broad and has always been integral to successful learning in higher education. For example, the definition published by the American Library Association (1989) shows that information literacy is about much more than the ability to use a range of ICTs effectively:

> To be information literate, a person must be able to recognize when information is needed and have the ability to locate, evaluate and use effectively the needed information… Ultimately, information literate people are those who have learned how to learn. They know how to learn because they know how knowledge is organized, how to find information, and how to use information in such a way that others can learn from them… they are people prepared for lifelong learning, because they can always find the information needed for any task or decision at hand.
>
> (American Library Association, 1989)

Information literacy, then, is essential to success as a student as well as being necessary in many other life roles 'not only to fulfil personal information needs, but also to function in the workplace, and to participate in society as knowledgeable citizens' (Bramley-Moore and Stewart, 2000: 4). A general view of information literacy as an essential life skill implies the acquisition of fundamental ICT skills alongside some broader dimensions of independence as a learner, including the social and ethical management of information. While information literacy is a necessary survival skill in the age of ICTs, the capabilities needed to be fully literate in a sophisticated multimedia learning environment include a mix of skills and abilities. These have been categorized by the American Library Association and the Association for Educational Communications and Technology (1998) under three headings:

- *information literacy*: accessing information efficiently and effectively; evaluating information critically and competently; and using information accurately and creatively;
- *independent learning*: pursuing information related to personal interests; appreciating literature and other creative expressions of information; and striving for excellence in information seeking and knowledge generation;
- *social responsibility*: recognizing the importance of information to a democratic society; practising ethical behaviour in regard to information and information technology; and participating effectively in groups to pursue and generate information.

(American Library Association and Association for
Education Communications and Technology, 1998)

Learning to learn about ICTs: their strengths and pitfalls

A great deal of information is only available to those who are able to use ICTs effectively and, while some students arrive at university with a wide range of ICT skills in place, others may need to be taught how to gain access to the online technology including their institution's intranet, conduct fruitful searches of catalogues and databases and review online journals. This means that, before being able to access information, students need to be fluent in the language and use of ICTs, especially those that are used in their institution.

Those students who are new to ICT in general or to the particular electronic media used in their courses could be said to be trying to learn two things at once: they are grappling with technology as well as with the challenge of completing assessment tasks, and could fail in their efforts to unlock sources of information stored electronically. Parry and Dunn (2000) found that frustrations with technology can be a factor in student dissatisfaction and can lead to students dropping out of a subject or an entire course.

Literature searches cannot be effective unless searchers have some background knowledge of the discipline and subject area so that they can enter particular keywords or phrases that will yield the information that is needed. They should have the ability to identify key authors, books, journals, Web sites and other sources, and be able to sort and classify all the information they have gathered according to the purpose at hand.

Internet search engines are sometimes the first 'port of call', after set texts, for undergraduates as they prepare assignments (SCONUL, 2003) because the process is so accessible and easy. However, this strategy raises issues of the reliability of information found through online searches. In the past, printed material passed through a well-established variety of quality assurance mechanisms. The books and journals on university library shelves were carefully selected for their relevance and credibility and, in any case, peer review is the cornerstone of scholarly publishing. On the Internet and World Wide Web, however, there is no such assurance of quality, so students must learn to apply informed judgement to help them determine the value of information found through online searches. Students now need to be able to evaluate material critically where once it was more common to use material that was already evaluated as to its merit.

Accessing and managing information in the disciplines

Information and ways of managing it are specific to particular fields; therefore students strive to learn how to research and present information in the way that is unique to their discipline. They need practice and feedback about how they are progressing to help them to become 'savvy', as Becher (1989) explains. They learn by observing and emulating experts, by feedback on formative and summative assessment tasks, and from immersion in the knowledge culture of the faculty.

Assessment is more effective in engendering learning when it reflects the nature of its knowledge base with tasks that are clearly linked to the curriculum. The context of an assessment task such as 'research a topic' is only meaningful when the topic is relevant to the students' level of learning and applied to their field of study. If these skills are assessed in isolation or out of context, students may not be able to transfer their learning to other contexts or related fields.

The examples that follow show that the kind of information to be accessed and the ways of managing and making meaning of information can vary according to different academic disciplines. The style of scholarly writing in each disciplinary field varies, and students' knowledge of their particular genre should not be taken for granted. Each field represented below would have its own way of structuring a piece of writing and of citing references to sources of information, as we have seen in Chapter 12. To do well in assessment tasks, students would have to develop the skills of information gathering and also of scholarly writing, argument and evidence in their field. These skills are not only about technical research, but include the investigation and observation skills needed to identify and classify the kind of information that is important, for example, in clinical settings (health professions), classroom education (teaching) or fieldwork (science or applied professions). Here are some examples of accessing and managing information in some disciplinary environments.

Sociology

In first-year sociology, students preparing to write an essay on comparative theoretical perspectives are required to show they have gained access to the full range of relevant theories and the influence of particular theorists. They need to demonstrate how they determine the influence of key theories they have selected and how they pictured the pattern of theoretical development before proceeding to compare and contrast perspectives.

For example, a first-year student could consult a sociological encyclopedia to find the names of well-known theorists and locate some key words and phrases relating to theories as a basis for a deeper search in the library catalogues, databases or search engines. The student could also do an analysis of regularly cited authors.

Visual arts

Visual arts students, preparing a rationale to accompany a sculpture for an assessment piece, have to be able to show that they have accessed comprehensive current and historical literature, that they know the key artists in the field and have seen examples of their work and that they can manage the information in such a way as to provide a credible rationale for the approach to be embodied in this piece of sculpture.

The rationale would include a section about influences and inspirations for the piece, some of which may be outside the established published literature especially if influences are very recent. The student might cite published literature alongside Web sites located, exhibitions visited (with catalogues) and other audio or visual material consulted.

Business

Bachelor of Business students in their first year could have an assessment task requiring them to locate literature outlining different models of organizational mentoring programmes and to categorize the programmes according to a continuum of managerial control or employee control of the process. Students would need to be able to search out the full range of literature that detailed cases of organizational mentoring programmes (including relevant full-text electronic journals and resources on the library shelves). Then they would locate the information within the journals and other literature, and organize the cases according to their place on the continuum of control.

Assessment methods

Accessing and managing information are foundation skills, as we noted earlier, and are, therefore, a crucial basis of all academic disciplines, so they will begin to be developed early and will be built upon during and beyond university studies. Most methods of assessment include locating and organizing information, often as a first step towards demonstrating other learning outcomes.

Early in a course, these skills can be assessed separately, but in later years of study they are usually not explicitly contained in marking schemes (although it is our view that they should be included). However, students probably achieve higher grades when effective searching skills are reflected in the quality of their work. Distance education students can be disadvantaged if they are not encouraged to search for information or if they are unable to explore other sources of information beyond a book of readings sent out with their study package. A problem too, from the student point of view, is the competition for printed and other resources in the university library. It is hard to demonstrate the ability to locate and use resources if they are insufficient and other students get them first.

One of the issues concerning the assessment of how well students access and manage information in a field of study is that the process is probably as important as the product of the search. Students are required to develop skills in the process of seeking, finding and handling information that are not always evident when the product of the search is the only assessment item. Many students, even into the later years of their studies, do not learn how to locate all the information they need, and the widely ranging reference list added to an assignment might sometimes be the work of a librarian rather than that of the student who presents it.

Essays

When they are clearly focused, well-crafted essay topics allow students to demonstrate how well they can access and manage information in a meaningful way. This traditional assessment method is used in higher education to assess many different skills in an integrated way.

While essays are effective when they are not overused, they should be well grounded in a relevant context or they may not achieve their purpose of enabling students to become familiar with how to approach information gathering in their field.

Students may be required to research a topic by finding information directly from laboratories, research centres, historical archives, indexed collections, homepages (of relevant individuals and groups) and library databases. They may also be encouraged to make contact with individuals in the field such as disciplinary specialists, curators, colleagues and their student peers in other parts of the world. If they are required to undertake searches of any kind, they should be taught the first principles of doing so, either formally in class time or in supplementary classes such as those conducted by reference librarians. Distance and online students can be taught online or through printed materials.

Discussions conducted online with key resource contacts can be structured as interviews in real time (using chat software), may be synchronous question-and-answer sessions or perhaps might use a Web form in order to collect data from the target audience that can subsequently be sorted into key themes and analysed.

For meaningful use to be made of the information gathered, the assessment task might further require that students collate the information, analyse it and present a synthesis of outcomes. This may take many forms depending on the knowledge area. Student reports may, in turn, be published through the Internet environment for inclusion in the growing disciplinary body of knowledge.

Essays and other assessment tasks that require students to navigate, retrieve, evaluate and use information are a natural progression from the inception of the World Wide Web. They require a plethora of information literacy and interpersonal skills in obtaining useful information. Use of subject trees, keyword search engines and directories of servers, collated by geographical location or interest groupings, forms the basis for the newly expanded knowledge domain of information literacy.

Case 13.1: Essay with a focus on information gathering

Later-year politics students were given the essay topic: 'Critically discuss the notion that local government in Australia is always about rats, rates and rubbish.' In order to undertake a critical analysis, students firstly had to gain access to comprehensive sources of information about local government in Australia, its legislative powers, responsibilities and activities. Secondly, they had to manage the information in relation to how much emphasis local government bodies place on rats, rates, rubbish and the other activities undertaken. Information such as legislation, geographical reach of local government authorities, emphases in Australian government operations and so on was available on the World Wide Web. Other information was available through library catalogues and databases. Students also had a textbook and several readings provided to them. The third step taken by these students was to plan and write their critical discussion.

Self, peer and group assessment

There is much informal learning that takes place as students learn with and from others in researching and preparing assignments and other assessment tasks. The skills of accessing and managing information are developed by benchmarking with co-learners as much as through teaching and the curriculum. Additionally, students working in groups are forced to self-assess their performance so that, through formative feedback, they refine their approach to locating and handling assessment tasks.

When self-, peer and group assessment is summative, there are often concerns about the reliability of grading because students are likely to be biased in their judgement for a wide variety of reasons. Students notoriously dislike taking on the role of assessor, but they can learn a lot about their subject area by analysing the worth of another student's efforts. If the marking criteria are clear these exercises can be very valuable. In addition to being provided with clear and explicit marking criteria, students find peer and self-assessment difficult unless they have been trained in how to assess their peers' and their own work against specific criteria and standards of performance.

Case 13.2: Self, peer and group assessment in social work
This example of a group project in social work has formative and summative components that include self-, peer and group assessment.

A group project, taken over a full semester, required final-year students to design a 'healthy breakfast' initiative for disadvantaged students at a local primary school. The initiative was a real-life one and the social work students would actually implement it with funding from a local community group. Each group of five students negotiated how the information for the project was to be gathered, and devised interview schedules. Individual students interviewed a number of school community members and also searched an agreed aspect of the topic through the library and on the Internet. This part of the project aimed to research similar initiatives and their outcomes. The information gained by each individual was organized into a database by the group to inform the development of a proposal for the 'healthy breakfast' community project.

The marks for the whole project were divided between tasks undertaken by individuals and group tasks. In this way the assessor was able to distinguish between students when calculating the final grade. Peer assessment was not awarded marks, but was a compulsory activity. Assessment tasks relating to information gathering and management were as follows:

- Self-assessment tasks (assessed by a diary/journal) required reflection on the way information was obtained and evaluated by the individual student.
- Peer assessment was used to evaluate the individual's reflection against negotiated criteria.
- Group assessment by the university teacher was based on how the group managed all the information individuals had gained and the quality of the database that was developed.

Inventories and annotated bibliographies

Inventories and annotated bibliographies may be used to encourage students to learn how to find and manage information in the context of their disciplinary field. Tasks such as these are valuable because they have firm boundaries, allowing students to focus their efforts. Such focus can make a task more manageable, whereas locating information for an essay can sometimes seem like finding out about the whole world and everything in it.

Case 13.3: Annotated bibliography in first-year science
A forestry course required students to undertake two field trips in the first year of their course. Their reports were assessable and included an inventory of forest resources. They were required to develop an annotated bibliography to accompany their inventory by the end of their first year. The bibliography was

developed progressively and assessed as a work in progress twice during the year. The task was compulsory, and in its first iteration formative feedback was provided. It was graded in the second iteration and attached as an appendix to the student's fieldwork report.

This assessment task was designed particularly to induct the first-year students into their new field. It was developed because the teacher, who was very experienced, had found that some students in each new intake were taking forestry without a grounding in high school science. The development of the inventory was made compulsory to ensure that students learnt how to relate what they found on field trips to the established literature in an accepted scientific manner.

Case 13.4: Annotated bibliography to support oral presentation

This assessment task accompanied an oral tutorial presentation. Students were asked to provide an annotated bibliography of the sources they consulted to underpin the theoretical framework for their presentation. The assessable components of the presentation were the bibliography and the slides that represented a synthesis of the presentation and were handed to the teacher one week after the presentation. The oral component of the task was not assessed, to alleviate the nervousness often felt by students when they give a presentation and also because it was only the written component of the task that was designed to meet the desired learning outcomes.

Case 13.5: Locating and evaluating the usefulness of resources from the Internet

Students in the study of 'communications' were required to prepare for the weekly lecture by completing a set of prescribed readings and also to find supporting extension materials on the World Wide Web. Students posted this material on to an online bulletin board for the class to share. This was also a means by which the teacher could maintain an up-to-date directory of resources.

The continuing nature of the assessment task became problematic. It soon became apparent that some students who were working ahead of the group had easily found relevant resources ahead of time, while some who were slower in accessing the resources floundered and were left behind to grapple with a search for the less obvious examples of relevant contributions.

Here the skills development process in the accessing and managing of information was in danger of suddenly being subsumed by the competitive drive to find something (anything) to post before it was posted by someone else. The teacher removed the mandate to post weekly and changed the task so that students were free to post resource sites whenever they were discovered. The requirement to explain the usefulness of each site posted was added to the task.

Information was thus accessed not as an end in itself but as a means of adding to the collective understanding in the class group. Assessment was amended to operate as follows:

Resource location and discussion activity (15%): Choose a topic from among the first five readings provided and either:

- find a Web site to support and extend the information provided in the readings;
- provide the URL (to the bulletin board);
- provide a summary of the Web resource and discuss its relevance to your chosen topic;
- engage in critical discussion with the class on the value of this resource site;

or:

- identify a reading (not already provided) to supplement discussion for this topic;
- provide a link (in the bulletin board) or make a copy of the article available for the class;
- provide a summary of the resource and discuss its relevance to your chosen topic;
- engage in critical discussion with the class on the value of this resource.

(adapted from Oliver, 2001)

Learning contracts

Learning contracts are written agreements negotiated between teachers and their students about individual or group learning projects. They specify what will be learnt, what activities the students will engage in and what the outcomes of the project should be. They are helpful in moving students towards being independent learners, as there can be more or less specific direction depending on a student's confidence level and degree of independence.

Learning contracts usually have an element of information gathering, so that students can gauge the existing knowledge in their topic before embarking on original research or project work.

Case 13.6: Learning contract to add challenge in creative design

Academic staff of an industrial design course were concerned that students were not developing the skills to access information beyond that which was readily available. The staff wanted their design students to gain access to a much broader range of information sources and to be innovative in their search for information and in their management of it.

To achieve this purpose the requirements of learning contracts were extended to add more challenge to the research design for the project. A new expectation was added to the pro forma that required students to identify the research strategies used in planning the design project. In this way students were challenged to delve more deeply and innovatively into a wider variety of possible sources of information and to justify their choice through their development and implementation of the learning contract.

Case studies and scenarios

Case studies and scenarios can place searching techniques into their disciplinary context. Students need to learn generic searching and information management skills, especially how to use the library and ICTs effectively, but then they should learn to apply these skills to the kind of information they need to locate in their particular field.

Case 13.7: Authentic scenarios and case studies online

Professional accountants are required to prepare corporate financial statements that comply with statutory requirements and professional recommendations. The preparation, presentation and audit of these published financial statements make up a considerable amount of the graduate financial accountant's work.

Assessment of the necessary skills was built into an ongoing process of participation in an online discussion forum for both on-campus and off-campus students in their final undergraduate year. In the forum students were invited to identify the relevant issues in a case study of their choice; consult with the reference librarian who regularly checked into the forum; engage in a search for up-to-date literature on this topic; search professional magazines, journals and books with both national and international focus; and utilize the archives of discussions to inform their final presentation submitted for marking and grading.

In such a way, based on realistic case studies and authentic information management procedures, students learnt about financial reporting as it occurs in the typical workplace.

Concept mapping

Concept mapping is a process of representing knowledge in visual terms by drawing networks of concepts or ideas (see Figure 13.1 for an example). The nodes and links within these networks represent the links between concepts. The most common reasons for using concept maps are to:

- clarify thinking about relevant concepts and their relationships;
- generate creative ideas through free association and brainstorming;
- formulate a research problem and all its elements;
- organize and plan the steps and stages of an integrated professional process;
- design complex resources such as long texts, hypermedia or large Web sites;
- represent and communicate complex ideas such as organizational relationships;
- support learning by explicitly illustrating the integration of new and old knowledge;
- assess one's knowledge and understanding or diagnose gaps and misunderstandings.

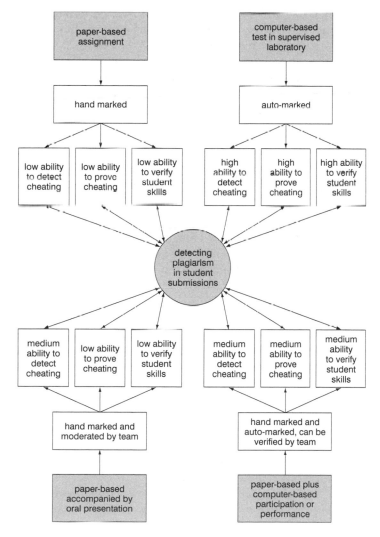

Figure 13.1 *Example of a concept map*

Case 13.8: Concept mapping for law

Using concept mapping as a form of assessment can measure the extent of a student's structural knowledge. An undergraduate law subject introduced students to legal research. Assessment was designed to allow students to demonstrate their ability to locate and use law reports, statutes and secondary sources. The academics involved knew that there was a vast amount of relevant information on the Internet. However, the volume of information was so great that sifting through it to identify relevant information, and then using it appropriately, was the main challenge for students.

A concept mapping exercise was designed around some legal scenarios, with situations that could only be addressed fully when students found and managed relevant information using efficient and effective Internet searching techniques. The students were required to display the outcomes of their search, using a concept map to illustrate further their understanding of the diverse elements for consideration and the relationships between them in terms of the scenarios provided.

Developing a research proposal

Development of a research proposal may be a useful and authentic assignment for students to undertake in courses where they may conceivably go on to carry out research of their own or assist in the investigative projects of others. Proposals for ethics approval or seeking initial approval from a research committee will be slightly different from proposals written to seek research funds. A clear explanation of the purpose of the assessment task will be required to enable students to pitch their proposal appropriately.

Case 13.9: Research proposal for a funding body

When final-year students of plant genetics were set the task of developing a research proposal, they were first required to state their research question – a description of the research problem and its importance. A literature review identified the need for their study. A key requirement was to provide a clear statement of the aims and objectives of the research derived from the literature and the gaps they found within it. Students' proposals had to describe their chosen methods and techniques to reflect a good understanding of appropriate methodology and high standards in procedures to be applied. An outline of the budget, resource needs and timelines was expected. The final proposal had to be well written and easy to follow.

Assessment of this research proposal was done with the target group in mind. So, in this instance, national research guidelines were used to establish standards and expectations.

Accessing a diverse range of information sources

The ability to locate information across a range of different information sources is extended when the skill is applied to non-traditional ways of gathering information. Students learn to recognize a wide diversity of information sources and how to handle them credibly and ethically.

Case 13.10: Searching for information across cultures

In exploring cultural issues associated with a minority group, students may access information that is often not accessible in the mainstream culture. In this example, an impression of sensitivity, cultural significance and respect for copyright are important questions in how to access and manage information appropriately. This task comprised:

- *Logbook.* Students kept a log of cultural issues for the target group throughout the semester as they were reported in the national or local media or in the students' own community. They collected as many press clippings as possible and developed an index of issues together with a dateline of events.
- *Information retrieval.* Using both library resources and electronic sources, students found information on the issues documented in their logbooks. They evaluated these sources of information in terms of their relationship to the issues in the index. Students needed at least five sources and 150 words of evaluation per source.
- *Interview.* Students had to locate an influential member of the target group in their nearest community or someone else who would agree to be interviewed on the issues identified. The experiences of the interviewee on the issues raised were then reported.
- *Essay.* An essay integrated previous work and permitted students to argue their perspective on the issues they had identified.

(adapted from Krendl, 1998)

Implications for teaching

The sets of skills needed to gain access to, and then to manage, a full range of information using a wide variety of sources and technologies should be kept up to date as much by academics as by their students, as we have seen. Many academics, in the midst of their busy lives, can be left behind by new ICTs relevant to searching for information. If academics do not possess these skills themselves, they cannot provide guidance to their students about how to locate the information they need.

Librarians are a wonderful source of expertise when teaching this learning domain. Reference and subject librarians are a veritable fount of knowledge about the common problems students face, and are usually keen to work with teachers to pre-empt them. Sometimes librarians find that assessment tasks set in the library are not well structured. These tasks may not direct student learning appropriately. Students sometimes prefer to go directly to reference librarians and ask them to perform the search that was intended to be the basis of the assessment task. Therefore, it is a good idea to consult a librarian who will then be able to work in a relevant and timely way to help students develop their skills.

As these skills are practical and based around print, electronic resources and information from interviewing or observing people, teaching that includes a lot of practical tasks using catalogues, databases, library searches and, if relevant, interviewing or observing people in the field or co-learners can provide the basis for monitoring progress, giving feedback and shaping students' searching techniques and ways of categorizing information to those that are appropriate in the subject or discipline area.

Many activities can be effective formatively as well as summatively. Paired or group problem-based activities are effective techniques to teach how to access and manage information in context.

14

Demonstrating knowledge and understanding

What is meant by 'knowledge and understanding'?

Every discipline has a body of knowledge at its core that shapes the academic and professional values and behaviours of its adherents. When students acquire the necessary underpinning knowledge in their discipline they learn to demonstrate that they have a command of important principles, facts, terminology, concepts, procedures and rules. Alongside 'knowledge' is 'understanding', that is, the ability to use knowledge to make meaningful relationships, to see significance, to make explanations, to identify causes and effects and to make decisions. Basic disciplinary knowledge is essential to higher-order learning, and though it cannot, in practical terms, be separated from how it is used, we deal with it independently because assessment tasks may focus more upon the knowledge itself than upon how it may be used. Biggs (1999a) calls this 'declarative' knowledge. It is this type of knowledge that we focus upon in this chapter:

> [Declarative knowledge] accrues from research, not from personal experience. It is public knowledge, subject to rules of evidence that make it verifiable, replicable and logically consistent. It is what is in libraries and textbooks, and is what teachers 'declare' in lectures. Students' understanding of it can be tested by getting them to declare it back, in their own words, and using their own examples.

> (Biggs, 1999a: 40)

Declarative knowledge is built up and continuously developed as students become increasingly sophisticated in their ability to do research and add to their store of disciplinary knowledge. Their understanding and the capacity to use the knowledge in more analytic, relational and abstract ways develops with intellectual maturity. Biggs (1999a) calls this more sophisticated and original kind of knowledge 'functioning' knowledge, because it involves higher-order thinking and application. We are concerned with 'declarative' knowledge here because, although there are many overlapping capabilities, higher-order skills are discussed elsewhere in this part of the book; secondly, desired learning outcomes may call for an emphasis in assessment upon declarative knowledge.

Well-developed declarative knowledge is the basis for functioning knowledge and intellectual inquiry. Ramsden (1992) found that students take more meaningful, 'deep', approaches to learning when they have a solid grounding in the knowledge base of their field of study: 'If there are gaps in your understanding of basic concepts, then it is obviously much more likely that your attempts to understand new material that assumes knowledge of those concepts will be frustrated' (Ramsden, 1992: 65). However, teachers, knowing the importance of grounding their students in the basics, can make the mistake of overloading them with factual material. Ramsden (1992: 137) also notes that loading students up with a large mass of facts and detail does not lead to knowledge or wisdom for two reasons: first, knowledge is not a fixed commodity, but is constantly evolving and growing; and second, when subjects have very heavy workloads students have no time to reflect, understand or think about how to apply the material, so they resort to 'surface' approaches to learning – namely, memorizing.

It is increasingly acknowledged that students learn more effectively when learning takes place within a context, is timely, and shows where their immediate topics fit within the whole curriculum, thus adding relevance and meaning. Measurement of how many facts are remembered does not automatically lead to the ability to use them in practical situations. Biggs (see, for example, Biggs, 1999a) identifies the integrated nature of knowledge and understanding and shows that effective learning develops through stages of increasing complexity when learners understand and can make sense of material, rather than when they acquire unrelated bits of knowledge.

Information and knowledge online

Today the word 'knowledge' is often allied to the broad concept of the globally based 'knowledge industries' involved with the interconnected world of ICT, which has the capacity to influence the acquisition of knowledge in every field. The Internet has been at the forefront of a massive global blow-out in the amount of information that is readily available but, while information is the building block of knowledge, it can be risky to equate information with knowledge in higher education or anywhere else. Like a food crop that needs to be processed to make a new product before it becomes usable and relevant, information needs to be understood, evaluated and used for a purpose.

The ability to appreciate what knowledge is needed and then to be able to retrieve and apply it is more and more important in the information age. For those with excellent information searching skills there is ready access to a great deal of material. Unfortunately not all students possess these skills in the early stages of their programme, thus rendering them underexposed to some of the relevant information of their field. The capabilities needed to access and manage information were discussed in Chapter 13, but we would emphasize the extent to which these abilities underpin those of knowing and understanding important facts, principles and procedures.

Knowledge and understanding in the disciplines

In most disciplines teachers need to establish that students have an adequate knowledge base before they can move on to more advanced learning tasks, but since disciplinary knowledge bases themselves are constantly evolving and changing students need to understand their discipline and its knowledge domain. This kind of understanding is often learnt through trial and error over a range of assessment tasks because the values and conventions of academic fields are often socially represented and many, if not most, as we have seen, are not tangible or explicit. Students may not be taught explicitly, but formative assessment with feedback from their lecturers can help them to become familiar with the expectations of their teachers and more broadly in their fields, and thus to be able to focus their efforts successfully.

Memorizing vs understanding

While it would be rare for professionals to have the need to recall fragments of knowledge in practising their discipline, there will always be a need for students in their early years of study to learn factual material. Assessment of basic knowledge is appropriate when students are learning new concepts, principles or rules that need to be embedded before deeper levels of learning can take place, but it is more likely to be usable when understood in its context according to the protocols and accepted norms of the discipline. A good example of this would be the learning of the periodic tables.

Traditionally, teachers and students have thought that memorizing facts, formulae and procedures, often by cramming, is a good way to prepare for examinations, but this is not necessarily an approach that will lead to long-term retention of knowledge. Memory without understanding has rarely been the most efficient way to store information for later recall. However, some students prefer to memorize the detail of factual material as a step towards understanding and making meaning of it, while others memorize formulae, schemas, definitions or summaries to help their performance in examinations (Cooper *et al*, 2002), and most students use memorizing as a strategy in one way or another during their undergraduate studies as a stage towards developing functioning knowledge.

Some students do poorly in examinations because, while they may know their facts, they cannot apply them. In a recent online discussion forum (Math Forum, 2002), mathematics teachers in the United States discussed knowledge and understanding. One teacher quoted from a student who performed badly on a science examination: 'I knew the formula; I just did not know I was supposed to use it for this kind of problem.' These teachers ask: 'Does knowing a formula but not how to apply it qualify as knowledge?' The consensus seemed to be that it does not. Students who are only able to 'regurgitate' factual information often cannot comprehend or understand the concepts associated with the material. While 'knowledge' can sometimes imply 'understanding', comprehension or understanding is a necessary condition for demonstrating it.

It is not only those who have failed examinations who have problems showing that they know and understand basic material. It is well documented (see, for example, Dahlgren, 1984; Marton and Säljö, 1984; Ramsden, 1984) that students often cannot demonstrate that they have retained factual knowledge even after performing well in examinations. This could mean that the examinations were not valid or that, although these students had knowledge enough to succeed at examination time, meaningful learning eluded them. They may have understood the rules and the formulae but not well enough to be able to apply them outside an examination setting.

When the disciplinary conventions are clear to students from the beginning of their studies, they are likely to express knowledge in a way that is consistent with the values and conventions in their field of study. Student reports of having muddled through a programme until they could appreciate what was required of them highlight the importance of teaching how and what to learn early in a course rather than having students memorize facts, procedures and so on in a way that isolates the knowledge from its application in the field. In some applied fields, for example chemistry, geography, physiology and pharmacology, the teacher may need to assess the knowledge base of the cohort before setting applied problems for the students to tackle. However, we recognize that in some applied learning environments both declarative and functioning knowledge are assessed in an integrated way.

Some ways that students can be asked to demonstrate a grasp of declarative knowledge, expressed in different settings, are shown briefly in the following examples:

History
In the study of history, knowledge is expressed through a personal insight based on evidential materials and existing perspectives. Students must demonstrate an understanding of the relationships between existing perspectives and develop an overall argument in an integrated way.

Declarative knowledge is demonstrated when students accurately describe historical events as perceived by particular historians, and demonstrate a personal understanding of relationships between perspectives on factual historical information. Functioning knowledge is demonstrated when students are able credibly to challenge traditionally accepted views and by the advancement of a more insightful perspective.

Veterinary science
Knowledge in the hard applied disciplines is more concrete, and facts are usually right or wrong. In veterinary science, for example, students must first learn factual material associated with such subjects as 'The principles of pharmacology and toxicology' before they can make meaningful use of them in clinical veterinary science.

Declarative knowledge is demonstrated when students accurately recall facts, principles, laws etc and understand how they fit into their studies of veterinary science by giving examples. Functioning knowledge is demonstrated when students can perform higher-order tasks such as problem solving in a clinical setting.

Assessment methods

Although knowledge and understanding can have broad meanings relating to increasing levels of sophistication, our approach here is narrowed to declarative knowledge, as the higher-order skills are well represented in other chapters in this part of the book (see, for example, Chapters 17 and 18). We concentrate here on assessing declarative knowledge also because its association with surface approaches to learning does not mean that it is not worthy of assessment.

Declarative knowledge fits within the early levels of the taxonomy of learning objectives identified by Bloom in 1956 (Rowntree, 1987). Bloom's taxonomy has six broad categories that are classified from simple to more complex levels of learning objectives (see below). Although this taxonomy has to be seen as overly linear, Levels 1–3 together generally represent the cognitive abilities needed by students to demonstrate the basic knowledge and understanding that provide the foundations of their field of study. Understanding can be taken to include both comprehension and application. Levels 4–6 represent the higher-order thinking that is discussed in other chapters of this part of the book. The six levels are:

1. *knowledge*: ability to remember facts, terms, definitions, methods, rules, principles etc;
2. *comprehension*: ability to translate ideas from one form into another, to interpret, and to extrapolate consequences, trends etc;
3. *application*: ability to use general rules and principles in particular situations;
4. *analysis*: ability to break down an artefact and make clear the nature of its component parts and the relationship between them;
5. *synthesis*: ability to arrange and assemble various elements so as to make a new statement or plan or conclusion – a 'unique communication';

6. *evaluation*: ability to judge the value of materials or methods in terms of internal accuracy and consistency or by comparison with external criteria.

(Rowntree, 1987: 103)

Levels 1–3 of Bloom's taxonomy (above) provide a framework for teasing out the abilities students need to demonstrate the acquisition of declarative knowledge. The framework should not be thought to be definitive, though, as it can be changed depending on teaching and assessing intentions. Rowntree (1987) felt that educators should not regard Bloom's taxonomy as prescriptive, but rather should view it as 'suggestive, illuminative and stimulating' (1987: 105). A framework such as Bloom's shows teachers the importance of assessing the full range of intellectual activities that their students should achieve concerning particular learning outcomes. Thus assessment tasks that encourage students to cram and regurgitate facts, definitions and so on in examinations without comprehension can be avoided. It is one thing to pass examinations by reproducing declarative knowledge, but, as we have seen, students need to take meaningful approaches to learning if they are to retain what they have learnt.

Another taxonomy of levels of learning development already considered in this book is the SOLO taxonomy of learning objectives (for example, Biggs, 1999a: 33–48). This taxonomy takes a more holistic, integrated approach than Bloom's does. The SOLO taxonomy shows that declarative knowledge builds into functioning knowledge as learning becomes broader and deeper in its context. Teachers choose appropriate levels of challenge according to the curriculum and the purpose of assessment schemes.

While the examples of assessment tasks below give snapshots of how declarative knowledge is assessed in a variety of ways, it is not our intention to promote teaching and assessment purely as knowledge transmission. In the early stages of an undergraduate degree programme and as they become more independent learners, students need to build their knowledge base, but it is often the case that assessment tasks are integrated and intellectually challenging in their contexts and across a range of the learning outcomes discussed in this part of the book.

'Objective' tests and examinations

Traditional methods of assessing declarative knowledge have included objective assessment tasks such as quizzes, multiple choice, true/false, matching or completion tasks. Objective tests are those for which students' answers do not need interpretation or the judgement of markers (Habeshaw, Gibbs and Habeshaw, 1993).

Objective tests are an efficient way to examine a wide range of topics in a subject, especially useful for assessing large cohorts of students. They can be marked quickly, manually or by optical reader technology. When they are well designed, they can be highly reliable (Habeshaw, Gibbs and Habeshaw, 1993) and valid. These types of tests can be written to allow students to demonstrate their level of understanding of declarative knowledge and, in the early stages of an undergraduate degree, it is often important to be able to test widely across topics in this way. However, before embarking upon the use of objective tests, it is crucial that you seek out an expert colleague or a good text on objective testing to ensure the tests are well designed.

Objective tests that call for an understanding of rules, principles and concepts as well as the recall of this material are more likely to encourage students to develop the capability to retain and apply knowledge after they have been assessed.

Quizzes, multiple choice, match-the-answer, complete-the-diagram, true/false and short answer objective tests can be used for:

- diagnosing students' level of knowledge and understanding at an appropriate stage of learning;
- self- and peer assessment exercises;
- formative assessment to allow students to diagnose and reflect upon their learning;
- summative assessment for grading purposes.

Computer-assisted assessment (CAA)

CAA has been used in many disciplines, for example a 1999 study in the United Kingdom showed that CAA tests were available in nearly every subject area. There is currently a bias towards science and technology subjects (CAA Centre, 2003). The term 'CAA' usually refers to examinations, tests or assignments that students perform at a computer terminal connected to an intranet. These are then marked and graded automatically. CAA is often used to test declarative knowledge through objective assessment such as multiple choice, true/false, matching or short answer tests.

However, if CAA is to provide valid and reliable outcomes for students, tasks and marking schemes have to be carefully designed because the construction of the kinds of objective tests commonly used in CAA is no easy matter and very time-consuming. This means that teachers, at least while they become confident with CAA technology, need access to expert educational designers and/or appropriate resources to help design tests and marking schemes and that fit with their higher education institution's computerized educational system and its capabilities. We would argue, too, that CAA tests should not assess declarative knowledge alone, unless they are for formative purposes. Well-designed CAA tests require students to demonstrate understanding and application of knowledge in an appropriate context.

CAA can be a boon for busy academics who need to monitor student progress throughout a subject or course because it saves staff time once tests, question banks and feedback have been prepared. Question banks can be designed to provide different tests for formative and summative purposes, and teachers can design detailed and specific feedback to be delivered automatically so that students can check their own progress. Suggestions for remedial work can be included with feedback, especially if students are able to retake tests or use CAA for self-diagnosis.

Some of the drawbacks of CAA are that it can be costly, that academic and administrative staff need training in the hardware and software involved, and that equipment failure can come at inopportune times, such as in the middle of examinations. However, its benefits outweigh these limitations and its use in diagnostic testing as well as for formative and summative assessment is well accepted in higher education settings.

Case 14.1: CAA (multiple choice questions) in a business subject

Business structures take a number of forms, eg partnerships, unincorporated associations, companies, cooperatives and so forth. In the introductory unit on business structures, students researched a topic, eg types of unincorporated associations, which include building societies and friendly societies, and the different aspects of each. A formative assessment task relating to the project was a multiple choice quiz to test students' knowledge of business structures.

The computer-based multiple choice quiz provided students with the opportunity for immediate feedback on their answers. On completion of several topics in their lectures (on-campus students) or their study materials (off-campus students), students logged on to the study Web site and were presented with one question at a time. They were required to select the correct answer from among four possibilities. Where they gave a wrong answer the software immediately provided them with reasons why the answer was incorrect as well as referring them to the relevant section of their study materials for further learning activities to reinforce knowledge.

It was possible to take this quiz several times, as the questions were served up randomly from the extensive item bank developed over a few years. If, after repeated attempts, students were still unsure of the reasons why they failed to pick the correct answer, the software provided further explanations and corrections to their misconceptions. When students were satisfied they had achieved their desired level of knowledge and understanding, they proceeded to the next topic and associated quizzes.

Although the formative assessment task was not compulsory, it was certainly in the students' interest to undertake these practice quizzes, as a selection of questions from this extensive question bank was then used for the exam component of the final assessment. This reinforcement of knowledge and understanding also worked well because of the incremental way in which students could develop their declarative knowledge base.

Computer-assisted diagnostic tests

Computer-based diagnostic tests can be undertaken before commencing a subject to identify gaps in the students' current knowledge. Guidance can then be provided. Alternatively, diagnostic tests may be given during the course of study to allow students to receive useful feedback. They may then be directed to learning support, or to revise specific content areas as in the case above. The benefit of completing such tests in a computer-based format is the speed and consistency with which feedback and suggestions can be given by the system, as well as the privacy in which students can face their own gaps of knowledge.

The three guiding principles found through researching the effectiveness of diagnostic tests are:

1. The test should validly assess what it purports to, ie reading skills rather than analysis, or writing skills rather than problem solving.
2. The outcome of the test needs to be of immediate use to students, such that they know what to do with the results of the test and can follow these up with actions.
3. Students should be able to learn something in completing the diagnostic test itself. For example, they learn about reflecting on their own learning needs, or about the value of questioning their taken-for-granted knowledge.

(Drew, Thorpe and Bannister, 2002)

Case 14.2: Self-diagnosis of academic study skills

A self-paced module on academic study skills was available to all students upon enrolment and prior to the start of each semester. Students worked through activities online in order to evaluate their own reading skills and writing skills. Feedback was provided on their progress for some activities while for others model answers were given for students to self-assess their achievements.

Once students completed this online programme, they were able to return to the exercises and resources throughout their programme of study for extra clarification, reinforcement or practice. They gained confidence and competence in their knowledge and understanding by working as they chose within the confines of the computer program.

Intelligent language tutoring systems

In the learning of languages, knowledge and understanding must be demonstrated in a range of ways – through effective reading, fluent writing, accurate listening and appropriate conversation. Each of these processes can further be broken down to sub-processes; for example, fluent writing is made up of planning, transcribing and revising. In the assessment of vocabulary and grammar practice, intelligent language tutoring systems (ILTS) can be used to facilitate students' progress and their achievement of meaningful interaction.

One of the most important considerations in assessment of language learning is the necessity for immediate and ongoing feedback and correction. Automated systems such as the one described by Heift *et al* (2000) provide sophisticated methods of effectively supporting the learning process.

Case 14.3: Learning French with the help of an automated tutor

Students of French provided their own 'natural language' input to the computer program, rather than selecting only from pre-defined answers. Students engaged with given activities by typing text-based answers and receiving a response from the interactive system. The ILTS used natural language processing (NLP) to analyse the students' input and provide feedback with respect to specific errors made.

A further enhancement of this interactive course support system included student modelling, which tracked ongoing performance, kept a record and adjusted the system decisions accordingly. For example, the level of feedback needed for the student was determined by the student model, and the difficulty of subsequent exercises was selected by the student model in response to previous performance.

Essays, reports and projects

Essays, reports and project work require description, explanation, analysis and argument. They are usually designed to test several learning objectives, including some about 'knowledge and understanding' (Hughes and Magin, 1996: 140).

Case 14.4: Demonstrating knowledge as a prelude to developing an argument

The process–performance paradox encountered in the human resource domain was presented to students as a mystery to solve: 'With the extensive knowledge available about staff selection and appraisal, why is it that HR departments keep getting it wrong?' For students to complete this essay-style assignment, they first had to demonstrate knowledge of the literature in the field, and then describe examples of practice to reinforce the point of view they finally presented.

The assessment of knowledge and understanding in this case was a preliminary requirement before students could successfully put forward a well-reasoned case. The marking criteria provided to students made it explicit that a sound knowledge of the literature, key models and concepts in the field was significantly weighted in the overall marks for this essay.

Producing an A to Z

Searching for information in order to develop a collated directory of information is a skill commonly required in client services. For practitioners in the field, it is not only useful to be able to refer to their own directory of relevant information, but in some cases this same directory may be extremely valuable to hand out to clients who may not otherwise find easy access to the specific details concerned. This task can be varied for appropriate use at different points in a study programme. Headings within the resource may be prescribed (early in the programme), negotiated (mid-programme) or autonomously constructed by students (final year).

Case 14.5: An A to Z of medicinal plants

An assessment task for final-year students in a phytotherapy course was to provide a detailed resource about the identifying features, cultivation, medicinal properties, extraction processes and dosage details of any plants in south-eastern Australia that they considered would be useful for prescribing in some way to their clients. Students were also required to demonstrate an understanding of precautions, contraindications, toxic dosages and antidotes for the plants they included in the directory.

Information about nutritional questions, treatment details, local resources and products available with a description of the strengths and limitations of each was also to be included.

The resource would be assessed for both its comprehensive scope and the quality of the annotations according to the criteria given.

Implications for teaching

Teaching declarative knowledge can be intensive, especially in the early stages, because students learn it through iterations of practice and feedback. Lectures are a good way to introduce new factual material because a well-planned and delivered lecture provides a focus for studies, identifies what is the core knowledge at each stage of a study programme and shows how it fits within the curriculum. Lectures help students to become familiar with the lecturer's own angle on the material and how he or she prefers it should be treated in assessment tasks. Some lecturers believe that they need to include a great deal of detail in lectures, especially when declarative knowledge is being introduced, but this can be counter-productive if students become overloaded and confused. Lectures that introduce new facts and concepts with explanations, examples and direction to further reading can be highly effective. Each lecture should probably introduce no more than three or four new concepts and should provide activities to allow students to process the new information by interacting with the lecturer and each other.

Quizzes, short answer and multiple choice tests on paper or with CAA can be used formatively to help students embed factual knowledge (see Cases 14.1, 14.2 and 14.3), and the dual aims of reducing teachers' marking loads and encouraging meaningful, reflective learning can be achieved through self- and peer marking of such quizzes. For example, the teacher could provide a list of objects, and students could work together to name them, or groups of students could match definitions to terms or classifications. Teaching games that involve meaningful repetition can be helpful, as can the progressive development of glossaries of terms, definitions, explanations and applications in a disciplinary context.

15

Demonstrating procedures and techniques

Introduction

This chapter addresses the assessment of skills that usually require performance to a predetermined standard of competence. Skills of this kind commonly take the form of procedures or techniques that can be observed and judged, and usually occur in applied and professional fields from medicine and the health sciences through to the visual arts and music. There is some overlap between this learning outcome, and that of Chapter 16, 'Designing, creating, performing'.

Rarely in higher education are skills assessed in isolation. In contrast to the vocational education sector, it is expected that the skills in undergraduate education are performed in their professional context, and involve significant prior knowledge and understanding of the purpose and application of the skill. Often assessment will include attitudinal factors in the performance, such as showing due care and diligence, or with appropriate flair, style or gusto, and so forth. They may also include a component of self-evaluation – students' assessment of their own performance, their strengths and weaknesses and areas to be improved.

What is competence?

The novice-to-expert continuum is particularly important in assessing skills, yet rarely are these defined or explored in the professions (for example, see Benner, 1984). Where exactly, along this continuum, can you reasonably expect students to be able to perform at any point in their progress through a programme? What is deemed competent? To a large degree, there will be professional expectations regarding abilities of graduates, although assessors will also need to make decisions about what is acceptable at various points during the programme. Some skills, such as developing competence in using a software package, can be acquired incrementally over time, and various levels of competence are acceptable. In contrast, critical skills such as the resuscitation of an infant can only ever have one acceptable standard of competence.

Whether we should expect all students to achieve the same level of competence as an outcome is another issue. For example, in music education or visual arts, students enter programmes with a wide range of ability and goals. The emphasis in these settings might be placed on individual development and improvement, and students may be assessed accordingly, rather than against the same measure.

Mastery learning, although not practised widely in higher education, is another interesting concept in relation to performance of skills. In this mode, students can have multiple attempts at acquiring the skill – the emphasis here is not on the time taken, but ensuring that every student attains his or her highest potential (Toohey and Magin, 1996). True mastery learning is undertaken in a self-paced learning environment with resources and tutorial support available, so it may be difficult to enact in traditional higher education settings with paced semester time-frames. However, the principle is a challenging one: Do we most value the students' best mastery of a skill or the system of ranking student performance based upon whatever competence can be achieved within a limited time-frame? If a skill is acquired, should we really be concerned with how long it has taken for the student to acquire it? The real strength of mastery learning is that it turns all assessment tasks into formative experiences in an atmosphere of continuous individual improvement.

Determining competence

There is little logic to norm-referenced assessment schemes when determining competence in procedures and techniques. Ranking of student performance, and arbitrary passing grades are of little use in explaining to employers and accrediting bodies what students can actually do. Student performance needs to be assessed against explicit standards of performance so there is no ambiguity regarding the minimum level of competence required and what the student has actually achieved. This will require the assessor to understand and articulate, with a high degree of professional judgement, the various degrees of performance, as well as what elements of the performance are valued and why. Again, the novice-to-expert continuum in the professions will be important benchmarks in devising criteria for bands of performance. Some assessors may decide that graded judgements of performance are not possible or desirable in their setting, because a skill is either demonstrated or it is not. In such cases, assessors may choose instead an ungraded result of either satisfactory or unsatisfactory. If the principle of mastery learning is being adopted, the result of 'achieved competency' or 'still achieving competency' might be more appropriate. Still other schemes may make distinctions between competence and the higher-order concept of achieving 'capability' or 'competence plus'.

Demonstrating procedures and techniques in the disciplines

Most procedures and techniques are embedded within their fields of professional practice so the use of these skills is highly context specific. The challenge in assessment is to ensure that the most lifelike and authentic conditions are created for the formative development and performance of these skills, which then are transferable to the workplace. It may require considerable effort on the part of assessors to create appropriate conditions for practising and assessing skills, and could involve role-play, simulations, field trips, laboratory work or professional practicums.

As mentioned earlier, it is rare for procedures or techniques to be assessed in isolation from the knowledge and understanding that drive their performance. Thus, in addition to actually performing a procedure, it may be expected that students explain why the procedure is appropriate in such circumstances, what other procedures may be relevant and how the procedure may differ according to changed circumstances. As students develop expertise, it is usually appropriate to assess multiple procedures and techniques in concert with each other or as part of a decision-making scenario, so that a more holistic picture of competence can be gained.

In each professional setting there is a further dimension of *tacit knowledge* regarding the appropriate performance of procedures and techniques. In nursing, for example, the insertion of a drip may be done competently, but without the requisite concern for the comfort of the client. A piano performance may be technically accurate, yet emotionally missing the mark. Adherence to the cultural rules and norms of a field may form an integral part of the assessment of students, and yet these norms may not be well explained to students or stated in marking criteria. Gerholm (1990) explores these forms of tacit knowledge and relates them to the development of the requisite intuition and *savoir-faire* to flourish within a professional community. Usually these forms of knowledge are acquired indirectly by students, through observation and modelling. They may be very subtle in nature and perhaps unconscious even to teachers themselves, yet the ability to master tacit knowledge will have a significant impact upon student performance. The idea of tacit learning provides a particular challenge to assessors to ensure that key qualities, attitudinal attributes and skills expected in the performance of a task are well explained to students, or that they are modelled and their underlying norms and values are discussed openly.

Assessment issues

Resulting from the discussion above, there are a number of issues in the assessment of procedures and techniques that need to be considered by assessors:

- *Devising and communicating a clear picture of what's being assessed.* Decisions about the type of techniques or procedures being assessed and the level of performance required will need to be made. These are based upon assessors' understanding of the appropriate cumulative development of skills over the course of study. Some techniques may only need to be assessed once during a programme. Other more complex tasks should be cumulatively developed over a whole programme. Expected gradations of ability over time need to be well communicated to students.
- *Integrating skills with underpinning knowledge and understanding.* The performance of procedures and techniques, without students being able also to provide a rationale for use, common variations and other underpinning knowledge, will be of limited use.
- *Ensuring the most authentic conditions possible.* There is little point in developing professional abilities such as these unless they are transferable to the workplace. Hence it is worth the effort to ensure that the most lifelike and authentic conditions are made available to students for practice and assessment.
- *Individual improvement or common mastery?* It may not be necessary or appropriate for all students to achieve a common level of competence. Consider models of mastery learning where students set their own goals relative to their individual interests and professional aspirations.

Teaching and assessing procedures and techniques *at a distance* have often been considered problematic, because the teacher needs physically to witness the demonstration of the procedures or techniques to measure achievement (unless residential schools or specially scheduled face-to-face events are organized for this purpose). Video demonstrations are sometimes employed as a means of both teaching skills to external students and assessing student performance, although it can prove cumbersome for students and unreliable from the assessor's point of view. However, as many distance education students are already in relevant workplaces or have access to such workplaces through their local communities, opportunities exist for workplace mentoring and assessment schemes (Morgan and O'Reilly, 1999; Morgan and Smit, 2001). Students appoint an appropriately skilled mentor/assessor with whom they practise procedures and techniques in their workplace (or authentic setting) until they have achieved the standards specified by the educational institution. The mentor/assessor is provided with detailed criteria and standards and verifies to the institution that the student has achieved the required standard.

Large cohorts may pose particular problems in assessing procedures and techniques, because of the level of individualized support required during practice and assessment sessions. *Peer and self-assessment* opportunities arise here as options that can help students monitor their own progress and provide constructive feedback to others, while taking some of the pressure off teaching staff in terms of individual monitoring. An effective scheme of this kind can dramatically increase students' opportunities for practice and preparation for final assessments, with the added benefit of a collaborative learning environment. Generally, it is important for students to learn to gauge their own progress in the acquisition of skills, and to benchmark their progress with others in the group. As always, criteria and standards must be very explicit and well communicated to students for meaningful judgements to be made.

Assessment methods

Observation of real or simulated professional practice

This is one of the most common methods of assessing skills, providing students with a lifelike but safe and supported environment in which to practise and be assessed. Many spaces across universities are commonly transformed into *de facto* surgical wards, recording studios, courtrooms, consulting rooms and so forth for these purposes. Increasingly, we also find virtual learning spaces that are dedicated for the practice of professional skills that can be demonstrated via computer applications or scenarios, particularly in domains such as information technology and the sciences. Field trips and professional practicums are other common methods of teaching and assessing these skills, offering the increased advantage of more authentic contexts, although sometimes more complex in terms of administration, insurance and supervision.

Case 15.1: Assessment of skills in a field trip

Interpreting a series of maps in a range of projections and scales, demonstrating the skills involved in the use of global positioning systems, surveying the topographical features of a landscape, interpreting aerial photographs and satellite images all belong to the skills set of the environmental scientist. For students to be assessed on these kinds of skills, they are presented with a number of activities to carry out in the field. Each skill can be associated with an authentic activity such as pinpointing the location of the field trip on an aerial photograph or satellite image, surveying the contours of the field trip site and finding one's way home using topographical maps.

A series of field trips are facilitated during semester where students are divided into teams and provided with the opportunity to practise skills. With the aid of checklists containing detailed criteria and standards, students collaborate and peer-assess each other's progress, with the aid of a tutor, and nominate when they are ready to be summatively assessed. They are allowed two attempts at any skill, which almost certainly assures that all students achieve the required competences by the end of semester.

Other written assignments during the course assess the knowledge component, but there is also a requirement that students are able to explain what they're doing and why, as they perform each skill. There are also tacit components to these assessments, such as treating expensive instruments with due diligence and leaving the environment in the same pristine condition in which it was found, which reflect core values of the profession. Students are warned that any significant breaches of these may result in automatic failure.

Role-play

Role-plays are excellent ways in which to support the development of procedures and techniques, and the ability to think critically and problem-solve as the role-play unfolds. They are ideal for assessing groups of skills where the student needs to select and demonstrate the appropriate response as events unfold. Role-plays of this kind often commence with a scenario. For example, a basic nursing skill is being able to safely lift a patient. A simple scenario is devised whereby the patient needs to be moved from a bed to a wheelchair, but is feeling faint and disoriented and is somewhat heavy. Students will need to assess mobility, apply appropriate lifting procedures, make decisions about the use of an electronic lifting device and show due care for the health and safety of the patient and themselves.

When role-plays are devised to test skill sets such as these, it is important to ensure that the scenarios are not too complex or ambiguous in terms of potential responses. The tasks must require clear-cut actions to defined situations. When seeking to assess more complex problem-solving and critical thinking abilities, other more effective assessment methods can be used that don't dilute the focus on correct and competent performance of skills (see Chapters 17 and 18).

Case 15.2: Assessing counselling skills through role-play
Counselling skills, procedures and techniques are assessed cumulatively during a programme using role-play as one of its key methods. In the first year, students are expected to master core listening skills, including attending, paraphrasing, clarifying and perception checking, as well as leading skills, such as opening, encouraging, focusing and questioning. Students form pairs and role-play as client and counsellor, practising these techniques with guidance, supervision, set scenarios and clear criteria. Videos are employed so students can later observe and evaluate their developing expertise. Students are assessed by submitting a videotaped interview of what they consider to be their best work, along with a written piece that critically reflects upon their efforts and relates theory with

practice. Students can be studying on-campus or by distance education to fulfil assessment requirements successfully.

Although the context for this assessment is not particularly authentic or lifelike, it is crucially important that basic counselling skills can be practised in safe, supervised settings where no harm is done. In later years, more sophisticated and authentic tasks are introduced as students' exposure to new theories and concepts becomes greater. Note that there is a clear novice-to-expert framework underscoring this assessment scheme.

Clinical assessments

Clinical decision making develops from clinical practice and diagnostic skills. However, in a student's progress towards such higher-order applications, the competent performance of clinical procedures and techniques in itself requires assessment and accreditation.

The first rule of practice is the same as for all body therapies: 'First do no harm.' When clinical placement is not available or is too premature for the novice student, simulations can be used to great effect in supporting learning and maintaining the principle of safety in care.

Case 15.3: Clinical assessment in physiotherapy

A student learning about treating back pain in pregnancy: 1) is given a scenario to review; 2) carries out the diagnostic activities with a volunteer client; and 3) suggests treatment options. In order to demonstrate the techniques used in these diagnoses and treatments, the student works with a volunteer such as a student peer or family member.

During assessment, the student is required to:

- ask questions about causes or precipitating factors, eg lifting, carrying, sleeping;
- demonstrate how to teach a pregnant client about her posture and body mechanics;
- suggest and demonstrate a series of appropriate stretching and strengthening exercises;
- demonstrate how to wear support garments such as a maternity back brace;
- apply a hot compress or cold pack;
- perform joint mobilizations and soft tissue mobilizations;
- develop and demonstrate a home exercise programme;
- demonstrate techniques that allow the client to manage her own symptoms;
- determine the factors that would indicate a referral to another specialist practitioner.

Each task has a designated level of competence and is assessed by observation with the use of checklists. Volunteers only provide feedback on areas familiar to them, such as the effectiveness of the student's communication, comfort during processes etc. Several elements of this assessment task take the student beyond simple demonstration of techniques. However, the competent performance of skills components is critical to the student's effective achievement of learning outcomes.

Problem-based exercises

Although problem-based assessment tasks are commonly used to test higher-order thinking skills (and are dealt with more extensively in Chapter 18), they are also employed for the demonstration of competence. The advantage in using problem-based tasks is that they enable students to perform skills in context. As the following case demonstrates, skills are the focus of the task, yet in problem-based tasks there will always be significant elements of analysis and relating theory to practice.

Case 15.4: Performing procedures in developing a database

This is a problem scenario provided to informational technology students to assess the accuracy of techniques and procedures in developing a database. The scenario concerns the operations of a yacht charter company that supplies on-demand charter boat services. All charter trip details are recorded, such as details of passengers and crew, expected departure times, destinations, duration of voyage, expected return times and prices. There are numerous complexities regarding information and differing access requirements of staff.

The assessment task requires students to develop a prototype database. An example of two different sets of test data (two different voyages booked) is to be used to indicate the system is working. Final reports printed out from the prototype database need to show that users can access the database to achieve their typical goals, but there may be several different designs that achieve this same end.

Although an essential element of the final submission is the inclusion of clear documentation concerning the operational features of the database, the major focus of this assessment task is the successful performance of database systems design procedures.

(adapted from Roche, 2003)

Artistic performance

A certain level of technical performance is required in any aspect of the creative and performing arts. While this is usually not the full focus of assessment, in the earlier stages of any undergraduate programme it is important for students to master the technical competence that underpins the higher-order demands of style and creative expression.

Although students entering a university programme should have achieved a basic level of competence in the area of artistic endeavour, such as an instrumental or vocal skill, they will be expected to demonstrate mastery of these skills with any performances they undertake during their first year.

Case 15.5: Technical competence with percussion in a group performance

For the subject Practical Studies II in music, a first-year subject, students of percussion were required to work in an ensemble, orchestra or band context to develop further their musicianship skills and competence in concert-style performance.

A selection from the learning outcomes that highlight the importance of technical competence includes:

- appropriate hand placement, body position and playing techniques for the percussion instruments (ie snare drum, bass drum, timpani, keyboard percussion, cymbals and auxiliary percussion instruments);
- correct care and maintenance of the percussion instruments, and knowledge of the necessary accessories;
- expertise in playing techniques for the snare drum, timpani and keyboard percussion instruments;
- appropriate performance techniques in assigned solos and ensemble pieces.

Assessment criteria for the technical aspects take account of the students' demonstrated mastery of tempo, rhythm technique and dynamics, and evidence of their preparation for performance, eg instrument in good order, sheet music on hand and annotations marked for a student's own reference.

(adapted from Sawyer, 2002)

Implications for teaching

The cases in this chapter provide but a glimpse of the variety of ways in which competence is demonstrated across the disciplines in higher education. However, we summarize below four key themes that are likely to arise for teachers irrespective of context:

- Competence in a skill is acquired by practice. The principal challenge for teachers is to provide maximum opportunities for practice with individual feedback upon developing expertise.
- There may be no absolutes or external measures of acceptable competence in a skill. This is particularly the case if the skill is assessed at differing points across a programme with staged development of expertise. In such

instances, teachers will be required to exercise significant professional judgement about what is appropriate and at which stage.

- Transferability of skills is a key issue. If the conditions under which the skill is assessed are not particularly lifelike, the likelihood of its transfer to real-life situations may be questionable.
- There is much tacit knowledge in the competent performance of procedures and techniques. It is important for teachers to be able to articulate all the qualities of performance upon which judgements will be made, and to ensure that these are adequately taught or modelled during practice sessions.

16

Designing, creating, performing

Introduction

The capabilities discussed here are combined in ways that bring individual innovation, imagination and creativity into play in higher education learning contexts. Of course they are not purely the domain of the creative arts and design courses. They are evident in all fields when students analyse situations or solve problems creatively, but this chapter has as its focus the kind of learning outcomes that are specifically about aesthetic value or individually creative design or performance.

Students tend to develop their aesthetic abilities alongside learning the theory and techniques that underpin the creative outcomes of activities and projects. In some technical design projects, students need to show they can use a particular technology or material efficiently as a first step to understanding its design possibilities. In the arts, students have to be able to follow instructions and learn techniques and procedures as a foundation for style or performance. In this way, the skills and abilities discussed here overlap with those in the previous chapter on 'demonstrating procedures and techniques'. The aesthetic dimension is added when techniques and procedures are applied innovatively, creatively, uniquely or as solutions to unorthodox problems. Here there is also an overlap with such cognitive abilities as problem solving and critical analysis.

Aesthetics are highly interpretive and individual to each person. Although there is much historical and contemporary evidence to show that creativity does not depend on a university education, the goal of many educators is to be able to influence students towards the development of their own creative ideas. However, many teachers in higher education settings believe that sound technique and knowledge of theoretical traditions are essential for creativity to flourish. Therefore one of the most demanding aspects of teaching students to be creative in higher education settings is to establish the balance between teaching technique and supporting personal expression.

What is creativity?

There are a great many notions of what constitutes creativity. Creativity can be a product of a problem-solving activity or it can be that 'aha' or 'eureka' moment, a flash of brilliance, a happy accident or perhaps talent determined by genetics or hard work. It can also be holistic, a blending of concept and feeling, analysis and intuition when feeling and knowing become one (Bensur, 2002). A creative person sees the 'rightness' or 'wrongness' of solutions based on heightened sensitivity to the problem (Wright, in Bensur, 2002).

Creativity can emerge when people are engaged in:

- imagining;
- visualizing;
- designing;
- analysing;
- making;
- creating;
- innovating;
- synthesizing;
- performing;
- solving problems.

(adapted from Nightingale and Magin, in Nightingale *et al*, 1996: 163)

Conceptions of creativity are widely disputed and definitions have various emphases depending upon the social, political or philosophical perspective at hand. For example, a farmer and an estate agent who view the same landscape painting would probably have different responses to it. The farmer might look at the landscape and think about the quality of the soil, and the estate agent would look at its position and sales potential. A motor mechanic could find aesthetic appeal in the design of a new type of vehicle engine at a motor show, and a member of the car-driving public might find the same vehicle aesthetically pleasing because of the smooth body design. There are other ways of thinking about creativity too. Some appreciate genres of taste and beauty for their own sakes; some have a preference for simplicity and functionality of design; for others creativity might derive from a particular style of art or performance or it may have some characteristic that is particularly satisfying for the individual.

Teachers often seem to have difficulty defining what they mean by creativity. They use words like 'flair', 'imagination', 'originality', 'intuition' or 'innovation' to describe creative responses in their fields. They amplify the descriptions with demonstrations and illustrations of what they mean through a variety of means, including models, debates, theoretical exposition, analysis of famous historical and modern creative work, monitoring and feedback on student progress. It seems that, if students are to trust academic judgements of their creative work, assessors need to be professionally credible and authoritative in their theoretical knowledge and in their standing in wide-ranging professional networks. One reason for the difficulty in articulating clear definitions of the artistic dimension of student work is that some concepts are not easily explained.

Eisner (1991: 6) coined the term 'educational connoisseurship' by taking the term 'connoisseur' as it is used in the visual arts, where a connoisseur is someone who 'depends upon the ability to see, not merely to look' in order to know, and applying it in educational settings. 'Educational connoisseurship' is a concept that has a grounding in professionalism, but goes qualitatively further to become the ability to 'help others learn to see what they might otherwise not notice' (Eisner, 1991: 69). This is perhaps the mirror image of the concept described earlier, that students tend to trust the judgement of assessors who are credible to them in their aesthetic fields. An educational connoisseur can help students appreciate creativity so that they are open to creative responses.

Designing, creating and performing in the disciplines

Creativity has different meanings in terms of practical outcomes in different disciplinary and professional settings. The fine arts and the performing arts have as their key goal the production of something that is aesthetically pleasing, as well as the conveying of a maker's or a performer's intentions. In architecture, engineering and information technology, for example, design that is pleasing to the senses is important, but the beauty of the construction of a building or the product of engineering or information technology design is not only reliant on emotions or senses. It also depends upon how creatively designers have solved design problems within the capabilities of their technologies. The aesthetic includes the way a problem has been solved to create functionality in a product. That is, the debate around the pre-eminence of form or function in creative activity is often based in disciplinarity.

In all disciplines, though, it seems there needs to be a blend of theoretical understanding, technical competence, critical analysis, problem solving and innovation for creativity to emerge. There is a wide diversity of approaches to teaching and assessing design, creativity and performance, each representing a different school of thought. Approaches can be more or less flexible, or they can be based on particular theoretical positions, such as postmodernism. Teachers might follow an apprenticeship model or take another approach. The following snapshots have been drawn from a range of settings to illustrate different ways of conceptualizing creativity in higher education:

Engineering

In engineering, creativity in design includes turning a client's expressed needs into a functional product. Prototypes and visuals are critical to a successful presentation of a design product. They are the means by which good design is illustrated. The visual is inseparable from the theoretical knowledge of design – it is not simply an organizational tool. Therefore it must show that the design is a workable and creative solution to the design specifications (Dannels, 2002).

Part of the aesthetic of the product of engineering design is that it should have appeal to a potential user; it should be a creative application of materials; it should provide a design for a product that fits specifications; it should be within budget; and it should yield a functional working solution to the design problem.

Music

Music composition students are expected already to possess a grounding in music theory and performance. As undergraduates they learn to create using stylistic models within a tradition, and through these they become inducted into the theory and styles of their musical tradition. They learn patterns and techniques and gain an understanding of musical structures within theoretical frameworks. Theory is often conveyed aurally by the teacher. The creative thrust of classical music as developed by contemporary classical composers should push the boundaries of the art form by creating ways of putting sounds together that no one else is doing.

Jazz improvisation involves years and years of learning routines, listening to and notating the improvisation of great performers, and analysing how to improvise within a musical tradition in order to gain insights. Then a performer can transcend existing patterns and spontaneously create a performance that is innovative and compelling.

Visual arts

Visual art in higher education is about students exploring such areas as art theory, politics, cultural theory or contemporary issues based on their knowledge of existing techniques, styles and movements in thought. They learn how to critique and understand genres of art. The concept of creativity is a higher-order activity that is not based purely on intuition, feeling, emotion and talent, but emerges from intellectual activity by, for example, combining two sets of knowledge to produce a work that shows an understanding of both – and rewriting them in an innovative, unexpected and perhaps emotional way. New combinations of established techniques and modes of production are valued.

Creative writing

Booker prizewinning novelist Ian McEwan began his creative writing studies with another well-known British author, Malcolm Bradbury, as his lecturer. McEwan has said that Bradbury taught him how to treat themes and about the structure of a piece of writing, but he learnt to be creative by having an audience and a purpose for his writing. Bradbury read his work, gave encouragement and left him to pursue his creative ideas free from limitations. McEwan felt he was free to pursue his own creative demons in his fiction predominantly through practice, encouragement and self-evaluation.

(from an ABC radio interview, *Arts Today*, January 1999)

Architecture

An architectural design project is an integration of conceptual design and technical knowledge and skill, including familiarity with building materials and client needs. Students would receive a set of design specifications and detailed description of the proposed building site. They conceive and explore design options. They frame and reframe the design problem and produce several iterations of sketches, working drawings and models. Aesthetic solutions to the design problem are those that take full advantage of the possibilities of the specifications and the site in a way that is functional at the same time as being innovative and aesthetically pleasing.

Assessment methods

There are particular tensions and difficulties that challenge assessors of aesthetic outcomes. While these are probably familiar to assessors of other learning outcomes, they are in sharp relief when one of the purposes of assessment is to identify and measure creativity. Nightingale and Magin (in Nightingale *et al*, 1996) identify several such tensions:

- How can assessors judge both technical competence and creativity to achieve a balance between these two categories of ability within a single assessment task? A related challenge is when and how to change the balance during students' progression through stages of technical competence in their course.
- How can assessors write assessment criteria that are clear and explicit for both students and assessors when assessment tasks are complex and multifaceted? There is debate about how specific assessment criteria should be in order to provide explicit guidance for students without stultifying their potential for creative expression.
- How can assessors agree on the quality of artistic work or a creative product when they come from different philosophies, schools of thought or allegiances within a discipline? It has been said that assessment of aesthetic work is highly subjective because it depends upon emotional and intuitive responses as well as on the professional and technical expertise of assessors.

It is difficult to separate out the aesthetic element of designing, creating and performing from the integrated cognitive and technical skills that culminate in a product or in the outcome of a technical or artistic process. Elliott (1995), for example, advocates a practicum model of music education that places the curriculum and assessment of musical achievement within its authentic professional environment. Elliott wonders whether music educators can organize music programmes in ways that are congruent with the nature and values of music as a diverse human practice. That is, he recommends assessment that meaningfully applies essential knowledge, skills and technique in a real-world setting. Similarly many engineering design projects are holistic where students work individually or in teams to come up with a design solution to a particular engineering problem and then apply their design by building a prototype of an engineering product. In music and in engineering, there are established standards for the aesthetics of performance or design, but there are also explicit standards for other aspects of the performance or the engineering product.

Systems of accountability for increasing the validity and reliability of assessment have become problematic in assessing art. Cannatella (2001: 319) asserts that while art assessment should be able to identify whether a work is 'good, bad or meritorious... the particular character and activity that goes into the making of art does not fit comfortably into any system of general assessment criteria'. Tutors need to know something about their students' intentionality for a work of art: the experiences, perceptions, thoughts and ideas that 'drive the work in order to understand the events shaping the decisions of it' (Cannatella, 2001: 320). The need for consistent marking in a learning domain that is individualistic and highly personal is the basis for the range of concerns about assessment in art.

A common solution to this dilemma and to the issue of the perception of subjectivity in assessing creative work is to use panels of assessors made up of academic staff who teach the subject, sometimes including external professional members of a panel.

Some of the grading criteria applied to creative work are difficult to express, so teachers describe expected standards of achievement in a number of ways: illustrations and exemplars including models, performance, the work of past students, collaborative work and self-reflection. You will notice that many of the cases outlined below include elements of self- and peer assessment used either formatively or summatively to encourage self-reflection and critical analysis. Students need to develop a conception of the expected 'standards of performance' to be able to engage in effective self- and peer assessment, so preparation for these methods of assessment include explanations of such standards, how they have been developed and how students should apply them to assess their own and their co-learners' work in formative and summative assessment tasks.

Designing and building a prototype

Design is commonly assessed as part of larger projects that require a design phase. Students need to show, for example, that they are able to devise a workable plan that meets a set of specifications in computer technology or that they can develop a credible design for a creative work of art, be it a sculpture, a piece of writing or a performance. Perhaps they need to show that they are able to use imaginative conceptualization in the design of an engineering project, or that they can work out how to go about solving a problem or a plan for a project in an applied professional setting.

In some courses, such as computer science or engineering, students may not consider their course to have a creative side. Some could see their design tasks as being about solving purely technical problems without any aesthetic element. Such an attitude can limit their learning of design principles, conceptualization and problem solving. An effective teacher would be able to help students appreciate the creative dimension of their field, so that they are more open to design possibilities. Therefore some assessment tasks are written with outlandish problems that of necessity require creative solutions.

Case 16.1: Designing and building a prototype in engineering

An assessment task in engineering was planned to test the design skills of final-year undergraduate students. The purpose of the task was to force students to think 'out of the box' to solve an unusual engineering problem. Small groups of students were given the task of designing a way to propel a raw egg (in its shell) up a slope without it falling off a plate. They had to build and operate a prototype to prove their design was a workable one. Those who received higher grades solved the problem by successfully propelling the egg up the slope in the shortest time-frames.

There were a number of possible solutions to this design task. It assessed student ability to solve problems creatively and it was also a realistic task in that the prototype needed to be functional and to be able to perform within a specified time-frame.

The skills of self- and peer assessment were integral to this task as the project was undertaken in small groups. Self- and peer marking schemes included criteria about teamwork in addition to those relating to engineering outcomes. Students received training and had practice in self- and peer assessment before beginning this assessment task. The teacher in this case took self- and peer assessment outcomes into account when determining the grade for each group.

Portfolios

'A portfolio is a structured collection comprising evidence and critical reflection on that evidence' (Baume, 2001). Portfolios of evidence are useful for both formative and summative assessment. Material in a portfolio can provide a review of student progress in the development of knowledge and technique, or it can include evidence of work to show academic or professional capability. A portfolio can track a design through drawings and critical reflections. It can also be a way to encourage students to organize the academic work that shows achievement and progression.

An important part of the value of portfolios in art and design is that the process of compilation over time can assist students and teachers to record a project or a work of art from its inception through to the finished product. How students progress in art, performance and design is an important component of assessment, and portfolios are a useful vehicle for students and teachers to track performance and to allow students continuously to review their work and reflect upon their progress.

Case 16.2: Portfolio of compositions

In the early stages of a musical composition course, students were required to keep a portfolio of their progress. The purpose of the subject was to teach students to write in the styles of their musical tradition before attempting a style of their own. They started by learning the techniques, structures and harmonies of Beethoven's sonatas, for example. Then they wrote a sonata in Beethoven's style. After they progressed through analysing other composers' work and composing in other styles, they finally directed, rehearsed and recorded a group of other music students playing their compositions.

The portfolio included written reflections on classes attended, notes on the students' insights into the musical styles they analysed, musical notation (of the music by the composers studied and their own original compositions) and recordings. It was compiled over the semester of academic study.

The portfolio was assessed progressively throughout the teaching period. One of the reasons for progressive assessment was to allow teachers to provide formative feedback during the semester, and another was to ensure that students compiled the portfolio progressively and did not rush around collecting evidence and writing reflections at the end of the period. Early formative assessment allowed teachers to identify problems and to focus tutorial assistance. Students were able to resubmit items that were judged to be unsatisfactory.

Insights and originality were determined by following the students' progress through the evidence and reflections included in the portfolio.

Producing a work of art, video or Web site

The production of artefacts is one of the most commonly used methods to assess design and creativity. These are usually whole-of-semester tasks, or even longer, which contain various submission points of work in progress for formative feedback. A final presentation is often accompanied by a written or oral piece that might be both analytic and reflective in nature. The analytical work explores theoretical considerations and how they have been applied in practice. A reflective piece may include elements of self-assessment, and reflections on the adequacy of the process and what has been learnt as a result.

Case 16.3: Web site for marketing students

Students undertaking an e-commerce subject applied their knowledge of marketing principles in the design and development of a simple Web site to support their chosen topic area.

This assessment task required students to design and develop a user-friendly and easy-to-navigate site that provided potential customers with enough information and attractive appeal to draw them into making a purchase. They could choose to include banner ads of their own design. Teachers had asked previous students to allow their Web sites to be shown to current students as exemplars and to illustrate grading standards (high distinction, distinction, credit and pass). Other exemplars were Web sites marketing a wide range of products and services, for example: subscription services, devotional services, music and holiday retail, DVD and other high-end commercial products. Alternatively, they could, if they chose, decide to advertise their own services as a precursor to developing their own business Web sites. Students demonstrated their sites in an end-of semester colloquium, which also entailed elements of peer assessment.

In this case, the identification of outstanding work depended upon the creative elements of the design (easy to look at, 'clean' design), effectiveness in achieving a marketing purpose (attracting interest, call to action) and the usability criteria such as ease of navigation and compliance with standards. Designing and creating a Web site for a marketing purpose was therefore to be assessed in both creative and functional terms.

Projects

Many professional disciplines involve the completion of projects and, aside from the creative disciplinary skills such as drawing, constructing, exhibiting or performing, undergraduate students also need practice in the cooperation, patience, persistence and determination required to complete a sophisticated collaborative project.

Roles may be assigned where benefits can be gained from understanding a multi-layered approach to the project, or alternatively students can be encouraged to work together, first recognizing each other's skills and talents and coordinating the project in order to make best use of each.

Case 16.4: Scale models in architecture

Early in their degree, architecture students learn to make scale models. The project in this assessment task required students to make a scale model and to design building plans for a large town. The town was to include a suburban area, a commercial area, churches and adequate public space including energy-efficient transport routes.

The assessment of this project included an appraisal of the quality of the scale model as well as the feasibility and appeal of the overall design. Self- and peer assessment were included in the marking scheme. Students rated themselves and each other regarding individual contributions to the model's aesthetic appeal and functionality. The teacher also rated each student, and the final grade was negotiated between the teacher and each student based on information from the three sources. Group marks were given for the effectiveness of the team in achieving the outcomes.

Performance

Performance is a branch of the arts that includes music, dance and drama. Students are judged on technique, the level of mastery of their artistic field, how they work to a public audience, communication and cultural expression. Performance is also learnt by studying the performance of acknowledged experts.

It is usual for students to enter performance-based programmes with widely differing abilities and prior experience. Teachers have to make important decisions about how to assess under these conditions. Will all student performance be judged against the same criteria and standards, or is it more appropriate for students to be judged on their individual progress and achievement? Is there room for individual students to negotiate their own achievements and to be assessed accordingly?

Responses to these questions depend largely upon the philosophy and obligations of the department. Most teachers are concerned both with the formative support and development of individuals on the one hand and with the necessity to maintain the highest possible outcomes as a whole on the other. Assessment schemes will therefore commonly reflect this balance.

Case 16.5: Assessing vocal performance

Vocal studies programmes admit students with a wide range of abilities and require them to perform in many different musical genres, each with different vocal demands. It is not unusual to find relatively untutored students with great potential mixed into a cohort with students who have received training since an early age and whose potential may have been significantly realized. Student performances are assessed using a variety of formative and summative approaches including improvement during term and final achievement at the end of each term. In these circumstances, a music department arrived at the following assessment regime in an attempt to achieve equity of opportunity.

In a portfolio-style assessment task, each student had a profile that documented personal and professional goals, plans for achieving them, and progress each term. Profiles were taken into account in making judgements about improvement, whereas final achievement was assessed against common criteria and standards for all performers. These two components were equally weighted in the final grade. Self- and peer assessment were utilized significantly in the formative components of the assessment, and a panel of professionals negotiated the summative component.

Visioning

Individuals have engaged in forecasting, dreaming, considering possibilities, watching trends and believing in the future since time began. In our lifetimes of rapid technological, sociological and spiritual change, a number of specialists in their fields came to see themselves as 'futurists' during the mid-1960s. These specialists represented disciplines ranging, for example, from mathematics, biology, education and engineering to sociology and history.

The syllabus in a futures studies course usually includes an introduction to specific methods such as trend extrapolation, polling, back-casting, cross-impact analysis, visioning and many more methods that show students how to apply new approaches to the problems of human life and the potentials of human possibilities. Futures studies is most effectively taught and assessed in a group context that utilizes the added richness of diverse multidisciplinary perspectives. It is an area of creative thinking that produces outcomes that are quite different from many product-focused areas in the creative arts.

Case 16.6: Visioning futures

'Re-imagining your own future' was an assignment given to a group of students in a futures studies programme. The skills involved in visioning were core to this activity as the theorists assert that there can be no change (personal, organizational or global) without first a vision. Learning about the creative process and the process of change, and applying creativity in thinking was the first step in learning about creative visioning. First, the whole class was introduced to the four key approaches in futures thinking: possibility; reciprocity; evolution; and values, vision and meaning.

Students were then formed into small groups. Each group was required to provide a mutually supportive context for individuals to undertake the following process:

- Identify personal values.
- Practise processes in futures thinking, considering and visioning possibilities.
- Discuss the concept of change, expanding possibilities and evaluating probabilities.
- Identify and evaluate values and preferred visions of the future.
- Personalize the future.
- Reassess the significance of future-consciousness.

Following the group activity, students submitted their own individual written piece of work that synthesized their imagined future. Assessment was based around the demonstration of creative thinking and original speculation, the production of a number of imaginative options, evidence of exploration of relevant theories, extensive optimistic visioning and evaluation of preferred futures, and a clear explanation of how the students would participate in their preferred future.

Reflections on the group activity were also required for submission and were assessed according to standards that had been developed relating to how the four key approaches (see above) had been implemented in the visioning activity. Formative self- and peer assessment of the value of sharing future-consciousness was included as an integral part of the assessment task.

(adapted from Dator, 1994; Lombardo, nd)

Implications for teaching

Of the many implications for teaching that have been raised in this chapter, there are two key themes that we would like to emphasize. The first concerns the acquisition of tacit knowledge, and the second is the considerable opportunities available for peer and self-assessment in designing, creating and performing as learning outcomes.

A central problem for many teachers in the fields of design, creativity and performance is how to articulate what they value and why. Many flamboyant terms, such as 'gusto' or 'flair', may be employed in an attempt to describe what is sought in student performance, but none convey a precise definition and each can be interpreted by each student quite differently. Teachers need to treat these terms as problematic, and must be able to unpack, discuss and provide exemplars of what they mean in the classroom. Students, as well, should be encouraged to arrive at some shared understanding through discussion. Discussions of values and giving expression to them are vital for students if they are to gain an understanding of how to improve, and to monitor their own development.

In his explanation of the term 'educational connoisseurship', Eisner (1991: 64) uses the analogy of wine appreciation to illustrate concepts of teaching creatively: 'It is a matter of perceptivity... the ability to differentiate and to experience the relationships between, say, one... quality in the wine and others. Like the interplay of sounds in a symphonic score, to experience wine is to experience an interplay of qualitative relationships.' Eisner goes on to infer that the ability to 'appreciate' (to experience the qualities of something and to understand them) can be taught. For example, 'teachers of literature can help people learn how to read a novel, indeed to learn the several ways in which a novel can be read... critics of film and painting help others learn to see what they might otherwise not notice and in the process increase their level of connoisseurship' (Eisner, 1991: 69). But language can be limiting. Terms are acquired 'from the perception of qualities that were conceptualised and then labelled' (Eisner, 1991: 67), hence the need for teachers to use exemplars and illustrations of what they mean by 'creativity', as we have discussed.

The need for values clarification relates to our emphasis on self- and peer assessment. It is an inevitable part of creative professionals' lives that their work will be subject to public critique. Unless students learn to develop a robust process of self-assessment, in which they are able realistically to appraise their own strengths and weaknesses, they will be vulnerable to the misguided flattery and criticisms of others. Indeed self-assessment is vital for the continuing development of an ability that is honed over time through practice and can be a continuing theme of any creative arts programme. Similarly, peer assessment – the ability to make sound judgements about the performances of others – is a vital skill for the creative professional, particularly in collaborative situations where constructive and supportive feedback is required. This is a sensitive task that combines skills in both judgement and communication, which should be taught and modelled by teachers to students during a programme of study.

Peer and self-assessment, of course, are not only of benefit to students. Many teachers express concerns about being sole arbiter of student achievement in assessment tasks where such high levels of aesthetic judgement prevail. Rightly, they are concerned that their own aesthetic sensibility dominates at the expense of diverse student creativity. Although panels of professionals may be assembled for assessment purposes, these may be difficult to arrange, given the frequency of assessment tasks. When the principles of peer and self-assessment are taught in a rigorous manner, including a conception of the expected 'standards of performance', they can provide an enormously beneficial input to the assessment process, and remove the pressure from the teacher as the lone decision maker.

Dunn, L, Morgan C, O'Reilly M, and Parry, S. (2004) The Student Assessment Handbook (New Directions in Traditional and Online Assessment) London: Routledge Falmer

17

Thinking critically and making judgements

What is critical thinking?

The ability to think critically and to arrive at sound judgements is a key outcome of any university education. It is perhaps the most significant marker of an educated person, irrespective of the number of courses undertaken or facts absorbed. As a society, we are generally comfortable with our ideas, beliefs and world-views. Without a commitment to critical thinking that tests and challenges these ideas, there would be little progress or reform. In the working world, the most consistently valued asset of an organization is the capacity of individuals to use their critical and creative thinking abilities to improve collective performance.

Critical thinking is defined by Paul (1993) as a 'unique kind of purposeful thinking in which the thinker systematically and habitually imposes criteria and intellectual standards upon the thinking'. The criteria of solid reasoning include precision, relevance, depth, accuracy and sufficiency. Paul argues that critical thinking also requires knowledge of the elements of thought, such as point of view, context and assumptions, and that the thinker must actively address these elements. In addition, thinkers need to evaluate the strengths and weaknesses of their thinking against relevant standards and theoretical frameworks throughout the process.

As useful as this definition is as a starting point, it implies that critical thinking comprises a series of generic, transferable skills that may be acquired by students in any context. If this were true, we would be able to assess critical thinking skills with standardized objective tests, regardless of the subject area or discipline. Such an assumption, of course, is hotly contested by those who claim that such skills can only be developed in higher education through

individual disciplines, with their own distinctive frames of reference, method-
ologies, language, logic and modes of argument. A critical thinker in science
will possess quite a different set of skills from those of a sociologist or
historian (Barnett, 1997; Brown, 1998).

There is middle ground in this debate, occupied by those who argue that
there are some broad, generic thinking skills and a great variety of specific disciplinary thinking skills. Broad thinking skills might include 'grasping the
meaning of statements; judging ambiguities, assumption or contradictions in
reasoning; identifying necessary conclusions; assessing the adequacy of definitions and the acceptability of alleged authorities' (Ennis, in Brown, 1998).
Arguably these are the sorts of skills that underpin a broad education in the
traditional, liberal curriculum, and they offer a terminology that can be recognized from various disciplinary perspectives.

Practically speaking, these distinctions between generic and disciplinary
thinking skills are not particularly useful for most teachers in higher education
who will already be located within a core discipline and who will be seeking
ways to teach and assess the development of a broad range of higher-order
thinking skills in their own context. More importantly, the challenge for
teachers is to move students from a dependence upon the thinking and judgements of others to arriving at their own valid judgements on the basis of their
own disciplined thought. Clearly, the ability to think critically and make judgements is a complex process that is difficult for students to stumble upon by trial
and error. Rather, these skills must be actively fostered and assessed by teachers
over a programme of study.

Critical thinking in the disciplines

What forms does critical thinking take in the disciplines? It is possible to
pinpoint quite distinct patterns of critical thinking in each of the four disciplinary groupings – sciences, social sciences, applied professions and humanities
(Becher, 1989; Kolb, 1981). What becomes more complex is the array of
different critical thinking skills required for the various specialisms within each
of these four categories. For example, within the applied professions, we find a
variety of disciplines such as law, medicine, architecture and nursing, each with
its own particular world-views and applied combinations of critical thinking
skills. Next there are differences within individual disciplines, for example postmodern critique of modernist or conventional thinking traditions. Students
will be expected to come to terms with a large body of critical thinking
conventions within their discipline, including:

● knowledge of theoretical perspectives, such as the scientific method or
  critical inquiry, and an accompanying understanding of key influences
  and milestones;

- how knowledge is made and reported in the discipline, and how it is reproduced at the undergraduate level;
- the conventions of structure and argument, for citation and acknowledgement, for the writer's position adopted in relation to the audience, and for the nature of metaphors in the field.

(Parry, 1998; Bazerman, 1981)

These are complex and widely variant issues across disciplines, with which students are often left to grapple unassisted, unless core or foundation units in programmes are provided to initiate students into their disciplinary culture. Here we provide some snapshots of critical thinking as they manifest in some disciplines:

History
Learning to think 'historically' is an important transition from the basic ability to recall factual knowledge and historical events. Traditionally, the skills of the historian include the ability to:

- identify and evaluate historical evidence;
- recognize biased and slanted historical writing;
- evaluate arguments generated by conflicting historical interpretations;
- generate historical hypotheses and causal explanations.

(van Veuren, 1995)

Postmodern critique tends to reject the approach and the skills of the traditional historian. It is argued that there is no objective 'past', that interpretation is subjective and ideological and that historical causality – why things happened – is complex and problematic and must assume a plurality of perspectives. Postmodernist historians are likely to reject the 'technology of research procedures' in favour of the deconstructive reading of texts, and history making that is explicitly local and personal.

Social sciences
A critical thinker in the social sciences is a person who is 'sceptical of simple or singular explanations to social problems, is mindful of the frequent mistakes people make in using numbers or statistics, actively looks for bias in oneself and others, and searches for underlying faulty assumptions'. Byrnes (2002) elaborates on these qualities:

- *assumption* – looking beyond widely accepted truths to see false assumptions or ignored factors;
- *scepticism* – a questioning of statements that offer a simple causal explanation for social conditions that are far more complex;
- *statistics* – viewing statistics as problematic, and not easily accepting numbers written or used by others as correct;
- *bias* – accepting that bias is present to some degree in all human perceptions, motivates much reasoning and contaminates many arguments.

Nursing

Thinking like a nurse, according to Heaslip (1996), is different from thinking like a doctor or dentist because of nurses' unique relationships with clients, and their distinct role in client care. As nurses engage in increasingly more complex clinical practice, there are greater demands upon them to demonstrate sound reasoning in the pursuit of safe and ethical client care. Students are required to reason about their role as nurses by critical reading, writing, listening and speaking:

- *critical listening* – to enter empathetically and analytically into the perspective of others;
- *critical thinking* – to exercise disciplined, self-directed thinking with a capacity to reflect upon the quality, accuracy and defensibility of the thinking;
- *critical writing* – to understand one's own thesis, how it can be supported and made intelligible to others, and what limitations, objections and other points of view need to be considered;
- *critical reading* – to enter actively into others' points of view, looking for assumptions, key concepts, ideas, reasons, justifications and implications;
- *critical speaking* – to convey effectively a point of view to allow understanding of that perspective, combined with self-monitoring and openness to dialogue and feedback.

Biology

In undergraduate biology, critical thinking means 'seeking reliable knowledge'. Students are often not well prepared to question the reliability of information or to analyse critically and challenge findings or procedures in the scientific literature. Ommundsen (1999) sets out a critical thinking schema that supports students to explore the fundamental rules of evidence that form the basis of credible investigation. In each case, the beginning student must ask: what quality of evidence would be ideal in this situation? Then students explore the evidence presented using the following four criteria:

1. *Outcome measure.* Was the claimed outcome actually measured?
2. *Control.* Was the outcome compared to that of an otherwise similar untreated group?
3. *Replication.* Was the outcome replicated?
4. *Randomization.* Was the outcome allocated randomly?

Small-group work would be used to allow students to grapple with the case examples and argue the merits of the case. Ommundsen (1999) provides further examples in developing scientific reasoning, such as critiquing poorly framed questions and redeveloping them as testable questions.

In these snapshots it is possible to identify significant differences in the way critical thinking is articulated that derive from the nature of the knowledge base. Indeed, there may be considerable variations within each discipline. The dilemma for students is how to know what is expected of them, particularly when there may be subtle distinctions between courses in a programme and between individual academics in the same programme.

What is evident in assessing critical thinking is the importance of teachers making explicit the nature of critical thinking skills required and the basis for them. Similarly, assessment tasks need to be purposeful in drawing out students' achievement of these skills.

Methods for assessing critical thinking

Critical thinking can be assessed, to varying degrees of effectiveness, by almost any form of assessment task, from essays and journals to multiple choice examinations. Yet if teachers really want to focus on the development of critical thinking skills, assessment tasks and marking criteria must be tailored quite explicitly for the purpose. In such instances, an essay should be valued first and foremost for its demonstrated critical reasoning and its sound judgements based upon evaluated evidence. A journal, while a more personal form of expression, will be similarly valued for its critical reflection upon key themes. Rather than simply testing declarative knowledge, a multiple choice exam may explicitly test one's reasoning methods, logical thinking and underlying assumptions. Whichever form the assessment task takes, the key to assessing critical thinking is to provide this particular emphasis, along with congruent teaching strategies and formative, developmental practice for the assessment.

Below is a series of assessment methods that are tailored to promote and support critical thinking. They are accompanied by cases or snapshots of practice in a variety of disciplinary fields.

Evaluative essays

The evaluative essay is a long-established and well-regarded way of assessing critical thinking, because it entails sustained and structured exposition of students' reasoning. There are many types of academic essays, including those that only require descriptive responses and do not call for a student's own point of view. However, an evaluative essay calls upon the student's capacity to assess, analyse and evaluate, and make informed and supportable judgements. It also assumes a knowledge of relevant theoretical perspectives and the underlying conventions and values in asserting an argument in the field. The argument must be represented in a coherent, logical form, with evidence that the student has weighed the evidence and made a reasoned conclusion.

The evaluative essay is a relatively higher-order intellectual activity, and is not one that we can expect students to be able to master early in their studies. It entails a series of micro-skills that may include purposeful reading, identifying points of view and bias, evaluating evidence, forming an argument, persuasive writing and so forth. It is important that we do not leave students to develop these skills on a trial-and-error basis. Rather, we must actively develop them, not only in our teaching but in assessments tasks that are heavily weighted towards the sequenced, formative development of micro-skills appropriate to the discipline. For example, teachers may elect to set assignments that focus on building blocks of the essay such as hypothesis formation or evaluative review of the literature. Over time, as students develop expertise in the micro-skills, the evaluative essay is more within their grasp.

Case 17.1: Development of thinking skills through essay writing

This is an example of a cumulative approach to essay writing throughout an undergraduate first-year core unit of study in the humanities. It places emphasis on developing the building blocks of the essay, with formative feedback at key points. Although the overall outcome of this unit is to introduce students to the history of the university, there is a concurrent agenda in developing students' thinking and writing skills and particularly in persuading the audience that the position adopted has merit and provides new insights:

- *Step 1 – annotated bibliography.* Students chose a topic or theme as the subject of their essay. The first submission point was an annotated bibliography of 10 key sources for the essay. Students were assessed on the quality of their sources, the accuracy of their descriptive overview and the incisiveness of their evaluation. These were an ongoing focus in class discussion during the first weeks of term, where the purposes and skills in literature reviews were taught.
- *Step 2 – developing an essay plan.* Students were then expected to develop a plan. It required them to make decisions about the argument they were adopting, the evidence that was to be evaluated in support of the argument, and the structure of the argument. The 'bones' of their reasoning were thus transparent and open to feedback before they committed to their final essay.
- *Step 3 – persuasive writing.* To prepare students for writing their essays, this task developed skills in persuasive use of language in appropriate academic form. It was an 800-word piece on a specified topic submitted to an online forum, thus allowing students to compare their efforts with others', develop technique and discuss the qualities and pitfalls of academic writing.
- *Step 4 – essay.* At the end of semester, students submitted their fully realized essay, based upon the developmental exercises in the prior three items. Although the earlier tasks had a strong formative role, each submission point was assessed and the final essay was only worth 40 per cent of their total mark.

Although this subject contains lively content, the teacher had been very purposeful in not seeking simply to test students' knowledge of the subject, although this was considerable by the end of term. Rather, the focus in assessment was upon critical thinking as demonstrated through the essay form. For the many hundreds of new undergraduates each semester who have completed this subject, it was a very worthwhile investment.

Reports

Reports are more applied in nature than essays, because they emphasize information. The purpose of the report is to provide organized factual information, analysis of a situation and, quite often, recommendations regarding further action. Report writers don't have to persuade the audience of the importance of the information or of the objective methods of investigating it. Instead, very precise reporting genres apply to disciplines, and students must reproduce whichever is appropriate. For example, a nurse's report on a patient's status would look very different from an environmental scientist's report on the biodiversity of a region, or an incident report by a welfare officer. Critical thinking skills include observing, investigating and organizing data into a logical presentation, making judgements about which evidence is relevant and formulating an argument or recommendations based on the information yielded.

Case 17.2: Assessing the critique of scientific method in botanical science

In the study of botany, reports may range from observations during field trips to complex studies of evolutionary processes. Critical analysis of the scientific literature is a key ability, and especially the ability to go beyond the face value of information and establish the relevance and appropriateness of methods and findings reported in the existing literature. In time, it allows students to participate in and extend the existing body of knowledge.

The task of critiquing report writing will commonly include the following elements:

1. Search for relevant articles, using keywords and search strings.
2. Refine the search to find articles of most relevance to the question.
3. Read to identify research methodology employed and rationale provided.
4. Critically assess the strengths and weaknesses of methods reported.
5. Report on the approaches that represent best practice and give reasons why.
6. Present the final report in accordance with scientific report writing conventions.

Critique of the scientific writing would thus provide students with practice in exercising their developing professional judgement as well as highlighting the variation inherent in scientific thought. Presenting such a critique as a report not only gives students the chance to write according to the accepted genre for their field but also provides the opportunity to make considered judgements and form points of view about existing knowledge and its adequacy. In some cases this exercise can also prepare students to pursue research questions of their own based on gaps or weaknesses noted in the literature.

Journals

Logs, diaries and journals may be used as a tool for developing and assessing students' thinking skills. In contrast to more formal modes of academic expression, journals are very effective in capturing more spontaneous ideas and more free-form responses to new ideas or experiences during study. They may also capture students' personal reflections on events or experiences during their learning, which may involve a series of iterations with discussion and hindsight. The act of 'critical reflection' is much favoured as a means of understanding one's experiences, ideas and values, as a precursor to finding new ways of thinking and acting. Teachers find journals valuable as an assessment form because they are able to see the growth of students' thinking and development of insights during semester. Another advantage of using journals is that many students find it easier to take a critical position if they are allowed to use the first person in their writing. This is particularly the case for those who are struggling to master the conventions of academic writing.

When assessing journals, the rationale, form and assessment criteria must be very clearly communicated to students, as they may be used for widely different purposes. If students are unfamiliar with the style and form of journals, it should be explained and modelled through exemplars, particularly to avoid the more rambling and incoherent of varieties. As marking journals can be a time-consuming experience, teachers may sometimes 'sample' the entries or ask students to highlight key entries to a specified word limit.

Assessing critical reflection through journals is dealt with in greater detail in Chapter 19.

Case 17.3: Journal of personal reflections

Within a graduate programme on teaching and learning in higher education, students were asked to maintain a continuous journal of reflection upon their practice and to note how it was informed or challenged by the theoretical perspectives encountered through the syllabus. Since students in this case were already practitioners within the educational context, it was highly relevant for them to be observing and contemplating the relationship between their own practices and the theoretical foundations in the area of teaching and learning (within their own disciplines).

Specific critical incidents were to be used as focal points for reflective analysis. Students were required to record evidence to support their interpretations as well as unravelling their tacitly held values and beliefs. Prompt questions were provided such as 'How might I learn from this experience and change my approach to a similar situation in the future?' Ideas for moving forward and benefiting from these reflective exercises were to be proposed.

This assessment task, having been ongoing over the entire semester, was submitted in extract form only, with a synthesis of learning attached at the front. Assessment of the reflective journals took account of the personal style of students' language when speaking of personal experiences and thoughts, and how this had been balanced by a shift in language to a more impersonal style when explaining the connections to theory.

Multiple choice exams

Although at first glance it may be thought that multiple choice questions are not useful for assessing higher-order skills such as critical thinking, there are many good examples of quizzes and tests developed for this purpose. Multiple choice exams can be effectively geared to assess the quality of thinking, and may contain a variety of questions concerned with the processes of logic, reasoning and thought. For example, when assessing the students' capacity to critique research reports, multiple choice tests will include questions such as:

> The greatest flaw in the evidence for this claim is:
> (a) Poor outcome measure
> (b) Lack of good controls
> (c) Lack of replication
> (d) Lack of randomization (Ommunsden, 1999)

Students' success in multiple choice exams will depend upon how well they are prepared for this kind of questioning. When faced with exams, students often adopt surface or reproductive approaches, accompanied by rote learning of content. Such approaches will not be particularly helpful in these types of exam where critical thinking and problem solving are required. The limitation of multiple choice exams as a method of assessing critical thinking is that they tend to be atomistic in nature, and are not really able to capture critical thinking of an extended or holistic nature.

Case 17.4: Multiple choice examinations in psychology

In psychology, well-designed multiple choice questions frequently form the basis for assessment of skills in reasoning and logic. Psychology is the study of the mind and behaviour, with the caveat that not all aspects of the human mind and behaviour are well understood. For the most part psychology students learn to find their own approaches to inquiry and reasoned thought, not only through becoming familiar with scientific method but also through the development of their own cognitive tools for argument, logic and critical thought.

Quizzes focus on a range of areas such as:

- *Inference or observation* – understanding behaviour from observation and remaining free from subjective interpretation. Questions test students' ability to analyse assumptions and identify biases.

- *Operational definitions* – identifying terms or concepts in operational terms. Students define the terms within a hypothesis that would require clarifying before the hypothesis itself can be tested.
- *Correlation* – the relationship between variables in a research study can be calculated in terms of correlations. Both positive and negative correlations show associations between variables without also showing a cause. Quiz questions would reinforce this understanding by guiding students to consider a wide range of possible causes.
- *Errors in thinking* – errors of logic and assumptions can sometimes be detected in the interpretations of research results. Questions would highlight erroneous conclusions and errors in thinking and methodology. Additional questions may invite students to propose changes to the methodology or flawed aspects of the research processes.
- *Faulty reasoning* – common fallacies in psychological thinking include simplification and overgeneralization. Students identify the fallacies in reasoning from a number of statements presented.
- *Thinking creatively* – Practising the skills of thinking 'outside the box' can be achieved by having students devise their own question bank of MCQs. In order to prepare some useful questions with a collection of credible distractors, students need to think creatively about common misconceptions, biases and errors of reasoning.

From this example, it is clear that assessment of the students' quality and capability of thinking critically and applying judgements in accordance with the disciplinary practices can be conducted using multiple choice tests and quizzes. As mentioned earlier, it is a method often used in the discipline of psychology and can also be applied to other areas where the students can focus on the development of their thinking processes over the duration of their course (eg nursing, theology and so on).

(adapted from Westra, Geoheagan and Flores, 1997)

Collaborative critical thinking

Group collaboration on thinking tasks is another very effective way of enhancing and assessing critical thinking skills, particularly if the concepts and practice of *metacognition* are introduced. Metacognition is a process of reflecting on one's own thinking processes while reading, writing and addressing problems, with the aim of sharpening and honing one's efficacy. As a solo activity, it may seem a little abstract, but it can come alive in small groups or in partnership with a critical friend. With a given issue or problem to tackle, students are encouraged to articulate the patterns of their reasoning, which are discussed using criteria such as precision, relevance, depth, accuracy and sufficiency. It is also important to articulate any underlying assumptions and points of view that may be driving the reasoning. Through a metacognitive process, students become aware of the gaps in their reasoning, and any need to broaden their perspectives in order to sharpen the process. It can be a fascinating and eye-opening experience for students to compare their own processes with others, particularly when there are marked differences.

Assessment of metacognition may take the form of a reflective journal or written piece where students record their developing insights during their discussions with the group or critical friend. There may also be collaborative products where an issue is thought through to a conclusion and the processes of reaching a conclusion are negotiated and documented.

Case 17.5: Collaborative exercise using metacognition

Using an example from the field of political economy, it is possible to see how collaborative methods can serve to deepen students' understanding of the subject area, context and their own thinking processes. Here is how one teacher frames the task:

1. Reflect back on your life and identify a moment when you became aware that you had been living in a closed cultural and ecological cocoon, i.e. you realised you had been operating in a narrow perspective or were making limited assumptions about the world... Describe the event. Write down as many details as you can remember.
2. Situate yourself at that time in your life in relation to your socioeconomic class, your family situation, your educational or work setting, i.e. write down as many context details as you can.
3. Now analyse all the factors, social, economic, political, family, educational, workplace (if applicable) and media that reinforced the ideology of your cocoon, and those which helped your breakthrough to occur.
4. When you have done this, discuss with your critical friend and see if you can deepen your analysis through dialogue and questioning. See if, with the help of your partner, you can identify the assumptions and values that underlie your story. This is not easy to do, as they often seem 'obvious' or are just 'common sense' – this is where your critical friend can play a crucial role. It would be useful if you could do the same for your partner – it is often much easier to identify others' assumptions rather than our own.

(Fisher, 1998: 10–11)

Assessment of this process has three different threads encapsulated in one submission:

1. a written piece that discusses the outcomes of the 'cultural cocoon' task;
2. reflections on the metacognitive processes involved and what students have learnt about their own thinking;
3. reflections on students' experiences as critical friends and how this has contributed to their learning.

Oral examinations

On-the-spot examinations such as vivas, presentations and performances demand a high level of focus from both the students and the examiners. Oral assessments are both feared and extolled because they require students to demonstrate their ability to respond coherently and dynamically to a given situation. They also provide opportunities for examiners to probe and pursue in greater depth areas where doubt appears, so that an impression of students' knowledge can quickly be obtained. There are many areas where instant response is required, from medical and nursing emergencies to public speaking and performance at interview, so oral exams may be very authentic and appropriate to real-life situations. (Oral exams are discussed in greater detail in Chapter 18.)

Case 17.6: Oral examination in political science

This is an oral exam involving a 30-minute presentation by each student to the two examiners, followed by 15 minutes of questions posed by the examiners. Students select a topic of particular interest and undertake analysis of the topic in the preceding weeks. One hour before the oral exam, they are given the following question:

> Using ideology critique, critically analyse the dominant political discourse in relation to a particular issue (eg civil unrest, human rights, sustainable economic development, terrorism, aid policies, non-violence, peace building and reconciliation etc) and then critically reflect on the underlying assumptions and values influencing your critique:
>
> - Provide a brief historical perspective.
> - Identify assumptions within the political discourse and how they apply to your chosen issue.
> - Identify ideological interests served by the dominant paradigm's approach to the issue.
> - Summarize your own proposals for peace making and reconciliation.

Although students are well versed in their chosen topic, this is a demanding task that requires students to 'think on their feet' to a high level. The assessment is primarily designed to test students' critical thinking skills in oral form, which is considered to be a key disciplinary ability in the political sciences. Marks are awarded on their demonstrated knowledge of the topic, the clarity and depth of their critical engagement with the issue, and the persuasiveness of their argument.

This is a labour-intensive assessment method and could prove difficult to facilitate with large cohorts. It is also an advanced assessment form that may only be appropriate for students in the final year of undergraduate study.

Classroom and online debates

Although debate is an assessment form that is commonly employed to test one's oral communication abilities (see Chapter 12), it is also excellent as a means of testing critical thinking. When debates are conducted online, the 'oral' component disappears entirely, making the task more overtly an exercise in critical thinking and reasoning.

Debating, from a critical thinking perspective, entails a variety of tasks, including:

1. identifying and summarizing the problem/topic for debate;
2. making explicit and presenting one's own or the team's perspective;
3. identifying and analysing other salient perspectives of the issue and arguing against the opposing position;
4. identifying, assessing and refuting the key assumptions of the other team;
5. assessing the quality of supporting data/evidence of the other team and providing additional data/evidence related to defending one's own team perspective;
6. interpreting the influence of context on the issue;
7. assessing the conclusions, implications and consequences of the opposing argument and proposing conclusions, implications and consequences to counter these.

(adapted from Washington State University
Critical Thinking Project, 2002)

Case 17.7: Debating maths online

Maths students are asked to debate the topic 'Prime numbers are best' in an online setting. The purpose of the assessment is to develop students' thinking and reasoning abilities. The class of 130 students is divided into 10 teams, each with 13 members (representing both negative and affirmative sides). Each of the 10 teams is provided with a group discussion area where they can declare which side they each will argue and then carry out their debate over an allocated seven-day period.

Prior to the debate event itself, each side of each team is also encouraged to use the virtual classroom (the synchronous area) for meeting together, exchanging views and developing some arguments on the topic. They must also agree on the order of speakers, who the 'whip' is, who sums up at the end of the week's debate, what their side's arguments amount to and so forth. Negotiation on the order of posting is also encouraged to facilitate a smooth progression through the week's developing debate.

It is a requirement that each individual student has a say during the week-long debate event. Apart from the first speaker (who is also the last speaker), each student must, to the best of his or her ability, refute the point made in the previous post and put forward an additional point to extend the side's argument.

The final summing up is done outside the small-group areas and in the whole-of-class forum. These final comments appearing in the whole-of-class forum will be a summary of the arguments for and against for 10 teams and thus comprise the fundamental arguments presented throughout the week.

An individual mark is given for completing the debate according to specified criteria and for the quality of contribution to the team's argument, particularly from a critical thinking perspective.

Implications for teaching

Summarizing some of the issues raised in this chapter indicates two of the major challenges facing teachers in developing critical thinking amongst students. The first challenge is actively addressing the inclination of many students to adopt surface or reproducing strategies. In most instances this will relate to issues of confidence and skill. The overall aim is to encourage students to move from reproducing the thinking of others to making their own judgements through their own disciplined thought. The second challenge is helping students to distinguish between critical thinking and subjective reaction, that is, thinking and evaluating on the basis of good evidence and in relation to relevant frames of reference. The concepts of good evidence and sound judgement must be fully explored in context.

To support students in this direction, it is necessary for teachers to:

- have a clear grasp of how critical thinking is evidenced in their own discipline and the various processes and forms it takes;
- offer as much formative development and modelling to students as possible in preparation for tasks that assess critical thinking;
- seek ways to develop a culture of curiosity and rigorous thinking in their classes.

The issue of tacit learning is a key theme in assessment and learning and it is referred to earlier. Teachers are not always able to articulate clearly the conventions of their discipline, although they certainly 'know it when they see it'. Every field of study has a knowledge base, the nature and values of which shape how the knowledge is expressed. Without having to put labels on the conventions they would typically expect, a teacher still needs to *show* students that these exist. The most effective way for students to find out how to think critically in a given field is to give them plenty of exemplars, and as much practice and formative feedback as is possible.

18

Problem solving

What is problem solving?

The ability to solve problems is an important professional and life skill with which we are all to some degree familiar. Problem solving is especially relevant in the applied professions, where problems form the basis of everyday activity in professional practice. It usually entails a familiar sequence of events, including:

- Recognizing that a problem exists.
- Understanding the nature of the problem and how it might be addressed.
- Developing a plan to address the problem.
- Acting upon the plan.
- Evaluating the outcome of the action – was the problem resolved?
- Reflecting upon the result – could it have been handled better? Could the problem have been avoided? Might the problem reoccur?

(Hayes, in Ryan, 1996)

Problems are often divided into two categories. The first category is *well-structured problems* – problems that are readily resolved if an appropriate step-by-step algorithm or procedure is applied. All the information required to resolve the problem is supplied to the student, and the solution is unambiguous in nature. These might be commonly found in disciplines such as mathematics, chemistry or computing science. The second category is *ill-structured problems* – problems that are often more complex, multifaceted and 'real-life' in nature, which may not have definitive solutions and for which not all necessary information may be at hand. Ill-structured problems are typically found in the applied professions such as medicine, nursing, social work, law, human services, architecture and so forth. Solutions to problems in these fields may well be contested by experts within the discipline, making professional judgement essential to success (Ryan, 1996).

Problem solving, as an academic activity, may take a variety of forms, but in this chapter we are principally dealing with ill-structured problems and the development and assessment of students' abilities in resolving these, while integrating relevant knowledge. Well-structured problems, involving step-by-step solutions, are dealt with in Chapter 15. Ill-structured problems are favoured here because they are more likely to support the development of professional judgement in learners that extends beyond their university programme.

Problem solving as pedagogy

How do graduates deal with the problems they face when starting their professional careers? Can we assume they have sufficient abilities to be proficient and safe in their practice? Do we have sufficient evidence that graduates are capable of employing decision-making processes to reach sound solutions?

Over the past 20 years, problem-based learning has captured the imagination of many educators as a way of fostering problem-solving and lifelong learning abilities, as well as preparing students for the complex world of professional practice. Problem-based learning is distinctive as a pedagogy in its use of problems as the stimulus for student activities. Rather than the content of a programme providing the structure to students' learning, problem-based learning starts with a problem – all learning then unfolds from this point. Often there is an unfolding sequence of problems throughout the programme that prompts students to engage with disciplinary knowledge in a meaningful and authentic way. Problem-solving and resource gathering abilities are fostered, often through collaboration in small groups and close tutorial support. Learning that occurs through this process is summarized and integrated into students' existing knowledge base (Boud and Feletti (eds), 1991).

Considerable expertise has developed in implementing problem-based learning (see, for example, Boud and Feletti (eds), 1991), although it is recognized that transforming a conventional programme to problem-based learning is a large undertaking that requires a shared commitment by staff. Problem-solving abilities can, of course, be developed without necessarily going to these lengths, with the use of problem-solving activities and case studies interspersed throughout the conventional curricula. In this chapter we will explore assessment in the context both of the problem-based learning approach and of smaller-scale individualized problem-based activities.

Problem solving in the disciplines

Problem solving varies in nature and emphasis, depending on the profession. A doctor or nurse, for example, works with problems relating to the health care of an individual client. An architect's problem might be related to design, given the difficulties of the site or troublesome requirements in the client's brief. In information technology, a problem may take the form of some particular troubleshooting required for a defective computer application. In most instances the problem solver is required to undertake a similar sequence of events to that outlined in the introduction above, although it is the context of the problem that vastly differs, along with the form that the problem solving takes. Let's explore some examples:

Optometry

Clinical problem solving, in an atmosphere of a rapidly developing knowledge base, is the foundation of contemporary optometry practice. Lovie-Kitchen (1991: 94) describes the problem-solving abilities of an optometrist specializing in low vision: 'Clinical practice in this optometric specialty requires the optometrist to be flexible and to adapt to the differing needs of individual patients in order to manage or solve their problems. The "solutions" may require prescription of optical devices, referral to other rehabilitation professionals or information to be obtained from any of a number of different sources.' She adds that, 'because of the wide variation in the nature of, and solutions to, the visual problems of low vision patients, the need to know facts, while important, seemed less crucial than the ability to solve problems'.

Mathematical science

Mathematical scientists pursue careers as 'problem solvers' in industry and commerce. In addition to the requisite technical knowledge, practitioners must be able to apply this knowledge to problems in a variety of settings. A consultant mathematical scientist must be able to work effectively in teams where good interpersonal skills are paramount. Problem-solving skills in this discipline therefore comprise a mixture of professional skills such as mathematical modelling and the ability to identify and analyse problems, combined with inter-personal skills such as understanding group dynamics, a capacity to work collaboratively, and written and oral presentation skills.

(Usher, Simmonds and Earl, 1991)

Philosophy

Philosophy does not have a professional context as such, although the abilities acquired through the study of philosophy, such as ethical thinking and moral reasoning, are increasingly sought after in an ever more complex and ambiguous professional and business world. Problem solving in this discipline may take the form of a difficult moral choice or ethical decision. Abilities include the capacity to identify fundamental presuppositions, analyse options regarding their moral worth and offer a disciplined argument for an appropriate course of action.

From these brief examples we can see that, while problem solving has some generic components and processes, the discipline will shape its form and purpose considerably. It is important that you're aware of what it means to be a 'problem solver' in your discipline and how it is commonly enacted in practice. This will enable you to be more purposeful in developing appropriate problem-solving activities and assessments that are valid, authentic and highly developmental for students facing the daunting task of entering their professions.

It is also important for you to be able to differentiate the varying degrees of complexity in problem solving from the novice to the expert in your profession. This will enable you to enact a staged progression of skills throughout a programme of study. In addition to problem-solving skills, another important factor that distinguishes the novice from the expert is the breadth of the knowledge base that can be drawn upon at any given time:

> The challenge for us as assessors is to differentiate between what is meant by the novice and the expert in our disciplines; nominate points on this continuum where we would like our students to be at different stages of a course; identify the standard of problem solving which we could reasonably expect at each of these points; help our students, through our teaching methods, to develop this level of ability; and choose appropriate methods to assess whether they have achieved this level of development.
>
> (Ryan, 1996)

Assessment methods

When assessing problem solving, many of the more conventional methods including examinations are less appropriate. For assessment tasks to have high validity and authenticity, they should require students to engage with applied, ill-structured case studies and problems in an environment that replicates professional practice as closely as practicable. Thus, many of the methods considered in this chapter are variations on a familiar theme. Regardless of the differing forms the assessment tasks take, assessors routinely want to see evidence of some or all of the following:

- understanding of the problem, clarifying where necessary;
- identifying what additional information is required;
- knowledge and concepts underpinning the problem;
- ability to generate ideas and workable solutions;
- justifying a choice of plan that is also morally and ethically defensible;
- ability to carry out the plan;
- evaluating the success or otherwise of the plan;
- evaluating the problem-solving strategy used;
- reflecting on own learning.

As raised earlier, the novice-to-expert continuum is central to the levels of performance that can be expected of students during their progress through a programme. In the first year, students' abilities to access and analyse information are only in the early stages of development. Their knowledge base to draw upon in problem solving may not yet be very significant. Assessment tasks at this point will more profitably focus on understanding the process of problem solving as evidenced through the work of others, along with assessment tasks that support the development of underpinning skills, such as accessing information, analysing and planning. It may not be until students are in more advanced years of study that they are able to undertake rich, multifaceted forms of problem solving. The following assessment methods tend towards the latter kind – rich case studies and ill-structured problems. Lower-order developmental skills in problem solving have been dealt with in other chapters in Part B, such as Chapters 13 and 14.

Problem-solving activities offer excellent opportunities for collaborative activity, providing development of such abilities as working cooperatively in teams, negotiating outcomes and managing conflict. These abilities are dealt with in much greater detail in Chapter 19, although they may also be an important by-product of problem-based learning.

Unfolding problem scenarios

The use of the 'What would you do next?' scenario is an effective and frequently employed method of assessing higher-order problem-solving skills. Unfolding scenarios, where the original problem evolves or escalates over time in response to initial actions, have the added benefit of complexity and authenticity in terms of professional practice. Thus, students are confronted with a problem, which they research, and they enact responses. They are then presented with the consequences of their actions or further developments in the case, to which they again respond. There may be a number of iterations of this cycle where students, individually or collaboratively, devise appropriate responses throughout the semester. Usually lectures, tutorials and other supporting sessions are organized in parallel to the unfolding scenario to ensure that students have sufficient support to engage in deep learning. When all the elements of the unit of study are combined to support problem-based learning, the experience for students is likely to be more meaningful.

Unfolding scenarios can be very effectively facilitated at a distance with the use of synchronous or asynchronous communications, or a combination of the two. Students may work in teams in dedicated discussion spaces where differing responses are debated and negotiated, and then be required to contribute their findings to plenary forums.

Case 18.1: Modified essay question – education

In special education courses, students learn about the teaching and management of children who have special needs, or who may be presenting in the classroom with certain behavioural problems. The end-of-term exam comprises three parts of an unfolding scenario, which are handed to students at half-hour intervals while answers for the former part are collected. The first part of the scenario introduces the case of a child who is exhibiting a variety of symptoms of problematic behaviour. Students are expected to analyse and discuss these symptoms and their relevance to known syndromes. In the second part, a diagnosis has been confirmed and students are to now meet with the parents who are upset and reluctant to accept the problem. Students discuss how to handle the interview and the range of issues to be discussed. Based on an agreed approach with the parents, a third part of the scenario then unfolds with added complexities.

The assessment task, of course, does not require trainee teachers to be expert psychologists, but seeks to develop students' reasoning and problem-solving skills whilst also testing their broad knowledge of the variety of situations that may confront them in practice. They are also encouraged to be creative and employ common sense in handling such situations. Hence the marking criteria for the exam are weighted most heavily in favour of their practical reasoning and communication skills, rather than a deep knowledge of syndromes.

Case 18.2: Collaborative problem solving – nursing

Legal and ethical issues are of increasing concern to nurses, and collaborative problem scenarios are effective ways of teaching and assessing critical thinking and clinical problem solving. A complex, multifaceted case study is used as a trigger, and students work in Web-based asynchronous groups for collaboration throughout semester. A problem-solving framework is presented that requires students first to undertake background research on the topics to assist in clearly articulating the nature and extent of the problems. Stakeholders and respective concerns are also identified. Concerns are then prioritized from a nursing perspective, data are identified that may be relevant to interpretation and finally a group position is formed regarding the series of problems. Assessment takes the form of both group submissions throughout the semester and individual reflections on the process and outcomes, submitted via journal. The two forms of assessment have equal weighting.

Where complex social issues are involved, it is not expected that groups will always achieve consensus. However, collaboration in problem solving brings a richer array of ideas and resources to the table, in the manner of a jury considering a verdict. Students argue their cases, and may or may not be persuaded by others, while always retaining the right to final dissent.

Role-plays and simulations

Role-plays and simulations offer a variation on the 'What would you do next?' theme, with the added engagement of students adopting roles in the problem or conflict. Role-plays and simulations may be undertaken in the classroom, over the Web or using the computer. Role-plays and simulations are often described in concert with each other as the presentation of a scenario, or simulation of a problem case, is frequently the commencement of a series of tasks for students to complete through one of several prescribed roles.

Students work in small groups to learn about their allocated role (for example, four students together develop one role or persona, which could be an individual, a government agency, a lobby group, a political party, a client etc). Students research the perspectives and underlying assumptions of their personae and prepare themselves for the ensuing interactions. A scenario is introduced that requires them to respond 'in role' through a series of escalating events. Use of communication technology such as discussion forums and chat rooms allows the process to occur over an extended period, providing additional time and intensity of focus for reflective participation and consideration of options for decision making and development of solutions. A debriefing phase is vital to analyse and reflect on outcomes.

Role-play is another form of assessment that takes considerable effort to establish and facilitate, yet offers significant rewards in terms of rich, engaging interactions between students, and a deeper understanding of the variety of perspectives that are often brought to conflicts in professional life. It also aids the development of some important micro-skills in problem solving such as recognizing a plurality of perspectives, negotiating and decision making. Marking criteria should be tailored to ensure that these micro-skills are being assessed in terms of discussions, role-play outcomes and individual student reflections.

Case 18.3: Role-plays in an engineering simulation

In an engineering-based context, small groups complete a four-stage simulation that includes:

- A *briefing* on the technical structure, the geographical and physical contexts of the role-play and the ICT interface itself.
- The *interaction* stage, which involves all personae responding to a given scenario that reflects contemporary events. For example, the scenario might be the release of a green paper outlining proposals for a technologically oriented development of the geographical region outlined in the briefing. From their role perspectives, participants respond to the green paper's call for discussion and adjust their responses as they gain a fuller understanding of all personae and their roles. These discussions take place over approximately two to three weeks.
- The *forum* stage, which is based around a number of public forums concerning the green paper proposals. Each of the forums should provide a different focus on the issues, for example a financial, ecological, social and political focus. Personae post comments and submissions in accordance with the terms of reference for each of the forums, and they comment on the postings of others. This occurs over a short period, eg 48 hours only.
- The *debriefing* stage, which is a vital part of role-play simulation activities where participants can make explicit what they have learnt and their

reflections on the process as a whole, as well as critical incidents along the way. This can be done either online or through face-to-face discussions within a tutorial setting.

Assessment of contributions to the interaction stage and the forum stage are graded as well as the debriefing essay.

(adapted from McLaughlan *et al*, 2001, 2003)

Oral examinations

Oral exams or 'vivas' (an abbreviation of the Latin 'viva voce') may be employed to assess a variety of learning outcomes, including oral communication skills and the development of personal attributes. Here they are used to test the ability to think quickly while employing problem-solving skills in given or evolving circumstances. Facilitating individual oral exams can be an intensive business for staff, yet their great strength as a form of assessment is the flexibility they offer in exploring students' reasoning capacity, knowledge and ability to apply theory into practice. Depending upon circumstances and the abilities being assessed oral assessments may be undertaken either individually or in small groups, and may also be conducted for distance students by phone or using synchronous chat software.

Oral exams may take the form of a dialogue between assessor and student whereby a series of questions or brief scenarios is put to the student. While questions may aim to sample students' breadth and depth of knowledge, the most important outcome is that there is a sound decision-making framework that is guiding students' judgements and responses. The assessor wants to see that students can think on their feet and give sound, composed, professional responses to problems. The assessor needs to be prepared with sufficient material to make each assessment individualized to some degree, while still assessing the same outcomes. Detailed, clear criteria and standards for marking are essential to provide transparency in relation to judgements on students' performance. Where there are multiple assessors running parallel sessions, it is also vital that effective moderation occurs to ensure the highest possible levels of consistency and fairness. Moderation may relate to issues such as how the oral exam is conducted, how much support or prompting is acceptable, the breadth and depth of questioning, shared criteria, interpretation of standards and so forth.

Oral exams are, of course, a relatively advanced form of assessment, most commonly applied in later years of study when students are being prepared for entry to their professions. Students usually find these kinds of exams highly stressful, as they only have a relatively small window of time in which to impress upon the assessor the extent of their knowledge and abilities. They may also fear that only a small pocket of knowledge – the one that happens to be their weakest – may become the focus of questioning. It is important for teachers to help allay fears and create a relaxed environment for such assessment forms. This is achieved by all the usual methods – allowing students opportunity to practise and rehearse for the assessment, and providing detailed, clear information regarding the rationale and scope of the assessment as well as the basis upon which marks will be awarded.

Oral examinations are also considered in Chapter 17, where a case is provided (Case 17.6).

Triple jump

The triple jump method was initially devised for medical education at McMaster University in Canada (Painvin *et al*, 1979) although it has been adapted recently for use in many more disciplines as an exercise in problem solving and managing one's own learning. It is often scheduled as an end-of-semester event that entails three stages:

- *Step 1.* A trigger such as an authentic case study is used. This may be in the form of a video documentary or piece of reportage from an actual event or situation, along with other primary source material, which together pose a range of professional issues and problems. Students are assessed on their ability to identify and evaluate issues and problems arising from the material presented.
- *Step 2.* Students are then placed into groups where lists are consolidated and prioritized, with each group member negotiating a particular issue or problem to be individually investigated and reported upon. Students are assessed here on their ability to work collaboratively towards an agreed outcome (via a written piece of work evaluating the group process and its effectiveness).
- *Step 3.* Students have a defined period (such as a week) in which to employ their own research and investigative skills in pursuing their topic. Their results may be presented in a variety of formats, including literature reviews, reports and plans of action, or a colloquium may be facilitated where oral presentations are given. Students are primarily assessed on their ability to plan and manage a project, as well as the rigour and quality of their findings.

(Toohey, 1996)

Clearly, if an assessment task such as this is offered as an end-of-semester event, it would be necessary to offer significant developmental tasks during term to help students acquire the necessary expertise in wide-ranging abilities such as problem solving, collaborative work and self-directed project work.

Rich case studies

Rich case studies are another variation on a familiar theme, where students are exposed to complex problems or data and are expected to discern issues and problems, use theory to interpret facts, evaluate possible courses of action and so forth. The distinguishing feature of the rich case study is that the problems that students tackle are static, rather than unfolding or escalating in nature. This usually means that they are less complex to facilitate than other assessment methods discussed here, and may be used readily in face-to-face, distance and online settings, as well as invigilated examinations as a final assessment event.

As the word suggests, 'rich' case studies usually have multiple strands of data, possibly using a mix of media, that are as lifelike and authentic as possible. They usually contain many potential issues or problems that students must order and prioritize before constructing an argument for a particular resolution or a plan to address the problem. Group work and debate of contentious issues are elements that can be added to the process.

Case 18.4: Case study assessment in early childhood education

This is an end-of-semester assessment in an education subject that is delivered online. The case study aims to draw together in a holistic way much of what is studied during term. Students have two days in which to complete the case study, which is made available online as a series of stimuli from a child day care centre. The case study revolves around three fictitious children and contains selected data, including:

- a brief profile of each child, taken on admission to the day care centre;
- written day book entries of child care workers relating particular incidents;
- photographs of children playing with each other;
- audio segments of speech and interactions between the children and also with their parents;
- crayon drawings by children.

Students are initially required to use their powers of observation and analysis to recognize issues or problems in terms of child development theory, occupational health and safety, and a variety of other issues. Students then plan, for each child, a series of relevant activities to support the child's development and well-being. Students are assessed on the accuracy of their observations and appropriateness of their plans, having regard to the theories studied during semester.

Self-directed problem solving

In many adult learning and distance education contexts, as well as in postgraduate education, students are often already immersed in their vocations and professions. These students may bring a rich fabric of experience to many learning encounters. When developing and assessing problem-solving skills in this context, it seems somewhat unnecessary to create 'authentic' problems when they have real scenarios at their fingertips – the array of issues, problems and cases that occur in daily practice.

Self-directed problem solving encourages students to use these individualized professional settings as the subject of problem-solving activity. Assessment will often take the form of a self-directed project in which students are required to identify and reflect upon a relevant problem, undertake background research, plan for and possibly undertake actions, reflect on outcomes and so forth. Although each student is working on an individual and unique topic, the group have in common a shared process that may incorporate elements of the action learning cycle, self-directed learning processes and reflective practice models. This will vary according to disciplinary setting and the teacher's personal preferences. However, the models and processes used should be explicitly taught to students during semester, with each stage unpacked and discussed. This may, in fact, provide a structure for all the learning activities throughout the semester. A shared process is important so that assessment submissions may be reasonably compared, but also because students can interact meaningfully with each other at each key point in the process, gaining peer feedback on their problems and potential ways in which to address them. In this manner, we strive to create a mutually supportive professional community of learners. Students may well be assessed on the quality of their interactions with others as well as the outcomes of their project.

Case 18.5: Collaborative, self-directed problem solving – education

In postgraduate teacher education, the subject 'Management of educational technology' is taken up by students wishing to advance their information technology skills in their own school environment. They identify an issue or problem that they are currently facing in the classroom or school administration that may be resolved by the application of an information technology solution. The following process is undertaken:

1. Students' first task is to articulate and discuss the problem with peers in an online discussion forum. If necessary they reframe their problem in the light of discussions.
2. From there they undertake research on potential solutions, with supporting study materials and Web links.
3. Potential options are then shared and debated within the group. Participants benefit enormously by discussing the ideas behind the solutions of others. Again options may be reframed during this process.
4. Implementation plans are then developed by individual students and submitted for feedback from teachers. Each plan includes specific criteria to be addressed, including rationale for introduction, relationship to any national goals or priorities, key learning areas, proposed impact on teaching and learning, potential community involvement and so forth.
5. Proposals are then piloted by students in their own contexts.

6. Results, outcomes and work in progress are shared at the end of semester, with individual reflections on the process and further ideas for improvement.

Students are assessed upon the documented outcomes of their project along with their contributions to the collaborative process at each stage. Depending on the scale of each project, it may not be completed by the end of semester. This is not considered a problem, as learning and experimenting will no doubt continue beyond the confines of the semester. As a final assessment, students submit an account of their reflections on the process, what they've learnt and how they might tackle other problems of this kind in the future.

Implications for teaching

There is a range of implications for teaching that have been touched upon in this chapter on problem solving, which we would like now to draw into focus. Perhaps the most significant issue for teachers is how to allocate dedicated time to developing their students' problem-solving skills while feeling that there is so much content to be taught. How can students solve problems if they don't have an adequate body of knowledge and understanding to draw upon? The tension between 'content coverage' and skills development is an ongoing issue throughout this book, as no doubt it is for many teachers in practice.

Moreover, many of the assessment methods presented here need some considerable time and thought in their development and facilitation – time that teachers may feel they don't have, when other more automated forms of assessment are readily available. Some may feel that there is little point in an individual teacher trying to introduce problem solving into an otherwise conventional, content-led curriculum.

Of course, problem solving is a core graduate attribute that is ideally taught at all levels of a programme, with collaboration and shared under-standing between staff regarding its application in incremental steps, in line with the novice-to-expert continuum, and its particular disciplinary forms. There are some excellent examples, in disciplines such as medicine and engineering, where problem-solving activities shape entire programmes of study (see Boud and Feletti, 1991, for example). Yet we don't live in a perfect world, and most teachers in higher education operate within the practical constraints of their own institutions and subjects. Interestingly, most of the cases provided in this chapter are examples of this: teachers seeking to promote active, applied learning, not as a whole-of-programme approach but wherever they manage to fit it in. The key to their success is that they not only assess using problems but their teaching *supports* the development of these skills by:

- modelling good problem-solving methods;
- providing students with the opportunity to practise the series of related micro-skills in an incremental way with feedback during semester; and
- prompting students to reflect upon their developing expertise and how these skills are transferable to other situations.

19

Managing and developing oneself

Introduction

The ability to manage and develop oneself is a learning outcome to which a great deal of lip service is paid in institutional rhetoric. We commonly read lofty statements in institutional plans and missions about the university's desire to produce graduates who are self-directing lifelong learners with the ability to manage their transition into professional life, to work collaboratively, to be self-evaluating, to make ethical judgements, to possess intellectual curiosity and so forth. Indeed, many educational institutions around the world are under increasing pressure to provide evidence that their graduates possess these key transferable skills and attributes. Yet of all the learning outcomes covered in Part B of this book, these abilities are perhaps the least tangible and undoubtedly the least well addressed in terms of teaching and assessment.

The abilities addressed in this chapter are largely attitudinal in nature. Some would argue that we cannot teach attitudinal qualities such as integrity or empathy in dealing with clients, or tolerance and concern for others. Even if we can model and promote these qualities by our teaching, critics would say that we can only assess them in superficial and inauthentic ways. Yet there are many teachers in higher education who are deeply committed to their students' personal and professional development and who are keen to impart important professional qualities and attitudes. Employers, in turn, are demanding graduates who are able to make a smooth transition to the workforce, imbued with appropriate attitudinal and personal qualities.

Although they are often interconnected in practice, these abilities are divided into four broad groups, adapted from Toohey (1996), that are considered in their turn below, along with their disciplinary concerns:

I Self-directing and lifelong learning abilities

Lifelong learning abilities are considered to be a key quality of graduating students, yet there is only occasional evidence of sustained development and assessment of these abilities in undergraduate programmes. Lifelong learning as a concept has appeared repeatedly in education circles and government reports since the 1970s, as a response to rapid social, economic and technological changes in Western society. At its basis is the idea that post-secondary education is necessarily a lifelong process for all adults, and not just a 'once-only' experience designed for young people. It has dimensions that are both instrumental (reskilling and competitiveness of the workforce) and humanitarian (personal fulfilment, enrichment of society and widest participation).

An undergraduate programme that promotes lifelong learning provides five key outcomes:

- a systematic overview of the discipline;
- an exploration of the discipline in context and with comparison to other disciplines and ways of knowing;
- opportunities for students to broaden their horizons and develop a rich repertoire of thinking, communicating and research skills;
- provision of some opportunity for student choice and flexibility in structure and learning approaches; and
- provision for incremental development of self-directed learning abilities.

(Candy, Crebert and O'Leary, 1994)

These are underscored by the core skills of information and computer literacy, which provide a doorway to the worlds of information and ideas.

Candy, Crebert and O'Leary (1994) contrast the above outcomes with a series of 'lamentable lapses' found in many undergraduate programmes, including overloading the curriculum; imposing too much detail at too advanced a level; making excessive use of lectures and other didactic approaches; failing to connect learning with the world of practice; using forms of assessment that encourage surface learning; not providing timely, useful feedback to learners on their progress; insufficient development of information literacy skills; and viewing the university as offering little more than vocational training. These lapses combine to produce graduates who meet the standards for professional accreditation but possess only short-term currency in the workforce, lacking the ability to be innovative, adaptive or self-directive in their professional futures. Those committed to developing lifelong learners recognize that students' undergraduate education will only ever be a part of their adult learning history. While bodies of knowledge may rapidly become outdated, students' motivation, academic skills and intellectual curiosity will continue to flourish as they move towards their next professional challenge.

At the heart of the lifelong learning movement is the pedagogy of self-directed learning, in which students are supported in incremental steps to identify and manage their own learning agendas and to evaluate the quality of their learning outcomes. Fully self-directing learners possess a rich variety of key skills including the ability to articulate their learning needs; define a problem or issue worthy of attention; plan, design and carry out a learning project; access and analyse information from differing points of view; reflect on project outcomes and evaluate their achievement against self-determined criteria. Underneath these skills are the attitudes of intellectual curiosity and professional autonomy. Once acquired, these skills tend to remain with people for life and may be applied in informal, professional or academic learning contexts. In undergraduate curricula the capacity for self-direction is ideally fostered incrementally over a programme of study as learners acquire the necessary foundations (see Brockett and Hiemstra, 1991; Candy, 1991, for example).

The facilitation of self-directed learning no doubt varies between disciplines. In some it may be argued that students must first master the basic declarative knowledge of their field before launching into self-directed activity. In others knowledge is functional from the very beginning. Self-directed learning is of course not appropriate in all circumstances but may be gradually introduced to a programme by providing opportunities for negotiated assessment tasks that encourage learners to demonstrate how they have achieved the learning outcomes in relation to their own particular needs, interests or professional circumstances. In promoting self-direction, teachers need to be able to reconceptualize their roles from content providers to facilitators of learning, or 'joint venturers' with students. Promotion of self-direction also assumes a willingness to shed some of their considerable power over what is learnt, when, the methods used and how it might be assessed. This of course may pose particular challenges to those who are wedded to set curricula, defined learning outcomes and a view that knowledge is fixed, finite and non-negotiable. Students, as well, may be initially reluctant to embrace the challenges of self-direction, preferring instead the structure and pacing that are most familiar to them.

2 Ethical practice and integrity

Most professions have codes of conduct and ethical standards of professional behaviour. However, these broad guiding principles or rules of conduct may offer practitioners only minimal support in dealing with daily ethical dilemmas of professional life. In recent years ethics education has become more critical, not only because of the increasing complexity of professional decision making but also because of a palpable loss of faith by the public in its institutions and the ethical conduct of professionals in business, government, the law, the research sciences and countless other areas of activity (Lisman, 1996).

In general terms, ethical thinkers are thinkers who have the ability to:

- identify and analyse the ethical issue or conflict of interest;
- demonstrate a sound understanding of cause and effect in their professional decision making;

- relate to an ethical framework that identifies core values that are consonant with the values of their own community and the expectations of broader society;
- justify publicly a course of action;
- advocate where appropriate on behalf of others.

These skills are closely aligned with processes of critical thinking, yet they differ in that they are founded upon variant frameworks of moral values, and there indeed may be little consensus regarding solutions to ethical problems. Most moral frameworks, though, are based upon fundamental principles such as beneficence (good intent, do no harm), autonomy (individual and human rights) and justice (natural justice and rule of law). As teachers, we might ask ourselves how these fundamental values are embedded in our teaching and assessment practices.

Although standard ethics courses are generally offered in university philosophy departments, undergraduates need exposure to ethical thinking and norms within their own disciplines. This may take the form of a dedicated professional ethics unit of study within a programme or, more appropriately, an embedded across-the-curriculum approach, where ethical issues are regularly discussed in context. Generally, students will need much more exposure than just the raising of ethical questions, which tend to promote simplistic, subjective responses. Rather, students should be introduced to a rigorous process of ethical inquiry with guided analysis and discussion, underpinned by a systematic framework. Teaching and assessment are mostly focused around case studies or vignettes through which students are encouraged to apply their reasoning skills, debate differing perspectives and points of view, and negotiate acceptable resolutions. Let's look at some brief examples of ethical thinking in the disciplines:

Social sciences
The social scientist needs a firm understanding of basic moral notions such as freedom and justice when analysing social systems and how society addresses social problems such as poverty and inequality. In the variety of professional practices of the social sciences, these issues will translate into a plethora of ethical dilemmas regarding fair treatment, conflicts of competing interest, and appropriate interventions. The social scientist will need to be able to identify the ethical issues, analyse the interests involved, determine who is affected by the decision and what stake those affected have in the outcome, and make an ethically sound, accountable decision.

Business studies
Business ethics range from a series of theoretical debates regarding justice and economic distribution in capitalist economies through to a series of highly applied ethical concerns such as consumer and shareholder responsibilities, rights and responsibilities in the workplace, environmental and social responsibilities, discrimination, whistle blowing, to name but a few. Business professionals and managers have the complex task of negotiating solutions that are legal,

moral, culturally acceptable, consistent with good business practice and yet affordable and minimally harmful or disruptive to their enterprises.

Law

Although ethical, legal and moral questions are often interwoven, legal ethics can be defined as something separate from the law. Ethical legal practice relates to the way in which lawyers conduct themselves with regard to the rights of their clients and the protection of the judicial process. It is founded on complex and contested concepts such as 'good faith' in one's approach to and performance of advocacy in an adversary system of justice. A lawyer's duty to a client may conflict with the lawyer's own ethical precepts. Should the lawyer offer moral advice on a course of action? Issues of access to the law may also occupy ethics discussions, along with the structure of the legal profession, the effectiveness of the system in dispensing justice, and the role of the profession as either an arm of governance or merely a service industry. It is generally agreed that legal ethics should be both taught as a discrete subject and also integrated throughout the curriculum, with extensive use of case studies and guided discussion.

(Armer, 1999)

3 Ability to be reflective

The issues and problems that confront professional practitioners on a daily basis are rarely straightforward or well defined. Frequently they are complex, ill structured and multidimensional, having no single or 'right' solution. With its focus on bodies of factual knowledge and tendency towards formulaic decision-making models, undergraduate education cannot adequately prepare professionals for such high levels of performance. In most cases it takes many years of experience and development to attain this 'expert' status within one's profession. However, Schön (1987) argued that undergraduate educators can sow the seeds for high levels of professional expertise by teaching and modelling the ability to be reflective. His models of 'reflection-in-action' and 'reflecting-on-action' – forms of learning by doing and reflecting on the process and consequences – enable practitioners to make new sense of uncertain, unique or conflicted situations going beyond available facts and procedures. A reflective professional creates a climate of intelligent practice and is more capable of change, innovation, creativity and management of complex issues.

Teaching and modelling the ability to be reflective is similarly as challenging as prompting self-directedness in students or fostering a spirit of inquiry. It commences with an attitude by teachers that the knowledge of their profession is not fixed or finite, so that learners can be encouraged to question orthodoxy and to dig deeper into subjects of interest. Teaching and modelling reflection also assumes an approach that is as experiential and active as possible, involving field trips, observations, experiments and practicums that provide students with the stimuli for meaningful reflection. This is underscored by a good working knowledge of the processes of reflection, as appropriate to one's discipline.

The processes of reflection are not always ordered ones, but reflection in learning should be intentional and can be supported by frameworks or models. Boud, Keogh and Walker (1985), for example, describe reflection in learning as a three-stage process:

- *Stage 1.* Returning to the experience – observing an event as it has happened and noting what occurred and one's reactions to it.
- *Stage 2.* Attending to feelings, including utilizing positive feelings and removing obstructing feelings. Positive feelings can motivate one to persist in challenging situations, whereas negative ones may create an affective barrier that prevents one from properly understanding the experience.
- *Stage 3.* Re-evaluating the experience. This may include processes such as making associations, seeking relationships and finding new meanings among the data, validating for internal consistency between new understandings and one's existing knowledge, and appropriating the new knowledge into one's own conceptual framework.

There are various models of reflective processes that will be very different in various professional settings, owing to the nature of professional values and cultures. Consider these two brief examples:

Engineering
While engineering design is based upon established principles of applied physics and proven rules and theories, consider the dilemma of the practising engineer who is experiencing a rapidly developing body of knowledge and changing societal expectations. These rules and theories do not always provide sufficient support when faced with new design challenges. Schön (1995) describes engineering design practice as akin to a 'reflective conversation with the materials of the situation' as the design process moves through phases of diagnosis, experiment, pilot process and production design. At each stage practitioners may be confronted with problems that require on-the-spot theorizing and experimenting, modelling the known with the unknown, and reflecting on similarities and differences, from which problems may be newly framed and further tested. The reflective conversation is a way of describing and making sense of new phenomena or unique situations.

Counselling
In the fields of counselling and psychotherapy, it is vital for practitioners to have a high level of self-awareness and a strong reflective core to their practice. This may take a number of forms. In a counselling session, for example, it is important for counsellors to be able to reflect on their interactions with clients, always alert to the possibility that they may be imposing their own value judgements or introducing their own emotional issues into the session. It is commonplace for counsellors to debrief with peers or supervisors, which takes the form of a reflective dialogue in which these issues are analysed. Like the engineer, the counsellor will be confronted with difficult problems that require on-the-spot theorizing, reflecting on similarities and differences drawn from past experience when considering ways forward.

4 Ability to work collaboratively

A consistently valued quality in graduating students is the capacity to be a 'team player'. Rarely do professionals work in isolation from each other. More commonly nowadays, they work in creative or multidisciplinary teams where a product, service or outcome is the necessary result of wide-ranging collaborative activity. Ironically, however, much undergraduate education encourages solo pursuits and, indeed, a competitiveness between students that is often underscored by assessment schemes where students compete for limited grades. Within this culture, it comes as little surprise that the development of collaborative skills and the assessment of group work can be problematic.

Effective collaborators have:

- a wide repertoire of communication and negotiation skills;
- an appreciation of the ideas and contributions of others in formulating a rich outcome;
- empathy for others and a tolerance of divergent views to their own;
- an ability to recognize and manage situations of potential or actual conflict;
- self-awareness and self-evaluative abilities.

The products of group work are mostly larger in scale and more complex than individual pieces of work and have the capacity to produce higher-quality learning outcomes for those involved. But a significant longer-term benefit can be achieved for students who are encouraged to use group work as a laboratory to develop their skills in collaboration and, with guidance and feedback, reflect on areas of strength and weakness. It may also be accompanied by some study of group dynamics and interpersonal communications and may usefully include peer feedback from group members during and after the collaborative process.

Difficulties arise in group project work owing to the culture of competitiveness (which of course is a very real concern to students) and the problems associated with allocating grades fairly to individuals. Poorer or less cooperative students may benefit from the diligence of others in the group, or may drag the group mark down by their own failures. Some teachers adopt the view that, in the 'real world', group project work will only be judged on the collective outcome rather than the relative merits of individual participants. Thus students must find ways to make their groups functional and cooperative in a rather dire 'sink-or-swim' manner. But, from a developmental point of view, the most effective facilitation of group work is that which puts equal or even greater emphasis upon group processes as upon products or outcomes. Within this model, there is room for students to evaluate their own and each other's contributions to the project, using explicit criteria to assist them in making informed judgements. This provides students with the likelihood of a fairer individual assessment, and also considerable insight into what is perceived by others to be the strengths and weaknesses of their group behaviour. Facilitating group project work can be complex, although there is excellent advice available that weighs the differing approaches (for example, Gibbs, 1995).

Teaching collaboration skills in any discipline is usually an incremental process. It may entail introducing small collaborative tasks in pairs, to familiarize students with processes of shared planning and cooperative effort. Controversial issues or topics are often selected for likely differences of viewpoint within each pairing. It is then necessary for students to negotiate their differences by clarifying mutual goals, establish a working relationship, which is more important than the short-term issue, and explore ways in which conflict or controversy can be turned to a strength. Students learn that conflict is fundamental to academic processes and may yield highly constructive dividends. Debriefing of how conflict and difference were handled in each pairing is a productive way for teachers to highlight the positive gains of controversy, whether they be in the domains of social competence, positive interpersonal relationships or academic rigour (Johnson and Johnson, 1994). As students progress through a programme, more complex forms of group work may be introduced, such as debates and large team projects. Students then face more complex challenges in planning, division of labour, communications, managing difference, the performance of individuals, time-frames, presentation and so on. It's important that teachers be explicit about the purpose of the group work to develop professionalism and to use forms of group work that are most commonly found in their own professional domains. Below are some brief examples:

Education

Although a great deal of the teacher's time may be spent in the classroom, an important shared activity between teachers is curriculum development. While each teacher has his or her own areas of interest and expertise, successful curricula must be greater than the sum of their parts, their elements working cohesively to achieve programme outcomes. School curricula will contain subject areas that are overlaid by developing key themes, core skills and national and state priorities, and that are mindful of local issues, children with special needs, parental input and a host of other issues. Unless teachers can effectively collaborate to bring the curriculum together in a meaningful way, their students may drift aimlessly through a series of unconnected islands of content. Teachers in a school must establish good working relationships, agree on an appropriate philosophical approach, understand and have respect for each other's disciplinary perspectives and be able sometimes to put aside their own enthusiasms in pursuit of common goals. Skills in collaborative curriculum development can be fostered throughout undergraduate teacher education (see the case studies in Toohey, 1996: 107–09).

Drama and theatre studies

For effective dramatic experiences to occur, actors must work together within group structures as they explore roles, character development and interactions. Professional actors must have excellent collaborative skills, which include welcoming individual differences and interpretations and the process by which shared meanings are negotiated. Drama in education is a sophisticated form of collaborative learning. Drama programmes develop collaborative skills from an early stage, using role-plays and improvisation to enable students to learn from and with one another with guidance and support from the teacher. Conflict or difference must be negotiated and can be employed constructively to fuel the dramatic tension of a performance. By involving students in dramatic situations, teachers are able to facilitate growth and the development of self-confidence in students and enhance their social literacy.

(Fairhead, 1990)

Assessment methods

Given the variety of skills, abilities and attitudes that are addressed in this chapter, there are many forms of assessment that may be usefully employed. Most of the more frequently used methods are considered here.

Ethical dilemmas and vignettes

Ethical dilemmas arise in most professional contexts where judgement is required. Where there are no clear-cut answers and the implications of any decision or judgement are complex, professional people such as lawyers, teachers, doctors, politicians, scientists and many others are called upon to back their judgement with a course of action and at the same time minimize undesirable consequences.

A change in an individual's established ways of thinking is difficult to measure. In assessing the development of an ethical thinker, it may be worth while using a pre-test and post-test approach if such a change is the desired outcome of the learning event. A variant on this might be to ask students to evaluate their own shift in understanding, attitudes and beliefs.

Ethical dilemmas as assessment items take a very similar form to unfolding scenarios, vignettes and rich case studies, which have been discussed at some length in Chapter 18. Here, of course, the ethical nature of the problem comes into sharper focus.

Case 19.1: Working through ethical dilemmas in science
Exposure to the professional standards, the various points of view within the class group and the perspectives espoused in the scientific media provides students with a rich array of possible ways to handle ethical dilemmas in science.

The question of enforcing compulsory vaccinations in the community was prescribed as a topic for student research and discussion in the form of an essay. Students were required to put forward all available points of view on the matter as well as citing supporting evidence from research. The final elements of the assessment task were to put forward their own point of view and to review how this had changed on the basis of their research.

Of course it is very difficult for teachers to provide definitive responses to ethical issues, especially since there are usually just a few set ethical standards in each specific strand of the scientific profession. In this case students' work will be marked on how thoroughly they have researched the issue and how well they have been able to use valid evidence to support their case. Self-reflection is an important element of their grade as they will need to have determined for themselves how they have kept an open mind during their research and how their point of view has ultimately emerged from their research.

Journals

Journals are particularly useful as a means of encouraging purposeful reflective activity throughout a semester. They may accompany a practicum or other experiential learning encounter. In such instances reflection is needed at various points: at the start, as students are anticipating the experience; during the experience as a way of organizing some of an array of encounters, experiences and feelings that have been generated; and following the experience where students can further reflect on these feelings and consolidate their position with the benefit of hindsight. The general goal is of reconstructing experience with a view to making order and sense of new ideas and information that they have retained (Boud, Keogh and Walker, 1985). Journals may also be used in non-experiential situations where they are useful for students to help organize their thoughts, reactions and feelings around new subject areas. For many, the act of writing is important as a means of ordering the array of random thoughts.

Students need practice to become effective as journal keepers. Thus it is sensible that there be multiple submission points so that teachers can ensure that the style is appropriate and that entries are on the right track. Teachers need to be very clear about the purposes of the journal, the form it is to take and how judgements are made about it. What kind of learning is it aiming to engender? How personal should it be? How analytical? How comprehensive and detailed in terms of coverage? How long should it be? What would a very good journal entry look like? How much of it will be read and responded to by the marker? How will marks be awarded? Guidelines in relation to all these questions need to be clearly communicated to students before commencing journal entries.

In general, teachers value journals because of the insight they lend to students' developing consciousness of complex issues and dilemmas in professional practice. They want to see that students are forming the ability to engage with problematic issues, understand their own personal responses, seek out and evaluate other viewpoints and respond in an appropriate and professional manner.

Case 19.2: Reflective diary

A graduate programme in leadership and workplace development required students to set out their own programme plan. Beginning in the first and only mandatory subject in the programme, students were guided to select their preferred pathway of 11 further subjects from a selection of over 20 electives (from a range of specialized areas such as organizational change, capability, career planning, professional profiling, leadership, action learning and spirituality in the workplace).

The reflective diary was prescribed as a method of initial goal setting, recording progress and subsequent follow-up, providing continuity as well as a focus for review and reinforcement of individual objectives. At the completion of each semester, students were to submit their reflective diaries as supporting documentation detailing their achievements, reflections and proposed pathway forward.

Reflective diaries were mandatory to complete in order to satisfy requirements, though they were not allocated a grade.

Portfolios

A learning portfolio is a collection of resources showing evidence of a network of projects that progressively work together over the course of study to enable students to:

- implement more effective professional practice with confidence and independence;
- demonstrate knowledge, understanding, skills and strategies in an authentic context;
- reflect on the conditions under which this professional practice works or does not work, and why;
- use prior and emerging experience to improve their own capacity to adapt to a diversity of contexts.

The portfolio may include a number of different items, including records of events or new situations, reviews, extracts from readings, diary entries, reflections on outcomes – indeed anything that has become the subject of learning. The key, however, is that this material is accompanied by a written piece that ties together and synthesizes what has been learnt, as evidence of meaningful engagement with the portfolio contents.

Case 19.3: Improving practice using portfolio evidence

In the case of a teaching portfolio, the student's inclusions can consist of an initial learning plan, map of aims and milestones, course reflections from subject to subject, progress reports, evidence of meeting course outcomes (self-determined, negotiated or prescribed) and evidence of learning activities or implementation of theories in practice, and transfer to the workplace.

Records of progress over time are in the form of reflective notes as well as including a range of elements such as tailored resources and models used in the applied context by students, lesson plans, audio and video recordings of performance and online archives of discussions that took place.

Students can often gain as much from completing the task as they might gain from the feedback and grades achieved. However, given the comprehensive nature of the submission it is only fair to provide a considered review of the work with some suggestions for future use of portfolios in professional practice. In some ways no grade is adequate for such a developmental and personal collection of works, but an acknowledgement of excellence or outstanding developmental achievement is very worth while.

Case 19.4: Portfolios to provide evidence of prior learning

In some cases portfolios can be used as evidence of prior learning. In this event, portfolio preparation is a process whereby students apply for credit for undergraduate and college-level learning that they have completed outside the formal classroom situation. Depending on the institution to which the student is applying, prior learning can be granted for a range of activities such as on-the-job experience, professional practice, vocational training, non-credit courses, workshops, seminars, online and hobby courses, sustained volunteer work, and community or personal development pursuits.

The students' process of evaluating their previous learning, matching it to current academic requirements, constructing the documentation and submitting the portfolio of prior learning is critical to gaining credit. This process enables students to assess their prior learning in the context of their own academic goals and thus connect past experiences with future educational and professional aims. Clarification of goals through examination of achievements and directions for personal development is further enriched by the exercise of critical thinking, writing and organizing the evidence. In highlighting the notion that much past learning may have been gained outside mainstream educational contexts, students are also reinforced in appreciating the value of lifelong learning approaches.

Learning contracts

Learning contracts are a key tool in promoting self-directed learning. They aim to provide students with an opportunity to undertake an in-depth study of a particular topic or area of practice with the broad guidance of an academic staff member. They develop students' self-direction and lifelong learning skills by supporting them to identify an area of personal relevance, set the learning outcomes, plan and conduct a project and negotiate the criteria by which the project will be assessed.

Learning contracts are usually submitted according to predetermined requirements and include such considerations as:

- the title of the proposed project;
- rationale for the project;
- a description of the project;
- expected learning outcomes;
- methods to be used;
- resources needed;
- time/task allocation;
- what will be submitted for assessment and how it should be assessed.

The proposal for a learning contract must usually be approved and signed by the unit assessor (and any other associated teaching staff such as workplace supervisors, where this is relevant). In the case of a learning contract for small research activity, consideration needs to be given to associated requirements, such as ethics clearance and project management. The most common area of negotiation between students and staff in the approval of a contract is the issue of scope. Teachers must be satisfied that the proposed project is realistically achievable in the given time-frame, despite the initial enthusiasms of many students.

A determination of student achievement is made from evidence that goals have been reached and specified learning outcomes have been demonstrated. Students' self-assessment can also be an appropriate way of completing the learning contract and sometimes it is helpful to have a staged approach to assessment, so that work in progress is provided with feedback through the study period. Where workplace supervisors or other external experts have also been involved, their input (if any) to students' grades needs to occur in accordance with prior negotiation.

Case 19.5: Learning contract in management

An undergraduate management programme was designed to include a subject on managing oneself in the context of the continuously changing management environment and recurrent uncertainty. Titled 'Today's manager', the subject required students to examine critically their own approaches to change and to develop a learning contract that outlined strategies for dealing with change more creatively. Some of the areas for change that students typically target are diet, exercise, stress management and time management – all of which can be achieved within the semester time-frame.

The contract was typical in form to the learning contracts in many discipline areas and the pro forma contained the following headings for students to address:

1. title of the proposed project (describes the learning goal);
2. rationale for the project (describes why the learning goal is personally relevant and challenging);
3. description of the project (describes the action plan, major steps involved, time-frames etc);

4. expected learning outcomes (describes proposed measures of achievement, supporting data and evidence of progress);
5. methods to be used (details of strategies to be adopted in reaching the desired goals);
6. resources required (specifies the literature, resources and equipment needed to pursue the learning goal);
7. time/task allocation (150 hours notionally allocated to this subject);
8. signatures of the subject assessor (required prior to commencement of the activities specified in the learning contract).

This series of steps, or similar, may be seen in learning contracts of all kinds. The main aim is to ensure students have thought through their project and have managed to keep it contained within allowable time and costs. Assessment of the proposal is commonly ungraded. However, the assessment of successful achievement of the substantive learning contract may in itself be a negotiated aspect. That is, as students are developing their own learning goals, they are also in a position to determine what might represent achievement with distinction, excellent achievement or satisfactory achievement. This is not always how the learning contract is assessed, though critical reflection is an important part of the process, and a component of self-assessment within the final project report would be quite a logical requirement.

Autobiography

An autobiographical work encourages learners to relate specific incidents in their personal histories to their sense of values and identity, and how this might impact on their professional lives and judgements. It is most likely to take the form of a journal or extended piece of writing, and may also include an abbreviated synthesis of what students have learnt from the experience. Autobiography may usefully accompany the development of ethical thinking, collaborative work and self-directed learning, as in each case one's attitudes and approaches have been shaped by significant life experiences. Mezirow's (1981) theory of 'perspective transformation' is influential in this process, in that students are encouraged to identify internalized ideologies and dependency roles that may hamper their development as professionals and as autonomous learners. The process of 'transformation' is a dynamic involving various stages of disorientation, reorientation and, finally, new ways of thinking and acting.

Autobiography is a highly personal assessment task – certainly it is much more than simply narrating a series of recollections of events and feelings. It is a challenging task to be able to step back from one's own experiences and to write a critical account at a meta-level. Careful thought needs to be given to its appropriate use and how it might be assessed. It may be appropriate, for example, to use ungraded assessment or to use it in a formative role only. If it is to be marked, clear criteria are essential. Clearly autobiography has interesting applications in the applied professions where self-knowledge and personal development are integral to the role.

Case 19.6: Lifeline of learning events

In this assessment task, education students are required to keep an autobiographical diary throughout semester. Students use the diary to note down their response to activities provided in their accompanying study materials. The first activity is to draw a lifeline of events and memories about learning. Students note the key events they remember, whether in a formal educational setting or not, and how the events impacted upon who they are as learners today. The diary grows as students proceed to investigate the principles of learning, experience and personal change.

This activity in itself forms a minor component of assessment but sits within an ongoing journal of reflection, and thus forms a core element in the process of understanding influences and circumstances affecting the students' approach to learning.

Case 19.7: Articulating professional values in journalism

Many professions entail complex and even contradictory value systems and inherent conflicts of interests. Journalists, for example, are regularly challenged by circumstances, their own values and those of their employers. In this assessment task, journalism students are posed the following question to be answered in the form of a reflective essay:

> Describe in autobiographical terms the significant intellectual and social values that have shaped your present aims to work in journalism. Reflect upon the relevance of these values and philosophies to your journalism studies to date. Discuss the origins of those values in your life experiences and how your values might contribute to satisfactions to be gained or constraints you might encounter when working as a journalist. Consider how you can represent your values through your journalism work and report from your own perspective on how you shall know the difference between being part of the solution or part of the problem in your future professional endeavours as a journalist.

The students' work will need to show depth of theoretical knowledge as well as a process of self-examination. Criteria for marking this assessment task will take account of achievement in both the writing skills and reflective skills required.

Group work

When the outcomes of a subject include the development of skills in teamwork and collaboration, group projects can be useful for developing a range of component skills, such as:

- sharing information and resources;
- collaborative decision making and planning;
- mutual assistance for mutual benefit;
- critical reflection, getting and giving helpful feedback and suggestions;
- engaging in large tasks that go beyond the individual's capacity to accomplish.

Group work may be structured along the lines of an authentic project that might be found in the relevant disciplinary area. Fieldwork placements can also be seen as a type of group project. In industries and professions such as information technology, film, radio and television media, social work, agriculture and many domains of science, staff work in teams to identify a problem, draw together information, develop or obtain resources and work towards solutions, products, responses or recommendations. In many of these contexts it is also the group that receives recognition for a product well developed or solution well conceived. To imitate this kind of scenario in an assessment task requires the creation of a simulated case or a 'real-life' brief in response to which students carry out their group project. Tasks may be divided and various roles allocated (such as researcher, reporter, writer etc). Each member may be contributing to an overall collection, or the group process may in itself be the most important feature of the task.

As discussed earlier in this chapter, the main issue around any group project is the equitable and meaningful allocation of marks. Facilitators of group work will need to think the issues through and devise a marking scheme that best represents the broad outcomes valued the most.

Case 19.8: Group design of Web site

Students preparing for employment in the multimedia and information technology industries quite often expect to be learning about teamwork. In the various professional areas of design, development and production of digital media and Web sites, the work is undertaken through discussion of the project and allocation of tasks across various members of a project team.

One university programme located in a metropolitan area is able to match the interests of local small businesses with the interests of small teams of students in a subject called 'Web site project development' for the design and production of a home page and multi-purpose Web site to support the aims of the business. Complex e-commerce requirements are beyond the scope of this subject.

Students are assigned into teams (rather than choosing to work with their mates) and each development team tenders for two projects from the list provided on the basis of a loosely structured brief, as would come from a client. Each team is matched with one project according to the strengths of their tender document and is introduced to the client.

The teams then undertake the consultation, planning, decision-making, problem-solving and communication activities in order to complete the Web site development project to prototype stage. Course notes, logbooks and instructions are provided online, as well as access to previous and/or exemplary projects completed at another time. Communication facilities online (e-mail and synchronous chat) assist with the planning and decision-making processes through the availability of instant archives.

Students complete the following:

- attending project team meetings;
- tender presentation;
- initial project scope;
- final project scope;
- design documentation and prototype;
- presentation of the design experiences to the class at the end of semester.

Industry-based requirements for graduates with skills in communication, teamwork, planning, decision making and problem solving help to determine the design of these kinds of authentic assessment tasks. The specific skills being assessed include the ability to work in teams (including both negotiation and collaboration), collaborative decision making, completion of clear and persuasive documentation, multimedia design and development skills, and oral presentation skills.

The allocation of marks occurs by allowing group members to report anonymously on their peers using a token allocation system. Using a total of 20 tokens, each student issues team members and him- or herself with the number of tokens that best represents relative contributions. The averaging of these totals enables individual students to achieve a mark that reflects their overall contribution to the project as a whole. The subject assessor also maintains a marking and moderation role to control for the rare dishonest students who might unjustifiably allocate themselves all 20 tokens. Systems of greater complexity for allocating individual marks within team projects can also be adopted if preferred.

(adapted from Woodcock, 2002)

Implications for teaching

The long-cherished notion that students will be imbued with appropriate qualities and attitudes by simply being exposed to the lofty world of higher education holds little currency these days. Universities and colleges today are more complex and heterogeneous institutions than could possibly have been imagined 50 years ago. Difference is the norm, and traditional notions such as integrity, autonomy, beneficence and justice are problematic, contested concepts – and rightly so. But it is understandable that teachers find teaching and assessing in this domain to be difficult and time consuming, with little ultimate evidence that their goals have been achieved.

How can we really know whether a graduating student will behave ethically in practice? Of course, we can't. Indeed, the burgeoning numbers of professionals now serving time in jail for a dazzling array of white-collar crime tend to reinforce this problem. However, teaching and assessing for particular attitudinal and professional qualities remain vital if for no other reason than that students understand what is expected of them, whether they choose to embrace these attributes or not. If students are taught to manage their own learning and to develop the habits of intellectual curiosity, then there is perhaps a reasonable chance that these habits will remain with them for life. If some students are not natural collaborators, perhaps they will never be, but hopefully they will manage such environments a bit better than before. These are the kinds of outcomes that, realistically, we come to accept.

There is certainly no escaping the fact that many of the teaching and assessment methods discussed in this chapter take considerable thought and effort. Facilitating self-directed or collaborative learning, for example, requires considerable planning and resources. In the introduction to this chapter, we referred to a series of 'lamentable lapses' in undergraduate education, such as overloaded curricula and didactic forms of teaching, which also tend to militate against developing these kinds of abilities. In many programmes, there is only room for token effort. It takes a conscious decision and commitment on the part of teachers within a programme to address certain qualities and attributes in a meaningful way, and to embed them throughout the curriculum in incremental stages.

Part C

Assessment in practice

Introduction to Part C

Part C of this book is about implementing assessment in practice to achieve the best possible outcomes for students and other stakeholders in the process.

In Part A we introduced a number of issues, themes and foundation principles that influence the assessment of student learning. In Part B we looked in depth at eight key types of learning outcomes, discussed what each means in its disciplinary context, considered how each might be assessed and explored appropriate assessment methods. Part C will focus upon good assessment practice, drawing on the issues and themes in Part A and the learning outcomes and assessment methods in Part B to amplify and illustrate our suggestions for effective assessment in practice.

In keeping with the practical nature of Part C, we have organized it into six chapters, each dealing with a stage in the assessment of student learning in higher education. As in Parts A and B, there are overlapping principles and concepts between the chapters of Part C. Our rationale for including these is to allow each chapter to be more or less self-contained:

- Chapter 20: Designing assessment tasks;
- Chapter 21: Developing marking schemes;
- Chapter 22: Communicating assessment tasks;
- Chapter 23: Marking and grading;
- Chapter 24: Evaluating assessment practices;
- Chapter 25: Dealing with plagiarism.

Part C is written in 'handbook' style and we have included short examples, scenarios, case studies and prompts as a guide to implementing assessment in practice.

Throughout this book we have asserted that the assessment of student learning is not an exact science, but that the principles we have discussed in Parts A and B have a bearing on the quality of assessment in higher education. We encourage you to reflect upon your own assessment practices as you read Part C and we invite you to adapt any useful ideas to suit your own assessment setting.

20

Designing assessment tasks

As we have seen in Parts A and B, assessment is a crucial issue in student learning and in assuring that the educational provider maintains academic standards. Grades allocated and feedback provided on assessment tasks drive students' progress through their programme of study. It therefore follows that the process of designing assessment is at the heart of the matter and can be considered a very important step along the way to good practice. Without full and creative consideration being given to the design of assessment there is the potential to affect adversely students' whole experience of learning.

Let's now take a step-by-step look at exactly what is involved in this process. Within each of the topics to be considered you will be prompted to pause for reflection and check how the issues may pertain to your situation. The topics covered are:

- context of assessment;
- diversity of students;
- whole-of-programme approach to assessment;
- aligning learning outcomes and assessment tasks;
- determining student assessment load, frequency and value of assessment tasks;
- improving validity and reliability in assessment;
- selecting methods of assessment;
- flexible design of assessment tasks.

Context of assessment

Find the assessment policies at your institution

In all educational institutions certain policies and procedures on assessment are clearly stated by an academic board or assessment committee. In large part these are designed as guidelines or reference points to assist individual staff members.

> Can you locate and read through the assessment policy for your institution?
> Any surprises?

Be clear about assessment policies prescribed by relevant professional bodies

Statements of policy are a means to ensure that consistency of standards is applied through student assessment across the institution. Where necessary, they will also prescribe the compliance requirements of professional, vocational and industry accreditation bodies. Accountability at this level is critical for establishing not only the graduate's credibility in the workforce but also the reputation of the programme and the educational institution as a whole.

> Does your assessment design have to conform to industry, vocational or
> professional specifications?

Make use of the diagnostic function of assessment

The diagnostic role of assessment has been showcased in Part B, so what needs to be appreciated in practice is that, when assessment takes place ahead of formal learning, it is being used to diagnose the extent of students' knowledge and understanding. If this process reveals significant gaps in knowledge, you will need to provide guidance and assistance for students to address this shortfall, before moving on to engage with the rest of the curriculum. An aspect of diagnostic testing that serves as a positive reinforcement to students is where you can help them become aware of what they already know. If you can help students to bring their prior knowledge to the fore, they can benefit by becoming aware of their own foundation knowledge and begin to build upon it.

> What is your experience with diagnostic assessment?

Design for a developmental function of assessment

The level of challenge that is presented as you design assessment tasks needs to develop incrementally. What you ask the students to carry out in their final year of undergraduate study will usually be more demanding than their assignments in first year. As students find themselves moving through a course of study, their need for basic encouragement makes way for a higher-order need for authentic application of learning and a lively discourse with their peers.

> How relevant is your assessment design to learners' needs? How do you
> know this?

Be clear about the association of your assessment with other subjects

The broader context of assessment also pertains to the prerequisite and co-requisite knowledge and skills that are assumed within a programme of study.

Since some subjects within the same course will cover the prerequisite knowledge, you need to keep the associated foundation subjects in mind when you teach. Students need to be aware of the prerequisite knowledge that they must carry as they proceed through the syllabus. When the subject you teach has a relationship to another subject that has been prescribed as a co-requisite, your responsibility is also to consider the overall amount of assessment and the due dates of each assessment task. You need to maintain fair and reasonable expectations of your students, and see your demands within the broader context.

> How many other subjects are your students studying concurrently, and when are these assessment tasks due?

Ensure adequate resourcing of assessment

The above discussion presupposes a level of resourcing for the assessment process. Without adequate resources – time, support staff and professional development – to support regular review of the course curriculum and the subject learning outcomes, your efforts to maintain fair and valid assessments will be made difficult.

> Before reading on, ask yourself:
>
> - Have you taken into account the broader context of your learners?
> - Can fulfilment of assessment requirements be applied by learners to a broader setting, such as the workplace or community?
> - How is the assessment process reviewed and resourced?

Subjects and their assessment requirements within the programme context

An arts programme has been very popular with off-campus students for many years because of its very open structure. So long as students undertake 24 units within three years they are able to qualify for the award. This flexibility of student choice has been a major attraction into the course, but staff have been frustrated by their inability to assume any prior knowledge in each of their subject areas. In a recent attempt at least to derive some standardization among the graduates of the programme, two subjects were nominated as compulsory core subjects. But in the spirit of flexibility these could be completed at any time in the students' three-year programme. After some animated discussion within the department it has now been agreed that the 100 per cent flexibility will be diminished in the interest of ensuring students build some foundation knowledge and skills in their first year. The course now runs with four core subjects as prerequisites to the rest.

Diversity of students

Knowing your students

Before you start planning your teaching session and assessment tasks, ask yourself:

- Who are your learners?
- What do you know about their cultural background, socio-economic status and living circumstances?
- What is their experience of university study, flexible learning and online learning?
- If you have taught this subject before, what has tended to be the age range of your students? Is it reasonable to expect a similar group this time?

Knowing your own personal perspective

Consider also the influences you might bring into your classroom: your race, gender, age, ethnicity, physical attributes and abilities. How might these impact upon your students when you meet them and as you guide them through their learning? Consider for a moment the time in your life when you first became aware of differences and how you reacted at that time.

Have you taken the time to reflect on your ideas of 'minority groups' and have these reflections undergone any change over time? How does your perspective on differences affect you today and how might they impact on your teaching?

Account for diversity in your assessment

It is easy to feel overwhelmed by the idea of having to take account of every student and his or her individual needs. Rather, let's start by considering a cohesive approach to the process of teaching and assessing for diversity. As the teaching session goes on, you may have come to know your students individually and gained a good sense of their personal circumstances. The difficulty with this in terms of assessment is that, by the time you have learnt about your students, the assessment tasks have already been set in place and little can be done to change them without fear of appeal from some members of the class.

- So what could you do to structure assessment that takes account of diversity? Find out very early in the session if any of your learners have special needs and, while making no assumptions, arrange for any appropriate supports or enablers to be put in place prior to assessments and exams.
- When considering using off-campus strategies, make no assumptions about access to libraries or community services. Allow for the

truly isolated students to negotiate the necessary arrangements so that assessment tasks can work in an equivalent manner for all students. Internet connection and access to computers cannot be assumed with certain target groups of students. What is the level of Internet access within your target group?

● How might these issues impact upon your choice of assessment design?

Assessing amid diversity online

Here is an example of how to take account of diversity among students in an online class. Tell the students:

● Everyone in the online class has both a right and an obligation to participate in discussions and, if called upon, should respond to achieve a mark for participation.
● Acknowledge the contributions of others with careful attention and an open mind.
● Ask for clarification when you don't understand a point someone has made, and before the due date of the assessment task.
● If you challenge others' ideas, do so with factual evidence and appropriate logic.
● If others challenge your ideas, be willing to change your mind if they demonstrate errors in your logic or use of the facts. Respond online for the archival record of your achievement of change.
● Don't introduce irrelevant issues into the discussion.
● If others have made a point with which you agree, don't bother repeating it (unless you have something important to add).
● Be efficient in your discourse; make your points and then yield to others.
● Above all, avoid ridicule and try to respect the beliefs of others, even if they differ from yours.
(adapted from UNC Center for Teaching & Learning, 1992)

Whole-of-programme approach to assessment

Consider the intended graduate outcomes for your programme

Assessment tasks are not designed in isolation from the learning context, and it is important to note that the disciplinary culture, the focus of the overall academic programme and the subject-specific learning outcomes will all play a part in determining the relevance of any individual assessment task that you design.

With these three layers of influence upon your practices – the discipline, the programme and the subject – your assessment tasks will always have several agendas to address. In many institutions you can find a statement of graduate outcomes, skills or attributes that define these broad areas of requisite achievement. See also the discussion in Chapter 4 on graduate attributes.

> Do you know of such a statement at your own institution, faculty or school?

Start by considering your disciplinary culture

As an educator you are steeped in a disciplinary area, and your teaching and learning practices will mostly be derived from the relevant professional values and tacit norms in that domain. Your first step is to take account of the full curriculum in the academic programme within which your subject is placed.

> Can you determine whether significant disciplinary outcomes will be covered within the programme as a whole?

Your subject in context

Once the overall aims for the whole programme are clear, each subject within the programme can be reviewed in order to establish its relevant portion of the overall assessment regime. While it is difficult for any individual staff member to undertake such a thorough review, this is ideally completed at the time of a regularly scheduled programme review. If such reviews have been overlooked or are overdue, you may be in a position to suggest a meeting with your colleagues to review the collection of subjects you teach with specific attention to the objectives and the assessment strategies.

It is at this point that your own syllabus needs to fit within the bigger context of the assessment regime. How many programmes do you know of where, despite the extensive range of global skills espoused, eg oral presentation, group work, information literacy and appreciation of cultural diversity, to name a few, the students' assessment tasks throughout their entire award rarely diverge from the essay format? Graduates may end up effectively writing over 40 essays to gain a qualification that will never require them to write another extensive narrative such as this ever again.

> Which of the overall graduate skills is your subject especially concerned with?

Assessment framework for your subject

Once you have considered the syllabus and course context into which your subject fits, the disciplinary context continues to play a part in the formulation of assessment, as mentioned in Part B. So, the assessment of the knowledge of concepts and techniques within the creative arts will take different forms from those within the applied professions of law or nursing, for example. With this in mind, the relevant content topics and learning outcomes in your subject will provide you with the basic framework of the demonstration of knowledge, capabilities and understanding that you need to design into an assessment regime.

> How might you design an overall assessment regime to include a number of smaller tasks that build on each other in an integrated approach to achieving the learning outcomes in your subject?

Process-oriented assessment

In addition to the content areas to be assessed, consider if you need to design for process-oriented learning outcomes that weigh up students' achievement in a range of more global skills such as:

- verbal and written communication;
- accessing and evaluating information;
- working effectively in cooperation with others;
- the application of higher-order critical thinking skills.

Using assessment for benchmarking self-development

And finally, in many cases an ideal assessment regime also gives room for establishing early benchmarks for change in students' attitudes, values, ideals and personal and professional principles.

> Before moving on ask yourself:
>
> 1. What is the relationship between the structure of your assessment design and the disciplinary culture in which the learner encounters it?
> 2. What does your assessment design contribute to the overall aims of the programme?
> 3. How have you ensured an alignment between the stated subject learning outcomes, the learning activities throughout the syllabus, and the assessment design?

Whole-of-programme assessment design

When an applied science degree was to be externalized, a series of consultations took place between educational designers and all subject coordinators to examine the graduate qualities intended from the course. These were then prioritized in order to see clearly where the emphasis in assessment needed to go. On the basis of these broad qualities, subject coordinators were able to see that they need not assess every skill or capability on the list. Coordinators of later-year subjects were able to rely on the assessment of information literacy, communication and teamwork skills in the prerequisite subjects, so they focused their assessment tasks on the higher-order challenges of co-authoring and drafting scientific papers, researching and presenting material using computer-based presentation tools, delivering oral presentations and peer review.

Aligning learning outcomes and assessment tasks

What is a learning outcome?

As you will be aware from the themes discussed in Part A, the first question to ask when developing a subject of study is 'What should the students achieve by doing this subject?' Learning outcomes are explicit instructions to the students in a subject about what should be learnt during the subject, the skills and capacities that must be demonstrated in relation to them, and the standards expected.

> Check your learning outcomes and focus on the verbs you have used. Will the students know what they have to do to achieve these outcomes?

Making learning outcomes explicit

An essential ingredient in students' overall success in the subject is that you tell them clearly what they should learn and your expectations of them on completion of the subject. It makes sense that you then examine whether each student has learnt, and can do, what you expect. As we know, students will perform with varying degrees of success. In Chapter 23, we will discuss how you can examine their performance and give them feedback, and provide guidance about how to improve.

If you were a student, you would want precise instructions about how to do well. You would want those instructions to be clear: explicit, unambiguous and written in simple language. You would want your university teachers to help you to learn well enough to be able to achieve the learning outcomes by the time you completed the subject. And you would want the assessment tasks to assess precisely what your teachers have assisted you to learn.

> Do your students know what you expect them to achieve? Do your assessment tasks assess what you have taught?

How assessment can go wrong

It is a curious and unfortunate reality that these principles of alignment are not always applied when learning outcomes and assessment tasks are designed and constructed. As a result, it is not unusual for educators to assess content and skills that are not stipulated in a subject's learning outcomes, as we discussed in Chapter 4.

When this happens, students will be confused because it will not be possible to work out exactly what they are expected to do in an assessment task *until after the assessment task is completed*, and by then it will be too late. If students are informed by reading the learning outcomes about the requirements of assessment tasks and the criteria against which they will be measured, then they will be able to learn strategically.

> Is the alignment of outcomes and assessments in your subject evident to you?

The purposes of learning outcomes

Appropriate learning outcomes are able to be operationalized and measured. These two qualities make them student-centred (see Chapter 4 – Valid assessment). In addition, learning outcomes signal clearly to students what they should be able to do upon completion of the subject. Within this, they should signal the areas of content that students will learn.

Learning outcomes:

- provide a limit to the content to be covered;
- provide focus and direction in the learning process;
- provide an intellectual framework for making meaning of the content;
- indicate what intellectual and/or practical tasks students should be able to perform;
- provide a guide to what will be assessed.

The purpose of giving explicit learning outcomes to students is to give a clear indication of *what* students should learn and what kinds of applications they should be able to *do* with the knowledge. John Biggs (1999b) observed that learning is *performative*: you need to be able to measure what the student can *do* at the end of the learning process. If you do not make this clear to students, they can have little hope of knowing how to do well in your subjects.

How to write appropriate learning outcomes

Appropriate learning outcomes should be consistent with what you assess, so that you measure only what has been stated as a learning outcome. In the example that follows you will notice that these learning outcomes do not limit a student's imaginative or creative capacity, and they are written so that they can be measured. Another feature of effectively written learning outcomes is that they permit judgements to be made about how well students have met the criteria. For examples of grading scales, descriptors and marking schemes, see Chapter 21.

This example is of a fictitious subject – interpersonal communication (IPC) in customer relations contexts. It illustrates how learning outcomes, and teaching and learning strategies are outlined for students, telling them *what to do* and *how to do* what is required.

Upon completion of this subject, students in IPC1 should be able to:

- correctly identify the main theoretical perspectives of DeBono, Bloggs and Billyo;
- examine customer service contexts and identify the relevant IPC issues;
- demonstrate a comprehensive understanding of the range of IPC techniques applicable to the customer service context;
- demonstrate the ability to work as team members and contribute productively on resolving IPC issues;
- write an evaluative essay in IPC that is appropriate to the conventions of the social sciences;
- demonstrate the ability to assess issues and devise solutions for problems in customer service contexts.

Teaching to learning outcomes: is your subject constructively aligned?

An essential feature of John Biggs's model of 'constructive alignment' is that the learning outcomes and the assessment tasks are closely aligned with each other. The learning outcomes represent the beginning of the subject, where students find out what the subject is all about. The assessment tasks measure what has been learnt. In the middle, the student has to do the learning, with the aid of teaching, guidance or some kind of direction towards being able to perform the learning outcomes successfully. Biggs coined the term 'constructive alignment' to represent a situation where the learning outcomes, the teaching and learning activities and the assessment tasks are all working in unison to support student learning – the subject is then said to be constructively aligned.

Assessing achievement of learning outcomes

There is a simple way to establish the quality of learning outcomes for a subject. Assessment, which is the primary focus of learning, is the key. Do the assessment tasks:

- measure all the main criteria called for in the learning outcomes?
- measure any skills or capacities that are not explicitly stated in the learning outcomes?
- measure more than the criteria stated in the learning outcomes?
- enable the students' achievements, according to what is valued in a subject in this course and at this level, to be measured?

If there is a concern about measurement, then the problem lies within the assessment tasks themselves. But if there is a concern about what is being measured, the problem is likely to be that the learning outcomes need review. Do either of these concerns apply to your assessment or stated learning outcomes?

What needs to be assessed?

Only the abilities stipulated in the learning outcomes should be assessed. Of course, within that, the subject assessor has options about how the abilities will be measured:

- Should all of the course content be assessed?
- Should the course content be assessed selectively?
- Is there too much assessment?
- Is there enough assessment?
- Are the assessment tasks appropriate?

These questions raise issues about assessment that are dealt with later in this chapter.

Be clear in apportioning the relative value of learning outcomes

The key to what needs to be assessed lies in the learning outcomes. By looking at a set of learning outcomes, subject assessors should ask whether achievement of each of the learning outcomes is measured in some way in the assessment regime for the subject. It may be that several outcomes are measured in one task, or it may be that one learning outcome is measured by a number of assessment tasks. The apportionment depends upon the relative importance in the overall subject of the ability being measured. From the student's point of view, the relative importance of the learning outcome will be evident from the weighting attached to it in the related assessment task.

You may recall the human rights law subject we already mentioned in Chapter 3. We use the same example here to show learning outcomes as they are developed from a statement of graduate outcomes:

The Law School seeks amongst other things to produce graduates who:

- are aware of gender and cross-cultural issues in law;
- are able to examine legal and non-legal issues critically;
- have substantive knowledge of a wide body of case and statute law;
- are able to express themselves clearly, creatively and concisely;

- are able to argue logically and objectively;
- have high levels of practical legal skills.

An assessor for a human rights subject in the law programme built upon these aims in the performance criteria, as follows:

In this subject (human rights) performance will be assessed against the following criteria:

- demonstrated awareness of gender and cross-cultural issues as they affect human rights in law;
- performance in examining critically a range of legal and non-legal issues that apply to human rights;
- substantive knowledge of case and statute law related to human rights;
- demonstrated ability to write clearly, creatively and concisely;
- demonstrated ability to argue logically and objectively.

The assessor then translated the criteria into grading standards for a specific assessment task. This process is discussed in Chapter 21.

Before moving on, ask yourself:

- In what ways does this assessment design succeed in assessing the explicit learning outcomes of the subject?
- How does your assessment design motivate learners to achieve the stated learning outcomes or to develop insight into their progress towards gaining the attributes of a graduate from your discipline?

Determining student assessment load, frequency and value of assessment tasks

Recognizing constraints

In considering the issues discussed so far in relation to designing assessment tasks, there are a number of constraints to take into account. These include:

- Inclusive of the examination period, a semester may be 16 weeks and a trimester 15 weeks. In some countries the study term is even shorter and in all cases the actual time available for assessment is less than 16 weeks. In most but not all subjects, the first assessment has to wait till the students are sufficiently into the subject to have something to assess. This is usually not before the fourth or fifth week.

- In planning assessment for a subject you need to allow time for marking and the return of material with feedback so that students can gauge how they are doing before having to submit their next piece of work. The time lag is exacerbated with distance education students, as you have to allow time for material to be mailed to you and, subsequently, mailed back to them when marked. This time may be reduced if you use fax or e-mail for assignments.
- In most cases your subject is not the only one the students are taking. A student taking a full load of four subjects may have to do between 12 and 20 assessment tasks in the teaching period! Does this matter? It means that students spend most of their time doing assessment tasks that tend to become the sole focus of their academic work. Is all this formal assessment really necessary?
- Finally, the more assessment, the more marking there is for you or other markers. Given increasing staff–student ratios, there is a case for being more economical with assessment.

Determining a fair student assessment load in a subject: how much assessment is enough?

The constraints mentioned above need to be taken into account in determining a fair student assessment load for a subject. In principle, a fair assessment load is one that ensures the learning outcomes for the subject are covered as efficiently as possible. This, however, assumes that the learning outcomes are themselves reasonable and appropriate, and that the assessment tasks are well focused and do not require disproportionate effort on the part of students. A fair assessment load will also be seen as reasonable by students if they get a fair return for their effort, not only by way of a grade and its relative weighting in the subject but also by way of useful and informative feedback.

For assessment tasks such as essays, case studies or reports, the subject assessor often prescribes the number of words within which the task should be completed. This is a useful but rather arbitrary guide. It implies that, taking into account all aspects of the assessment task, an adequate answer should be in the order of a certain number of words. There is, however, wide variation in the number of words required within a standard undergraduate or college programme. For a subject, the range can be from 3,000 to 10,000 words. Institutions need to address the issue of justification of word lengths, as the variations exist within schools as well as between them.

The question needs to be asked: is there any need for students to write, say, 4,000–5,000 words in total for all assignments in a subject, excluding examinations? How much is enough? The answer may be: enough to demonstrate the students' grasp of the requirements of the assessment task in relation to the marking criteria (see Chapter 21).

In trying to establish a fair assessment load the following questions may be helpful:

- Are any of the learning outcomes redundant?
- Are any of the assessment tasks redundant?
- What do students and staff say is the amount of time and effort expended on each assessment task in this subject?
- How many assessment tasks are required of students in this subject?
- Are all the assessment tasks essential?
- Do the assessment tasks reflect a suitable sample of the subject content?
- Is any of the content in this subject assessed elsewhere in the course?
- Where students are provided with choices (eg essay topics), are the choices comparable in terms of difficulty and subsequent marking?
- What is the overall workload of full-time and part-time students in the course?
- Is it feasible to set formative assessment tasks, eg 'work in progress' assignments, or is formative feedback combined with summative assessment?

Deciding the frequency of assessment tasks: how often should students be assessed?

Frequency depends on what kind of subject you are teaching. A laboratory-based or problem-based subject may require students to complete experiments on a weekly basis and have their work checked. A practice-based subject may require students over a semester to demonstrate competence in a range of skills consecutively or concurrently. A conceptually based subject may require students to write essays or reports, present seminars and undertake examinations. The principle of parsimony applies, that is, as few assessments as possible to meet the learning outcomes of the subject and provide feedback to students.

The following questions may be helpful in thinking about frequency:

- Do students have sufficient time to prepare each assessment task adequately?
- If you were to reduce the number of assessment tasks would the students be disadvantaged? How?
- Do students, both on-campus and off-campus, receive feedback on early assignments in time for learning to occur before another assignment is due?
- What opportunities does your assessment design provide for learners to obtain feedback on their progress, without penalty?
- What are the implications of failure – does it mean wasted effort or encouragement to improve?
- What opportunities have you in place for students to resit or resubmit?

Determining the value of assessment tasks: how much is each task worth?

How do you arrive at the value you assign to each assessment task? If you have, say, two assignments and an examination, why assign 20, 30 and 50 rather than 30, 30 and 40? One reasonable justification for a smaller mark for the first assessment task is that the assessment is usually early in the study period when students are finding their way into the subject, it is often shorter than the second, and timely feedback may allow students to be more confident about their next assessment task. Complexity, effort and the relationship of assessment tasks to learning outcomes are considerations when you determine the value given to each task.

The impact of conflation of marks needs some attention here. Conflation can occur when different markers or different assessment tasks impact upon the overall spread of marks in the group. For example, one marker who is consistently 'harder' in the allocation of marks will impact upon the whole group of marks by drawing the range of marks below what might otherwise have been. Or one assessment task may be found to be inadequate in discriminating the poor students from the better students, leaving the majority of students with a similar mark, in which case it has little impact upon the final grade. In standards-based marking schemes this may be of less significance than in the case of norm referencing (see discussion on these approaches in Part A).

The following questions may be helpful in thinking about the value given to each assessment task:

- Is the value (usually percentage weightings) assigned to each assessment task commensurate with the complexity of the task?
- Is the value assigned to each assessment task commensurate with the amount of effort required for students to complete it?
- Is the value assigned to each assessment task commensurate with the importance or degree of complexity of the learning outcomes related to the assessment task?
- Have I had the opportunity to engage in moderation of marks together with the team of markers? If not, is there a way to organize this for the future? (See Chapter 23 for more details.)

Fair reward for group work

In your subject it might be appropriate to allocate students to small groups to work on all or part of an assessment task. The learning outcome(s) might reflect the need for collaborative activity, critical analysis, problem solving or some other type of learning that is appropriately accomplished in groups.

Collaborating in groups is a time-consuming and difficult, albeit rewarding, activity. Group members must find time to get together, coordinate research, learn together and rework drafts of their essay, report or project.

The frequency, time allocation and percentage weighting for assessment tasks involving group work itself or the product of group work should be recognized and commensurate with the amount of time and effort involved.

Improving validity and reliability in assessment

As assessors we are not only concerned with what the student said or did in an assessment task, but we are concerned with the 'truth' of the raw data of assessment and what to 'make' of it in terms of grading the student's work. The 'truth' of assessment depends on the validity and reliability of the assessment method, while what we 'make' of it depends on what type of measurement we use (for example, norm-referenced assessment or criterion-based assessment). Assessments should be both valid and reliable.

Defining validity

As we outlined in Chapter 2, validity is concerned with whether the assessment method actually measures what we want it to measure. An assessment task is valid when it corresponds to the purpose of the test. Assessment tasks are more likely to be valid if they align directly to the learning outcomes for the subject. Validity is as important as reliability, as without validity a reliable test will consistently measure performance inaccurately, eg a speed-reading test will consistently measure speed of reading rather than comprehension. But whether or not a task validly assesses a particular outcome depends upon what the student does, not what the designer of the assessment intended.

It is helpful in this regard to use the same language in the assessment task as in the objective. For instance, if an objective to be tested is stated as 'the ability to critically analyse…', then the assessment task should ask students to 'critically analyse…'. Markers must of course be clear about precisely what this means and reward appropriate efforts by students (see also Chapter 21).

Checking validity

The following questions may help you in checking validity:

- Do the learning outcomes accurately reflect what you want students to learn in the subject?
- Does each assessment task align constructively with particular subject learning outcomes, content and learning activities?
- How might you increase the sample of learning outcomes and content areas included in any single assessment task?
- Are you using assessment methods that are appropriate for the learning outcomes specified?
- Have you employed a range of assessment methods?
- Is the percentage weighting appropriate to the learning objective and the task?
- Are there any implicit marking criteria that are not articulated to students?

Is a portfolio assessment valid?

If you are considering using a portfolio-style assessment for an introductory subject in the social science domain, ask yourself: 'Could students present a good portfolio but not understand the nature and scope of social science as a disciplinary area? Could students fail to present a high-quality portfolio but still understand the range of perspectives within social science?'

Of course, the answer to both is 'yes', so it's a good idea to give explicit instructions in how the portfolio is required to demonstrate students' awareness of the range of social science perspectives (through supporting critique, for example). You can use the portfolio in association with other types of assessment, such as online discussion participation or oral presentations as a means for students to demonstrate their conceptual understanding.

For a description of portfolio assessment, see Chapters 16 and 19.

Defining reliability

Reliability refers to the consistency with which the same assessment task under the same conditions will produce the same set of results. The closer the level of correspondence in the results obtained from repeated applications of an assessment task, the greater the reliability and precision of measurement. Reliability is increased when the assessment task consistently measures the 'real' level of attainment regardless of who administers it, which learners are tested and who marks the submissions. For more discussion on reliability in marking, see Chapter 23.

Setting standards

Validity, reliability and the ways we judge student performance are all related to how we establish standards. The concept of standards has been identified as critical in higher education. Standards can be expressed as 'an agreement between examiners', 'a common understanding of quality as manifest in their subject'. A common understanding of quality can take the form of standards derived from criteria embodied in learning outcomes. For further discussion, see Chapter 3. We also discuss setting standards in Chapter 21 and marking reliability in Chapter 23.

Setting standards and preparing a team of tutors to help with marking

In a large first-year core subject, the marking is done by casual tutors, who are not always the same people from year to year. One of the ways in which this subject assessor hopes to achieve greater reliability among her group of tutors is to work with them and develop a marking sheet or scoring rubric. She then works with the team through several examples, and together they agree on the selection of a few exemplars, each representing the achievement of a different score. They discuss what distinguishes these from each other. Following this preparation, the team of tutors is usually able to complete the marking of all 500 or so papers, requiring only the confirmation of the assessor for a handful of borderline cases.

Selecting methods of assessment

There is a wealth of assessment methods used in higher education to assess students' achievements. How do you choose?

It is particularly useful to think first about what qualities or abilities you are seeking to engender in your learners. Nightingale *et al* (1996) provide us with eight broad categories of learning outcomes, which were covered in detail in Part B. Within each category, you will have found suggestions for some corresponding methods that are particularly suitable. You might recall the evaluation of research literature as an assessment of critical thinking skills, the group work to test problem solving, and the open-book exam that assessed the skills of accessing and managing information at the same time as testing content knowledge. These are just a few examples of the case studies of assessment methods as they align with the range of learning outcomes and disciplinary contexts in Part B. When you identify the abilities that students need to be able to demonstrate to achieve particular learning outcomes, you will be able to choose appropriate methods of assessment.

Assessment methods that best measure achievement of the stated learning outcomes

The primary rule is to choose methods that most effectively assess the stated learning outcomes of the subject. If your objective is to develop oral communication skills, then a written assessment will clearly not be an effective measure. Similarly, if you are wanting to develop critical and analytical thinking, an assessment emphasizing memorization will negate your efforts. Assessment methods need to be closely aligned with your aims and learning outcomes, as otherwise your teaching and learning goals will not be realized. As we know, students will take their cues from the assessment. Moreover, misalignment of learning outcomes and assessment tasks may also cause confusion or anxiety in students, and may lead to their adopting a surface approach to their learning.

Assessment methods that are aligned with the overall aims of the programme

A secondary rule is to choose methods that are aligned with the overall aims of the programme. This may include the development of disciplinary skills (such as critical thinking or problem solving) and support the development of vocational competences (such as report writing, team skills etc). Hence when choosing assessment items you have one eye on the immediate task of assessing student learning in a particular subject, and another eye on the broader aims of the programme and the qualities of the graduating student. Ideally this latter task is something that you do with academic colleagues so there is a planned assessment strategy across a programme.

If you haven't already looked at Part B, you would do well to browse through the various examples of assessment methods provided within the context of the range of learning outcomes.

> When you are designing assessment tasks, do you allow students the opportunity to develop their exam techniques or to master the format for assessable tasks, eg written reports, reflective journals, exemplary portfolios?

Flexible design of assessment tasks

Flexibility in higher education is represented in many ways and at many levels, as our discussions in Parts A and B have shown. Not only can higher education institutions today provide flexibility in enrolment, pedagogy and learning environment, but they are also doing their best to facilitate cross-institutional collaboration and accreditation.

In certain settings, students have the benefit now of flexibility in the timing of when they can complete an assessment task – before, during or after formal learning. The flexibility of mode of delivery has also increased in recent years because of the increasing use of the Internet and World Wide Web in assessment.

> Does the online environment offer flexibility for your assessment scheme? Does the introduction of online technologies to support the assessment process enhance student learning in your subject?

The following considerations may help you in reconceptualizing your assessment for greater flexibility:

- What does flexibility mean for you?
- What might be the benefits and motivations inherent in such a change to your usual ways of assessing?

- What might be gained or lost by moving some or all of the assessment process into the online context?
- Would you say that the online context offers additional opportunities or constraints for applied and holistic approaches to your assessment?
- What types of online assessment tasks might be relevant and realistic?
- Alternatively, which assessment approaches might be best supported in the offline context for your subject and thus enable greater flexibility?

Flexibility for whom?

In some cases it appears that the student's and teacher's perspectives may be somewhat exclusive of each other – to devise a learner-centred solution to flexibility does not necessarily also result in reduced workloads or greater efficiencies for teachers, as the time and resources required for negotiation of tailored tasks to enhance authentic learning experiences would be prohibitive in large classes. The question is: why would you want to make your assessments more flexible? The point of considering flexibility is to highlight the importance of designing your assessment task to suit the circumstances of your class size, subject area and learner characteristics.

Students negotiate assessment details

Many busy adult learners have reported that flexibility in assessment has great appeal. There are possibilities to negotiate the nature, scope and form of the assessment task. You might allow negotiation on individual versus group work, or the context of the task. If students are in a workplace, a more authentic learning task can be devised and the assessment of outcomes can be matched to the students' own desired outcomes or, indeed, those of their workplace. Student-centred flexibility is not solely about the online context.

Designing assessment tasks at a glance

- Design assessment methods that are aligned with the overall aims of the programme.
- Ensure you have accounted for any requirements set by professional bodies.
- See that your assessment tasks are aligned with the stated learning outcomes.
- Use assessment methods that best measure achievement of the stated learning outcomes.
- Rely on as few assessment tasks as possible to meet the learning outcomes of the subject and provide feedback to students.

- Be fair in how much you ask of your students and how much value you ascribe to each task.
- Check the validity of your assessment tasks by asking whether they measure what you intend them to measure.
- Select methods of assessment in association with the abilities you wish to foster.
- Take account of flexibility of assessment tasks and diversity of students.

21

Developing marking schemes

If assessment defines the curriculum (Ramsden, 1992), so marking schemes define assessment. In Part A of this book we discussed that assessment frames the curriculum for students and directs their learning. The term 'marking scheme' means a document that is the explanation of how student work will be assessed; therefore it is important that marking schemes are well designed to include the marking criteria and the standards that teachers use to calculate marks and grades.

'Marking schemes' (in Australia and the United Kingdom) and 'scoring rubrics' (in the United States) are designed to show how the products and processes of student performance in assessment tasks are measured. We will use the term 'marking scheme' here to mean a scheme that describes assessment criteria and standards of achievement. Copies of marking schemes are usually provided to students before they attempt assessment tasks. Markers can then use the same scheme to record marks and provide feedback on each student's work, and return the completed marking schemes to individual students as explicit feedback on their performance.

Marking schemes can be straightforward if there is a right or a wrong answer, or a right or a wrong solution to a problem, for example in the case of multiple choice, true/false or other objective tests (see Chapter 14 for some information about objective testing). In these cases students need to know the structure of the test, the kinds of questions that will be asked and the weighting of marks to be allocated to each item. But when assessment tasks are flexible and open-ended, as is often the case in problem solving, critical analysis or evaluation for example, the development of marking schemes can be complex. Teachers sometimes find it hard to explain their marking criteria and students can tend to misunderstand what they are being asked to do.

Marking schemes should be aligned with desired learning outcomes and particular assessment tasks to go some of the way to overcoming the 'guessing game' where students try to unravel the mystery of how assessment judgements are made (see Chapter 20). When marking criteria are made explicit they also provide a framework for reliable marking and accountability in assessment. The term 'reliability' was defined in Chapter 20. By 'accountability' we mean that assessors are able to account for how their judgements were made, and that they have evidence to justify marking and grading decisions to stakeholders in student assessment, as we discussed in Part A of this book.

In this chapter we will firstly look at some of the terms associated with marking schemes especially in relation to criterion-referenced and standards-based assessment, and then explore some issues you will need to consider when you develop marking schemes. We will provide some practical examples of ways others have approached the task. The chapter is organized as follows:

- criterion-referenced and standards-based grading systems;
- marking schemes and scoring rubrics;
- developing marking schemes;
- ensuring that the marking schemes are open, fair and defensible;
- developing marking schemes with workloads in mind.

Criterion-referenced and standards-based grading systems

As we said in Chapter 3, proponents of criterion-referenced and standards-based assessment systems seek ways to increase the fairness and accountability of assessment practices. Grades are awarded according to how well the individual student has performed against specific criteria and standards of achievement. For this reason criterion-referenced assessment is often criticized as being reductionist. Some academics argue that it reduces complex professional judgements to a series of discrete, observable, lower-order tasks (Morgan and O'Reilly, 1999).

When standards for each grade or level of performance are collegially negotiated and used as a basis for assessment decisions, the charge of reductionism may not be justified although there is a need to develop processes further to achieve transparency about how grades are awarded. As we have discussed throughout this book, subjectivity and the exercise of professional judgement in marking are always present and must be accepted alongside the very real concern for accountability regarding assessment of student performance. In Chapter 23 we will consider some of the issues of subjectivity in marking, while in this chapter we will be more concerned with the reliability and transparency of assessment schemes.

In many higher education institutions, it is a requirement that students are told how their work will be assessed, that is, the marking criteria should be made explicit to students at the beginning of a course and for each subject. However, there is a lot of debate about the precise meaning of the words 'criteria' and 'standards', as you will have seen in the discussion of the mixed messages about assessment terminology in Chapter 3. Sometimes the words are used together to mean the particular principles or standards by which student work is judged, or they are given separate meanings (see the definitions below). One thing is clear, though, and that is that many academics are somewhat confused about how to make standards explicit to students, often because they do not understand the assessment system themselves. Barrie, Brew and McCulloch (1999) found that, while most academics in their study could describe the characteristics of performance, it was the standards or fixed levels of achievement that were hard to define. The difficulty comes in the attempt to be explicit about both the characteristics of student performance and the standards by which it will be judged.

Generally, the following definitions apply:

Criteria: the desired characteristics of student performance in an assessment task, for example 'evidence of wide reading'.

Standards: levels of achievement by which performance is judged. Specific descriptions are provided to distinguish between, for example, 'exceptional', 'outstanding', 'good', 'satisfactory' and 'poor' in relation to specific assessment tasks. Descriptions like these are also developed to describe grade levels generically (for example high distinction, distinction, credit, pass, fail).

We have shown in Chapter 3 that criteria and standards are not separate and clear cut. Some criteria, especially those around disciplinarity, are not always explicit. They are best developed collegially with understanding of what can be expected of students at the different stages of development within a course. The goal of clarity in marking schemes is often only achieved after several iterations of design and redesign.

Marking schemes and scoring rubrics

Marking schemes and rubrics are designed to be either 'holistic' (see Example 1 below) or 'analytic' (see Examples 2, 3 and 4 below). Biggs (1999a: 152–53) argues strongly for holistic marking schemes because he believes that each assessment task is an integrated whole and that judgement should be about total student performance rather than its isolated parts. Holistic marking doesn't ignore the detail, but it is about knowing students in all their strengths and weaknesses (Rowntree, 1987).

Holistic grading as described by Rowntree and Biggs is what we call standards-based assessment and is discussed at length in Chapter 3. For a good example of standards-based assessment, see the descriptions of a range of standards for a subject in law (high distinction, distinction, credit, pass, fail) in Chapter 3.

Analytic marking schemes that allocate marks or percentages to each part of a task and then add or average them for a result can skew student results in a way that does not happen if a marking scheme is holistic or standards-based. A difficulty with analytic marking schemes is that of weighting, or giving a higher proportion of marks to more important aspects of a task than to those that are less valued. A single element of the task might have a disproportionate effect on the final result. Biggs (1999a) considers that the amount of time taken on each part of a task is the only valid measure of difference. Analytic schemes that show the weighting of topics can be very helpful in some ways, though, as they show students where to allocate their time and effort.

Teachers seem to find it difficult to articulate standards at the various levels for standards-based grading. Analytic marking schemes appear more straightforward and 'fair' because results seem to be more easily scored. As we have seen, all marking decisions have an element of subjective judgement, and we would argue that numerical outcomes give only an illusion of objectivity (see Examples 2 and 3 below). Some analytic marking schemes, though, show the subjective nature of judgements more clearly (see Example 4 below).

Pitching the level of challenge

It is commonplace that students within a cohort have a wide range of abilities and this should ideally be reflected in the spread of assessment results. If there is not a reasonable spread of results, perhaps you should consider:

- whether the assessment task includes too much or not enough challenge for this particular subject at this stage of the programme;
- whether the marking scheme appropriately reflects the pitch of the task;
- whether the marking scheme is designed in such a way that student performance is accurately reflected in the results.

It is suggested that you remain alert to ensure that assessment tasks are pitched appropriately and that marking schemes reflect this in the way they are structured. Of course different cohorts of students can have specific traits that mean there is not always a spread of results. Alternatively, the distribution of results might be positively or negatively skewed because the cohort is very able or not very able (see Chapter 3). So, although we suggest you remain vigilant about the range of results within cohorts, we also believe you should not normalize results when there is good reason for high or low attainment across the cohort.

Example 1: Marking scheme with clear descriptions of standards at each level of achievement

In this marking scheme for an assignment task on report writing, the description of the standard for each level of achievement (excellent, sound etc) in a particular assessment task includes the characteristics of performance (criteria).

Writing a professional report

- *Excellent*:
  - Used a professional report format (see example in study notes).
  - Graphics are descriptive and clearly support the document's purpose.
  - The document is clear and concise with appropriate grammar used throughout.
- *Sound*:
  - Used a structured, though not totally professional, report format.
  - Some supporting graphics are provided, but are not always clearly explained.
  - The document contains minimal distractions.
- *Needs improvement*:
  - Unstructured report format, or rambling in style.
  - Ambiguous graphics.
  - The document contains numerous distractions in all or some of the following forms: flow in thought; graphics; language structure.
- *Inadequate*:
  - Did not use a report format.
  - There seems to be no organization of the document's contents.
  - Graphics were either not included, irrelevant or not explained.
  - The document was difficult to read and understand.

Example 2: Analytical scheme with differential weighting applied

This is the same report-writing example with an analytical marking scheme. Here the characteristics of performance (criteria) are explicit and the highest possible level of performance (standard) is embodied in the criteria. The marks can be added to give a score out of 15, and the weightings show students where the assessor places emphasis within the assessment task.

In this example, there is greater potential for a spread of marks than in Example 3 below, because the teacher has identified where student performances are more likely to vary and has allocated marks accordingly.

> ### Writing a professional report
>
> - Used a professional report format (see example in study notes) (3 marks).
> - Provided descriptive graphics that clearly supported the document's purpose (6 marks).
> - Structured the document in a clear, concise style with appropriate grammar (6 marks).

Example 3: Analytical marking scheme with a Likert scale

In this version of the marking scheme for the report-writing task, instead of a designated number of marks for each item, each has a 5-point scale. The marker circles the point on each scale according to student performance on the item. This scheme is still numeric in that the points on each scale can be added to give a score, but the topics are evenly weighted.

It is important to take care when designing a marking scheme with evenly weighted items to ensure that each is of equal importance so that results are true to the purpose of the desired learning outcomes and of the whole assessment task. Results should reflect overall student performances on the assessment task. A problem can arise when student performances are not able to be differentiated clearly enough in their results.

> ### Writing a professional report
>
> | | Inadequate | | | | Excellent |
> |---|---|---|---|---|---|
> | Used a professional report format (see example in study notes | 1 | 2 | 3 | 4 | 5 |
> | Provided descriptive graphics | 1 | 2 | 3 | 4 | 5 |
> | Graphics support the document's purpose | 1 | 2 | 3 | 4 | 5 |
> | Clear, concise structure | 1 | 2 | 3 | 4 | 5 |
> | Appropriate grammar and spelling | 1 | 2 | 3 | 4 | 5 |

Example 4:Analytical marking scheme including qualitative marking

In this type of analytical marking scheme the qualitative nature of the scheme is more visible than in the previous examples. The assessor puts a mark to show where the student's work falls on each continuum. This scheme does not give marks, but allows the assessor to make a judgement about the quality of the student's work and to give specific feedback on the different criteria.

Writing a professional report

Used professional report format_____Did not use professional report format

Descriptive and relevant graphics_____Graphics unclear and irrelevant

Document was clear and concise_____Document was unclear and difficult to read

---

Which type of marking scheme to choose?

In many higher education institutions generic grade descriptors have been developed to denote particular standards of achievement (for example, high distinction, distinction, credit, pass). Individual marking schemes are derived from these standards to achieve grading consistency.

In some institutions individual faculties develop specific marking criteria and grade descriptors to relate to individual assessment tasks. In these settings, results may be derived solely from judging student performance against the standards. Others, in addition to standards and marking criteria, may have a system of scaling of grades to ensure that, for example, only a small percentage of high distinctions or distinctions are awarded within any cohort. This is known as cohort referencing and ensures that the so-called 'bell curve' of results (a few high results, most in the middle range and a few very low results) is maintained. The reason for this is to attempt to replicate a range of results that, for a statistically normal population of similar students, would be spread in this way.

Choosing the appropriate type of marking scheme depends on the assessment regime that applies in your institution and on the assessment task itself. Standards and criteria are usually part of the 'constructive alignment' process that we have discussed throughout this book. The desired learning outcomes, assessment tasks and marking schemes should align as to the expected characteristics and standards of student performance.

Developing marking schemes

Assessment tasks and their marking schemes are usually designed together, although we are dealing with them separately in this book. In some cases, though, you might not have been involved in the design of an assessment regime and need to become familiar with marking schemes. In other circumstances, the assessment design may include marking schemes that are negotiated either within teaching teams or with students. Whatever the sequence of events, early in the process you need to unpack each assessment task to identify its purpose, how it fits into an assessment regime and how it aligns with desired learning outcomes (as discussed in Chapter 20).

Ask yourself:

- How does this task fit within the overall assessment regime for the subject?
- Which of this subject's learning outcomes are to be achieved with this assessment task?
- What skills and abilities are being assessed through this assessment task? What levels of ability are represented in the learning outcomes and the assessment task? Are all the skills and abilities of equal importance in the curriculum?
- What are the teachers' intentions regarding the way this task should be performed?

These and any other relevant questions will need to be answered before you begin to develop a marking scheme.

Aligning marking schemes with assessment tasks

Some teachers feel that there is a straitjacket being wound around them when they are asked to develop specific marking schemes. They would argue that focusing on outcomes rather than processes makes it difficult to reward the unanticipated creative outcomes that sometimes occur with higher-order achievement. These are valid concerns, so it is helpful to be aware of possible pitfalls when developing marking schemes, two of which are:

- Marking criteria should reflect the level of desired learning outcomes in the assessment regime, but sometimes they are written at a lower level for easier marking. For example, the assessment task might call for critical analysis while the marking criteria show description and recall.
- Analytical marking schemes might reduce the integrity of the assessment task by dividing the whole into discrete parts, as shown in Examples 2,3 and 4 above, making it harder to apply professional judgements and holistic standards.

If you are to avoid these problems, you need to plan marking schemes carefully and ensure that they are aligned at the same performance level as the assessment task. The wording of an assessment task shows the level at which it is to be judged. We are assuming that the tasks themselves have been written at the appropriate level to align with desired learning outcomes, although it is worth while to check the alignment. The SOLO taxonomy (Biggs and Collis, 1982), which we have mentioned often in this book, is a good guide for decisions about whether a marking scheme should allow more or less flexibility in student responses and how judgements should best be made. Bloom's taxonomy of learning objectives (discussed in Chapter 14) could also help in aligning performance with assessment tasks and marking schemes.

Doing away with the mystery of performance criteria

Another objection to explicit marking schemes is that, when the mystique that surrounds the marking of student work is stripped away, academics become more vulnerable to students who have a greater understanding of assessment and the increased confidence to question grading decisions.

Perhaps the difficulty comes when we are trying to move from an individualistic method of making judgements to a more accountable criterion-referenced, standards-based system, or it might be that the learning outcomes to be assessed need a flexible assessment regime that seems hard to document in explicit terms. See, for example, the assessment tasks in Chapter 16.

Students have difficulty with vague marking criteria, and misunderstandings can and do occur when there is guesswork involved in matching actual teacher expectations with what students perceive them to be. Well-written marking schemes can help teachers and students to have the same understanding about the meaning of assessment tasks and how performance will be judged.

Should the process be assessed? Yes, when it is the purpose of the task

Science students had an assessment task at the beginning of their first year that required them to provide some library references to sources of information. The aim of the task was to allow students to demonstrate that they had learnt the fundamentals of information searching.

However, the marking scheme related to the results of the search, and many of the students simply went to a reference librarian and handed over the task, and the librarian did the searching for them. Those students did not learn searching skills. It would have been better to develop a marking scheme that was explicit about the purpose of the assessment task (that is, include criteria and standards about the process of the search as well as the product of it).

Developing marking schemes collegially

Marking schemes are more likely to be clear, understandable and explainable to students when they are developed collegially. The language of standards and criteria is also likely to be better aligned with assessment tasks when it has been debated and negotiated with colleagues through a benchmarking process. In subjects with large numbers of students and multiple assessors, a process of negotiation can help the assessors to reach common agreement about how judgements will be made, thus increasing the reliability of the grading of student performance. We discuss collegiality and moderation of results further in Chapter 23. The following cases show how working with colleagues can improve marking schemes.

Uncovering a hidden criterion

Recently a university teaching team (subject assessor and three casual tutors) met to discuss how to translate an assessment task (an essay) into a marking scheme to be sent out to distance students early in the semester. The idea was to promote marking transparency. The assessment task had been designed by the subject assessor to measure the relevant learning outcomes for the subject. However, when the team discussed marking the paper, it emerged that 'academic style' would be assessed, even though it did not appear in any of the learning outcomes for the subject. The teaching team developed a marking scheme that included 'academic style', gave it to students before they started the assessment task and planned to review the learning outcomes for the following year.

Assessing creative performance

The marking criteria in an assessment of musical performance included the following characteristics of a high-quality performance: 'Musical nuance to indicate phrase structure is consistent and sensitive.' There was a panel of assessors in this case. Before the student performances were assessed, the colleagues on the panel negotiated what each criterion meant in relation to each standard of student performance (high distinction, distinction, credit, pass). In class, teachers discussed with students the agreed meaning of words like 'nuance' and 'sensitive' with examples and illustrations showing how they could be demonstrated in the particular musical tradition of the performance.

Higher- and lower-order performance combined

Marking criteria and standards written as simple checklists are probably more appropriate for lower-order skills, for example students' ability to define and describe knowledge in their field or, in later years of study, having the ability to show they have acquired some new knowledge.

As we have discussed, flexible, holistic marking schemes for assessment tasks that target the higher-order skills are complex and difficult. An additional complexity is that many tasks designed to assess higher-order skills are set in realistic contexts and are necessarily ill structured. The marking scheme in the next case included both quantitative and qualitative measurement.

Combining objective tests with open-ended criteria

In the subject advanced biomechanics, human movement undergraduates were required to learn a body of new information and also to apply it by solving technical problems. The assessment task was a project assessed by a written report. The marking scheme reflected both the lower- and higher-level abilities and performance. It included, among other criteria, a checklist to assess 'knowledge of relevant information' and a continuum to measure 'original thought, critical reflection'.

Expressing criteria that are usually tacit

Another of the challenges for academics in writing explicit marking criteria is to learn how to express the sometimes tacit elements of their professionalism that must be acquired if a person is to be accepted as an expert in a disciplinary field.

Frogs must stay in the pond

Student performance on a field trip in environmental science was assessed on a pass/fail basis. Before embarking on the trip the first-year undergraduate students were given the marking scheme to be used by their tutors to assess their performance. The document showed clearly what they should do to collect samples in the field and how to write up their field notes. Afterwards, one of the tutors said that a core element of student performance was that they should leave the environment as they found it. If students did any harm to the environment, such as not returning a frog to a pond, they failed the assessment task. However, this piece of information was not written on their marking scheme or explicitly conveyed to students by members of the teaching team. The tutor said students should have absorbed the information through their studies because it was an accepted ethical stance of environmental scientists. It was suggested to the tutor that the marking scheme be revised for clarity to add this important element of assessment.

Ensuring that marking schemes are open, fair and defensible

It has been said that if marking schemes are too explicit students become 'spoon-fed', they can be inhibited from achieving their own personal learning goals, and assessment can become a less academically rigorous process. These criticisms represent potential dangers for the reliability of marking schemes and have to be considered. However, judgements of the 'I know good work when I see it' kind and other less accountable methods of making decisions about student work are no longer defensible in higher education where judgements, as we said in the Introduction to Part A and at the beginning of this chapter, usually have to be justified to students and other stakeholders in the process.

Explicit marking schemes help assessment processes to be seen to be open, fair and defensible. At the same time they are not necessarily proscriptive.

Why increase openness and accountability?

- Making assessment criteria and standards clear and available to students is a characteristic of student-centred learning environments. See the Introduction to Part A for a discussion on this development in higher education.
- Publishing marking schemes to students before they attempt assessment provides opportunities for students to focus their studies and organize themselves for success. This is particularly helpful for open and distance students who do not have ready access to academics for consultation or co-learners for benchmarking standards.
- Providing students with marking schemes before they begin to prepare for assessment does not reduce the academic rigour of the assessment outcome when assessment tasks and marking schemes are developed with care and aligned with learning outcomes.
- Standards-based marking schemes are not necessarily proscriptive, and can be developed to assess higher-order thinking like critical analysis and problem solving. However, it is true that students are steered along a path outlined by specified learning outcomes.
- Individual projects or negotiated assessment tasks allow students to direct their learning towards their own goals.

Open, fair and defensible?

A group of humanities students discussed their results after a reflective journal had been marked and returned to them. They had not been given a marking scheme for the journal and discussed between them what the assessment criteria might have been. After looking at their marks and the feedback on each of their papers, one student thought that most of the marks had been allocated for analysis of topics in the journal, while another considered that reflection on the analysis had been weighted more heavily. They went to their teacher to try to clear up the mystery. A marking scheme had actually been negotiated by the teaching team of three people, so the teacher of this group was able to let the students into the secret of how judgements had been made. The students went away grumbling that 'it wasn't fair'. They agreed they could have achieved higher grades on the assessment task had they been let into the 'secret academics' business'. They considered a formal complaint to the university. The marking scheme in this case was probably equitable because it had been negotiated within the teaching team to meet learning outcomes, and each student's work was marked in the same way. It was defensible for the same reason, but it was not open and public to the students before they attempted the assessment task. It was unfair in that students were not able to see in advance the standards and criteria upon which their work would be judged.

Invigilated examinations

The invigilated examination is not a method in itself. Exams consist of a range of assessment tasks such as essays, objective tests or problems. These kinds of tasks are also set as coursework assignments. The difference is that the tasks are undertaken by students in a closed examination situation with an invigilator (a person who has the authority to supervise examinations) to ensure that the work they submit is all their own.

The same principles of openness, fairness and defensibility apply to examinations, but this is the least accountable of assessment types. It is rare for students to be given individual feedback on an examination performance, and in some cases they do not receive a result, because the results for all assessment tasks in a subject may be aggregated in an overall grade for the subject. It could be argued, though, that examination marking schemes should be as open and public as coursework assignments.

Developing marking schemes with workloads in mind

The changing landscape of higher education (see Part A) has had several impacts on teachers, one being that of increasing their workloads, so while it is important to develop marking schemes that are fair, open and defensible it is also important to devise practices that minimize the workload associated with assessing students.

It is time consuming to develop effective marking schemes, but it is time well spent if they are developed with the idea of reducing the amount of time taken to mark student work and to provide feedback on its strengths and weaknesses.

Some practices to make life easier are:

- Prepare marking schemes that can be used as attachment sheets to be completed and returned with marked work.

- Give students a blank copy of all marking schemes with their assessment tasks at the beginning of the teaching period.
- Ask students to prepare questions for clarification about the marking scheme before they attempt the task. This will pre-empt misunderstandings.
- Allow space for individual comments at relevant places on the marking scheme.
- Prepare a glossary of assessment terms used in marking schemes to be attached to the blank marking schemes for students.
- Prepare a numbered bank of frequently used feedback comments to which you can refer students (see also Chapter 23).

Developing marking schemes at a glance

- Developing marking criteria is a complex task. It requires professional judgement, and is not a mysterious process. Judgement should be made against specific standards and criteria.
- It is never the aim of marking criteria to be obscure or to 'trick' students; neither is it the intention to 'spoon-feed' them or to reduce their individual level of intellectual effort.
- Consider the purpose of assessment tasks, especially the level of skills and abilities to be demonstrated to make sure the marking scheme is at the same level. It is fairly common to test lower-level skills at the expense of higher-order ones because they are easier to mark (Ramsden, 1992).
- Negotiate the meaning of assessment tasks, marking criteria and standards with colleagues before developing marking schemes.
- If it is possible and practicable, negotiate marking schemes with students.
- If this is not possible, encourage students to ask questions for clarification to achieve common understandings.
- It could be necessary to be proactive in checking that the understanding of open and distance learners matches the purpose and intention of teachers and that marking schemes are clear.
- Consider the tacit elements of professionalism, and make sure that they are explained in marking schemes.
- Use plain English where possible and explain technical terminology.
- Checklists are useful for showing how well students can identify or describe factual material.
- Open-ended marking schemes allow students to make their own meanings in assessment tasks but they are harder to write unambiguously.

22

Communicating assessment tasks

In prior chapters we discussed the importance of students' *perceptions* of the assessment task, and the impact this has on how they go about their learning. If students perceive that they are being assessed on their ability to recall or recite facts, then they will prepare for that assessment by rote learning, regardless of our own intentions. Although we may intend that students engage deeply with the subject matter, our communication of the task, along with our intentions, may have been less than explicit.

Unfortunately, many well-designed assessment tasks can be undermined at this stage. What we assume to be a concise and pithy statement of requirements can, from students' perspectives, seem a patchwork of confusions, and may be read in a number of different ways, according to students' prior experiences and expectations. During the early phases of students' academic careers, they are still trying to unravel the mysteries of what is expected of them. Students are required to master the conventions of a range of genres, from formal academic essays to more personalized reflective journals. As discussed earlier, they must master many of the tacit expectations of the discipline, including language, tone, argument, referencing and all the other elements of disciplinary discourse. As if that was not enough, they must also negotiate the whims and quirks of individual markers who, as we know, often have their own particular preferences.

When we view assessment tasks from students' perspectives, we come to see how much more complex they are than we might have anticipated. To a significant degree, the problem is ameliorated by the development of detailed marking criteria, which convey to students a range of expectations. The other key issue is how effectively and thoroughly the task is communicated to students.

How do we manage to get this so wrong at times? Of course, no one sets out to write a poor assessment task, but some of the more common communication problems arise because of:

- *Hurried preparation* – many assessment tasks suffer very simply from lack of time spent at the drafting stage. This may result in insufficient information, or ambiguities in meaning, or simple but vital errors and omissions.
- *Attitudes about 'spoon-feeding'* – some assessors express concerns that providing supporting information for assessment tasks is akin to spoon-feeding or making it too easy. Such sink-or-swim approaches to assessment reflect rather antiquated notions of academic rigour, and deny students useful developmental opportunities.
- *Our own lack of clarity* – sometimes we are not totally clear about what we ourselves are expecting. By leaving tasks open to a range of responses, we may think we are being flexible, yet we leave the door open for students to get it very wrong.

This chapter provides an approach to drafting and communicating assessment tasks that leave little to chance. The aim is to minimize the possibility of students taking inappropriate or mistaken pathways, and also to minimize the potential flood of enquiries that teachers endure when assessment tasks lack clarity, particularly when large cohorts are involved.

Consider the following assessment task, a journal, as an example:

Assessment task 1 – Journal
Develop a journal over semester, recording your responses to and reflections upon a minimum of eight key issues that you have encountered in this subject. Your journal entries should demonstrate that you have engaged thoroughly with the issues. The journal should be submitted in the final week, and should be no longer than 3,000 words.

Marks will be awarded on the coherence of your responses and reflections, the quality of your writing and presentation.

Although this may be a relatively commonplace assessment descriptor, from students' perspectives there are a number of problems immediately apparent. For example:

- What is the overall aim of this assignment? What is it that the assessor really wants?
- How do I get started? Which issues should I pick? Do I decide which issues are the 'key' ones? Should they all be of the same length? Should I be making arguments? If so, how thoroughly? Or should I be mostly summarizing the issues?

- What are 'reflections'? Are they simply my personal feelings on the subject? Do I need to use a formal academic tone? Should I use academic referencing?
- What would get me a pass in this? What would I have to do to get a really good mark?

More experienced students have usually discovered the answers to these questions. Gradually, by a process of trial and error, students are able to unravel the mysteries of what is expected of particular tasks, in their particular disciplinary settings. Less experienced students, however, may struggle with these kinds of issues for some time. Depending on the quality and timeliness of support and feedback, they may not persist if they are consistently getting it wrong.

We mentioned in Part B the concept of 'cue consciousness' (Miller and Parlett, 1974), which is a significant contributor to our understanding of how students become savvy in their disciplines and in their assessment work. Cue-conscious students are more alert to, or actively seek, cues from their teachers and tutors regarding the appropriate approach to a task and how to maximize their grades. There are parallels to be found in Entwistle and Ramsden's (1983) findings of students adopting a 'strategic' approach to study, and in Lockwood's (1992) 'assignment focused' learners. It is clear that some students are better than others in understanding what is required of them. This, of course, does not necessarily mean that they are better students or adopting deeper approaches to learning. Rather, they become adept much faster at negotiating the assessment system.

Without the benefit of other students and teachers at hand, distance education students may be particularly disadvantaged in relation to cues (Morgan, 1993; Morgan and O'Reilly, 1999). Without face-to-face interaction, it may take them considerably longer to clarify expectations, with assignment feedback being perhaps the only form of 'dialogue' they experience with academic staff. Distance students who are nervous or reluctant to make contact with teachers or tutors will find this particularly difficult, and may be left to languish for some time in their own confusion.

We argue that it is important to provide appropriate and timely cues to students, particularly in the early stages of their study. The provision of these cues is, in fact, an important part of our teaching role and should not just be left to chance, or only for the cue-seeking student to discover. In the sections below we consider some of these key cues in assessment tasks, which are adapted from the work of Morgan and O'Reilly (1999):

- providing a rationale;
- explaining terms;
- explaining the form;
- suggesting methods of approach;
- information overload.

Providing a rationale

What is the logic of your assessment task and how effectively is it communicated to students? If you are assessing Web-based discussions it may be that you really want students to engage with and master this medium because you highly value the kinds of rich discussion and collaboration that occur. You need to be very explicit about this. Similarly, if you believe that the most worthwhile learning occurs through the use of authentic work-based problems and you are seeking to prepare students for professional life, then your tasks should be accompanied by a compelling rationale of this kind. Although the tasks we set may have a very clear logic, we do not always communicate this to students, assuming perhaps that they will naturally understand. As Gibbs (1995: 8) puts it: 'Students need to be on the inside of the logic of the course, believing in its rationale, not tagging along, feeling bewildered and jumping through hoops.' If you are successful in communicating your rationale, then it is more likely that you will engender a climate of joint venture with your students, rather than a climate of 'them and us'.

Let's reconsider the journal assessment task provided earlier, now with the benefit of a rationale:

Rationale
This assessment task has three aims:

1. We would like to check your understanding of key issues that have arisen during semester, including your ability to provide a brief contextual overview of each issue and introduce relevant arguments from the literature.
2. We want to see that you have really thought about these issues yourself and that you have evaluated the arguments and evidence for each issue. As a result of this, it is expected that you are able to make some judgements about the relative merits of arguments and evidence presented.
3. We would like to promote the habits and practices of critical thinking and reflective practice using the journal form. We believe that these abilities are critically important for future success in professional practice.

We encourage you to identify what you believe to be the key issues. We also encourage you to take your own stand on the issues, but they must be backed up by sound evidence and argument, rather than just your own beliefs.

A rationale of this kind has the capacity immediately to clarify a number of issues and concerns for students. Moreover, it communicates your intent and values.

Explaining terms

Taxonomies of learning, as we have discussed in prior chapters of this book, provide a window to the subtle and complex world of academic learning. They are usually represented as a hierarchy of activity, from lower-order tasks such as describing, relating and summarizing through to higher-order activity such as evaluating and synthesizing. These are the key terms that are employed in assessment tasks. Often we find key terms that have only minor shades of difference in meaning, such as 'analyse' and 'interpret' or 'evaluate' and 'criticize'. It is likely, when teachers provide their own interpretation of these terms, that they will differ, perhaps quite significantly.

From a student's perspective, terminology poses a number of problems. How can it be expected that students will understand and relate to the language of assessment, if there is no firm agreement amongst assessors themselves? Of course it is unrealistic for all teachers to have shared understandings on the meaning of terms, which is why it is important that we unpack and articulate what it is we expect, in our own particular context and disciplines. Defining and explaining terms, or at least how we interpret them for the purposes of the task, is another important role in teaching that should not be left to chance.

Let's again consider our worked example, this time adding some support with regard to terminology:

Terminology
There are four main activities that are embedded in this task:

1. Identifying key issues and providing an overview of the issue. By 'overview', we mean locating the issue in context – why it is an issue and for whom.
2. Evaluating the arguments and evidence for each issue. By 'evaluating', we mean weighing up the strengths and advantages and weaknesses and disadvantages in each of the arguments advanced.
3. Reflecting upon the issue. This means introducing your own views, based upon your own experiences and observations, and how this may have altered as a result of your reading and discussions in this subject.
4. Making a judgement upon the issue, based upon your evaluation of evidence and your reflections. This may be a definitive or qualified judgement, or you may decide that further evidence is required before judgement is appropriate.

With clarification of this kind, there is a greatly reduced opportunity for ambiguity or confusion, and greater likelihood that students will adopt appropriate learning strategies.

Explaining the form

As we have discussed at some length in Part B of this book, assessment methods take quite different forms according to the discipline and also according to the particular outcomes you are seeking. Hence the essay may be focused upon higher-order activity such as evaluation and argument, or lower-order activity such as describing and reporting. In the humanities, assessment methods take different forms from those of the sciences. This is another area, clearly, where students may experience confusion unless guided appropriately. Let's continue with our worked example:

The journal form
The journal method of assessment has a range of purposes. Sometimes they are personal and 'chatty' in tone and are used for recording ideas, reactions and experiences. In this assessment task, however, the journal is being used for more formal, structured academic activity. Each of your eight journal entries should be around 350 to 400 words of structured writing, with referencing to others' work as necessary. Each entry should demonstrate that you have engaged with key readings on the issue. Spontaneous responses are not sought. The use of 'I statements' is quite acceptable, although they must be substantiated. The completed journal may be presented in a folder or binder and should be word-processed and double-spaced with each new entry commencing on a new page.

Suggesting methods of approach

Experienced students usually have developed preferred methods for approaching assessment tasks. For example, some may prefer initially to read and take notes; others prefer to read, discuss and write in more eclectic combinations. There are, of course, many variations and no one right way, although clearly some approaches may be less effective than others. Students tend to develop their own methods of approach based upon their perceptions of the task at hand and their preferred style of learning. But for students who are only just starting out, it can be very difficult even to get going, with little in the way of experience to guide them.

Offering suggestions for ways of approaching the task can be very useful for both experienced and inexperienced learners. For those who have developed certain approaches, suggestions are useful as a means of benchmarking. Can I improve or refine my approach? Should I experiment with a new approach? For those with little experience, suggestions are useful as a way of developing their own style of learning and tackling tasks. Offering methods of approach is another way to encourage deep, appropriate learning. Although it would be inappropriate to attempt to impose particular strategies or methods on to students, particularly if they already have developed their own successful methods (see Morgan, Dingsdag and Saenger, 1998, for example), suggested methods of approach offer to students suggestions for good practice and may also provide further cues for students wanting to clarify what is expected of them.

Let's once again consider our worked example, with some suggested methods of approach:

Suggested approach to this assessment task
It is strongly suggested that you work on this task consistently throughout semester, rather than leaving it to the last week. If left too late in the semester, you will simply not have enough time to do it well. The following hints may be useful for you in getting started:

- As you read, what key issues have you encountered? Make notes. What is the issue? What is the context? Why is it important?
- As you explore the issue, note the authors' central arguments. What evidence is there to support the position adopted? Is it convincing? What counter-arguments can you find?
- What is your own reaction to the issue? What is the basis for your reasoning? Is it sound? Are you persuaded more by one of the arguments?
- Start drafting your journal entry. Using the format above, express your thoughts in a clear, logical manner, with each paragraph building on the former.

Note: You are welcome to check in with your tutor once you have completed your first journal entry to gain feedback. This is particularly important if you are not feeling confident. Use the feedback to redraft as necessary.

Information overload

Having argued in this chapter for the provision of detailed supporting information accompanying an assessment task, we should balance this with some caution regarding the potential for information overload. Too much information or dissection of what is expected in a task may be just as disconcerting to students as too little. When students are commencing their study, it is likely that you need really to focus on just one or two developmental aspects, leaving other components to be developed in subsequent assessment efforts. For example, you may set an essay primarily as an exercise in structuring argument. In this instance your supporting information, and marking criteria, will be weighted heavily towards this aspect, rather than trying to evoke a high level of student attainment in all aspects of the essay form.

As students gain experience with assessment tasks and forms, too much information and direction could in fact have the reverse effect. It may limit students' horizons and stifle their interests in extending themselves in novel or creative ways. The information and support we provide to students should always be strategic, based upon issues such as students' progress through a programme, and the particular emphasis you want to provide in a task. This is really a matter of judgement by individual teachers, ideally within the context of a whole-of-programme approach to assessment that develops students' abilities in planned, incremental steps.

Communicating assessment tasks at a glance

- Communication problems arise from hurried preparation, lecturer attitudes about 'spoon-feeding' or the individual teacher's lack of clarity.
- The logic of the assessment task should be provided to the student in the form of a rationale.
- Terminology needs to be consistent and clear. Give students explanations of assessment terms they might misunderstand (eg 'overview', 'evaluate', 'reflect', 'judgement').
- Assessment tasks take different forms. Explain the form (eg journal form, essay form).
- Students learn by experience. Inexperienced students benefit from suggestions about how to approach assessment tasks.
- Too much information can be as disconcerting to students as too little. We suggest taking a whole-of-programme approach to balance the level of communication to students.

23

Marking and grading

In the end, the summative assessment process comes down to the marking of student work and the awarding of results, usually grades. All the good and careful work leading to this point (designing learning outcomes, assessment tasks and marking schemes or rubrics) can be undone if marking is not carried out in such a way that the result is a true reflection of students' performances on assessment tasks.

Marking and grading are the culmination of the assessment process for students. Preparing for assessment is where most of their energies are applied, as we have seen, and, although they can approach assessment tasks with trepidation and anxiously await their results, they will usually accept their assessor's judgement if they believe it to be fair. Teachers dread marking and grading for other reasons. This work comes either in the midst of teaching and administrative duties or at the end of a teaching period when, although their institution winds down for a time, markers must work under pressure to return marked work to students in a timely way and with sufficient feedback to assist their learning. At the end of a teaching period marking is combined with the job of finalizing results against looming deadlines. The work must be completed within a limited time-frame, yet it must be done well for reasons of fairness and consistency. Assessors have to be able to justify their marking and grading decisions to their students, their institution and the community.

In many higher education institutions much marking is contracted out to part-time or casually employed staff who attend the campus infrequently if at all. Casualization in higher education is increasing, as we noted in Chapter 4. Part-time and casually employed staff can miss the valuable collegial networking that takes place at meetings and other less formal gatherings of their disciplinary group where there are debates about teaching and assessment. They are rarely involved in the development of subject guides, learning outcomes, assessment tasks or marking schemes. Without these experiences, staff can become isolated and marginalized and might be unaware of important aspects of marking practices. This is particularly true of those who are employed to mark the papers of distance and open learning students. It is very important to ensure, as far as possible, that these staff members are kept up to date about assessment practices and that they take part in as many activities around assessment of students as possible. Your institution may have devised ways to reduce the isolation often experienced by casually employed academic staff.

Bearing the foregoing issues in mind, we will discuss the practice of marking and grading under the following headings:

- assessment systems;
- marking practices;
- multiple markers, reliability and consistency;
- feedback to students;
- awarding final grades;
- record keeping.

Assessment systems

When students receive a mark of 35 out of 50, what does this mean? Is it a 'good' mark or a 'poor' one? It depends on students' previous marks and their expectations of the current piece of work. It also depends on the assessors and their expectations of particular students alongside their perceptions of the assessment task. A mark does not mean anything out of its context. Results are interpreted in different ways depending upon the markers' vested interests. Occasionally students consider themselves to be 'distinction' students on the basis of previous results and are outraged when a lower grade is awarded. And sometimes students are thrilled with results that are over and above their own expectations. Results, including the unexpected, have to be able to be justified to the students within the framework of an assessment system.

Type of assessment regime

In Chapter 3, we discussed three assessment regimes in some length. In brief they are:

- *norm-referenced assessment regimes*: students are ranked in order of results whether or not explicit standards are used in the judgement of performance, and the grade depends upon rank order within a cohort;
- *standards-based assessment regimes*: student performances are measured against criteria and standards, and the grade depends upon actual results; and
- *criterion-referenced assessment regimes*: all criteria in each standard are explicitly identified.

Although norm-referenced assessment has a long history in higher education, it has, in recent decades, begun to be replaced by criterion-referenced or standards-based systems because these latter make explicit to students what performance standards or criteria are. They also hold the promise of higher levels of accountability and marking reliability. Both of these systems involve determining student grades for each subject over a range of assessment tasks.

As we explained in Chapter 3, assessors usually find it useful to have a conception of what the norms might be in grading a cohort, so that major deviations from what is expected alert markers to check their marking practices.

Grades

Each higher education institution has its own system of reporting results. Typically they consist of grades (such as high distinction, distinction, credit, pass, fail) and each grade represents a predetermined level of achievement.

Pass/fail

Some courses and some subjects, though, are assessed on the basis of pass or fail. Students pass when they meet the requirements of the course or subject and they are deemed to fail if they do not meet these requirements. This system can be used:

- to determine whether or not students can operate technology or equipment to a satisfactory standard;
- to identify whether they can perform essential procedures, for example in a laboratory;
- to record a result in some kinds of flexible individual projects where students determine their own learning outcomes within a very broad framework.

A pass/fail assessment regime might operate for a whole subject or for part of a subject while other assessment tasks are descriptively graded as shown above. Many of the skills discussed in Chapter 15, 'Demonstrating procedures and techniques', are appropriately assessed on a pass/fail basis.

Combining pass/fail and descriptive scoring within a subject
Bachelor of Business students had three assessment tasks for their subject 'Introduction to human resource planning'. All three tasks were compulsory, but only the third was graded to discriminate between levels of achievement. Students who satisfactorily completed all three tasks were awarded the grade achieved on the third. Students had to:

1. identify and list at least 10 resources (hard copy and online) relating to theoretical and practical models of human resource planning in

> organizations, using library catalogues and databases and Internet search engines (carried out in small groups, and assessed on a pass/fail basis);
> 2. produce a group report that categorized the models from the first assessment task (assessed on a pass/fail basis); and
> 3. submit an individual essay that critically analysed the information from the first two assessment tasks, and argued for an individually designed model (graded according to level of achievement).

Students aim for a grade

In some subjects it may be appropriate to include an element of student choice in the assessment regime. Students may choose to do particular assessment tasks to achieve a 'pass' grade, or to do further tasks to achieve a higher grade.

> ### Core and optional tasks
> In the information handout for an introductory humanities subject, students were provided with the assessment tasks and marking schemes for the subject. Assessment consisted of a core task and a range of optional tasks. Students who chose to do only the core task were eligible for a 'pass' grade. Those who chose to do additional assessment tasks were eligible to aim for a higher grade.

Marking practices

Studies about marking reliability tend to show that when several teachers mark the same student's work they score it differently (see, for example, Gibbs, 1995: 4). In academic development programmes, too, there are often widely differing values about standards and marking criteria among those academics present (Brown, Rust and Gibbs, 1994). We discussed these issues in Chapter 3.

This situation occurs when subjective professional judgement is used in marking such assessment tasks as essays, reports, reflective journals, art and drama or musical performances. It is less common when there is a right or a wrong answer such as in objective tests that include, for example, multiple choice or true/false questions. To some extent the differences can relate to disciplinary values. Brown, Rust and Gibbs (1994: 9) suggest that the similarities and differences in the way teachers mark student work 'have little to do with the knowledge the authors [of the work] displayed'. It has more to do with the values, experience and expectations of the marker.

Validity and reliability in assessment are explored in Part A and in Chapter 20. In this chapter we are concerned with ways to increase reliability in marking practices. Some of the threats to reliability, all involving bias of one sort or another, include:

- *'Halo' or 'horns' effect.* Markers might have formed global impressions of students that influence their marking. Previously formed positive (halo) or negative (horns) impressions can influence an assessor to distort other information without having a conscious intention to do so. This effect can also refer to the influence of others' work on the judgement being made. For instance, if a marker has read several poor essays in a row and then comes to one that is somewhat better than average, it may receive a much higher grade (a halo effect) than if the same essay was read immediately after an outstanding piece of work.
- *Tendency towards the average.* Markers can 'play safe' and score the work of all students towards the middle range of grades. They never award high or low grades, thus hoping to avoid the accusation of having made serious errors of judgement. This kind of bias can denote lack of confidence in marking ability.
- *Personal preferences.* Markers might have a particular 'bee in their bonnet' about how assessment tasks should be performed. For example, if they prefer essays without topic headings, they could score essays with headings less favourably than those in the style they prefer – whether or not this is specified in the marking scheme.
- *Stereotyping.* Another type of bias is to make judgements about students on the basis of appearance or behaviour.
- *'Hard' or 'soft' marking practices.* It is sometimes almost a badge of honour for teachers in higher education to be 'hard' rather than 'soft' markers regardless of standards and criteria set out in marking schemes. Those who are considered to be 'soft' markers are traditionally frowned upon as lowering standards, although both 'hard' and 'soft' marking practices indicate bias.

It is an accepted part of the nature of human beings that they are subjective in their judgements because of their individual ethical and moral values, their past experiences, their passions and, for some, their professionalism. Teachers are not immune from bias or from getting 'bees in their bonnets' when they assess student work.

Some examples of different types of bias follow, with suggestions about how the situations could be managed. We do not argue that anyone can eliminate bias in assessment but, when teachers are aware of the possible threats to fair or equitable marking and attempt to overcome them, unfair bias can be reduced.

Stereotyping can cause bias

A lecturer marking the work of a particular student was very surprised at the high level achieved because he had considered that this student 'did not care about her studies and wasn't trying very hard'. He had formed this opinion because of her somewhat unconventional appearance (rings through her nose, eyebrows and lips) and because, although she usually attended class, she rarely contributed to class discussions. He went back over the assessment task and took some marks away where he thought he had been too 'soft' in the first instance. Fortunately, this lecturer was concerned enough to discuss the student's work with a colleague who re-marked the paper according to the marking scheme and judged it to be at the higher level of performance.

'Horns' effect?

A student who received a lower grade than he had expected told others in his group that the teacher had 'marked him down' because he had 'spoken out' with controversial opinions that the lecturer did not like. Is this an example of 'horns' effect, or is it an example of a student who does not want to acknowledge a poor performance in an assessment task? It could be either. In this case the lecturer had a well-developed marking scheme showing standards and criteria and was able to defend the decision with reference to how each student's work was marked.

However, another version of this scenario could have ended differently if the lecturer had not devised a specific marking scheme and was left without the means to show that the result was a defensible reflection of the student's performance on the assessment task.

We are assuming that neither of these lecturers showed bias, but in yet another version of the scenario the student could have been right.

Tendency towards the average

An inexperienced marker using an analytic marking scheme for a series of 10 examination questions, each worth 5 marks, awarded no more than 3.5 marks to each response that had included all or most of the characteristics of a right answer because it was her view that no student should ever get full marks. Also she was worried that she might have missed a key fault in some of the answers. No student gained a very high score in this examination, although some had answered most of the questions with complete accuracy.

Using self- and peer marking

Many assessment tasks are suitable for self- and peer marking for both formative and summative purposes. Objective assessment tasks (such as multiple choice, true/false or short answer questions) are often used as practice tests marked by students themselves or by their peers. Practice tests have been shown to improve performance in summative tests (see, for example, Sly, 1999). The improvement might occur because of the feedback gained from the practice tests and also because, through practice, students become familiar with particular types of tests.

Self- and peer assessment may also be used to engender reflection and deep understanding in higher education programmes, and are appropriate to assess learning outcomes that require higher-order thinking and performance, for example 'designing, creating, performing', 'critical thinking' or 'problem solving' (see Part B for examples).

Students find self- and peer assessment difficult although they report that the benefits to their quality of learning outweigh the drawbacks (Hanrahan and Isaacs, 2001). The study by Hanrahan and Isaacs found that students consider that marking their own and their peers' work is hard when they are unsure of standards, and that it is difficult to be objective in self- and peer marking activities. They also found it uncomfortable to have their peers read their papers and worried about them being overcritical. Some of these problems can be addressed with training on giving and receiving feedback, standards and marking criteria.

Another good reason to include self- and peer marking is that it can reduce your marking workload in the following ways: 1) if self- and peer assessment are part of the summative assessment regime, you may only need to do random spot checks of the results once you are confident students know how to apply standards and criteria; 2) students learn from their own experience of marking how to approach other assessment tasks, thus making their responses easier to follow and easier to mark.

Computer marking

Computer-managed learning (CML) tests and activities can be designed to provide formative feedback to students by automatic computer marking of tests. Results of practice tests can be made available to both teachers and students for diagnostic purposes (Steven and Hesketh, 1999). Feedback can be included with the results as part of a CML package. An advantage of using computer-marked testing for formative purposes is that students receive their results immediately and can act on the feedback (Chapman, 1999). Another advantage is reduced workload for teachers once the programmes have been designed.

Computer-assisted assessment (CAA) is normally used for summative assessment and usually includes objective tests such as multiple choice, true/false, short answer or match-the-answer questions. These are also marked by the computer with the results returned to the teacher. It is important to consider all aspects of the assessment task before you choose CAA. See Chapter 14 for information and examples of this type of assessment.

> For simple assessment criteria it is possible to completely automate the assessment, but for more complex criteria total automation may not be possible or desirable. Human examiners and computer-assisted assessors are complementary; they have different strengths and weaknesses.
>
> (Dowsing, 1999: 133)

Multiple markers, reliability and consistency

Marking teams consist of two or more people involved in marking an assessment task. You might be a member of the part-time or casually employed higher education workforce, or you might be a new academic in need of assistance to achieve reliability and consistency in your marking practices (see also Chapter 2). If you are a member of either of these groups you will find the collegial support of other markers to be extremely beneficial especially when the team includes experienced teachers, as they can provide leadership and guidance by taking on the role of managing the team for consistent marking.

There have always been part-time and casually employed staff who mark student work, mostly for sound educational reasons. For example, some part-time markers are practising professionals with valuable knowledge of current disciplinary practice. Assessment panels that include expert practitioners are common in some disciplines such as architecture, engineering, the fine arts, music and drama (see Chapter 16). Postgraduate students often take on marking duties to eke out their allowances and to become inducted into academic life. In some settings where marking is outsourced, a permanent teacher who is the official assessor of a subject briefs markers on how to mark student work. The part-time staff then do all the marking for the subject, although it is the official assessor who is accountable for the consistency and reliability of results.

One of the effects of the trend towards academic casualization in higher education is the increased difficulty of attaining consistency by teaching teams with multiple markers, some of whom are not on-campus very often. This is highlighted in the current academic climate as the proportion of part-time and casual markers to permanent teachers increases, exacerbating the existing challenges inherent in arriving at consistent, reliable marking outcomes when there are multiple markers of the same assessment task.

Teams of markers can include those who are:

- experienced permanent members of the academic staff who work together and are able to meet frequently;

- markers who are geographically remote from each other because they are based at different campuses of the same university, or are members of different institutions in jointly run educational programmes (perhaps in different countries);
- part-time and casually employed markers who are employed for short periods specifically to do marking, and are not paid for additional hours to consult closely with other team members;
- practitioners in a disciplinary field who are engaged as markers because of their expertise, but who are not experienced in assessment and marking practices;
- newly appointed teachers without experience in assessment and marking practices;
- postgraduate students who are experienced as students, but inexperienced as assessors.

Moderation of marking

In optimum conditions all members of a team become involved in negotiating marking schemes and are available to debate the intricacies of how student work will be judged. But in the current pressured educational world this is difficult to achieve unless everyone concerned intentionally works toward the achievement of reliable and consistent marking practices. One of the ways to achieve this is to moderate the outcomes of marking exercises.

The term 'moderation' in assessment means regulating the marking of individual markers to achieve consistency in the application of standards of performance and marking criteria. This needs to be done even when all members of a marking team are using the same marking scheme. It is not sufficient that each member of a team is provided with a copy of the marking scheme because, as we have seen, different interpretations will result in inconsistent marking. When there are multiple markers, moderation can take place by using:

- face-to-face meetings;
- telephone conferencing;
- e-mail messages;
- online discussions (either synchronous or asynchronous).

Before the marking period, it is suggested you seek the answers to the following questions and if the answer to any of them is 'no' it will be in the interests of marking consistency to attempt to fill the gaps:

- Are students aware of how all the judgements will be made before they attempt the task?
- Have you debated the underlying values implicit in the assessment task and how this task fits within the whole assessment regime?

- Is there common agreement about standards and marking criteria?
- Have you decided how to approach unexpected but appropriate student answers to specific questions?
- Have you agreed about what to do when a student comes up with an 'out-of-the-box' creative solution to a problem that is outside the marking scheme but should be acknowledged and rewarded?
- Do you recognize and try to avoid errors of bias as individuals and as a team?

A lot of the work of moderation takes place before the marking period, as implied by the suggested questioning above. If marking practices are agreed within marking teams, moderation of results at the end of marking periods is made easier. It is more an exercise of fine-tuning than one of major re-adjustment. Here are some suggestions.

Markers compare results after marking the same paper
At the beginning of a marking exercise, the coordinator of a marking team chooses a paper at random and, after removing student identification, copies and distributes it to each member of the team. After each person marks the paper according to the agreed marking scheme, they debate the variations in marking (face to face or electronically), finally coming to agreement about marking approach.

Spot checking at random
The coordinator of a marking team 'spot-checks' marked papers in each grade range for consistent application of standards and criteria. If inconsistencies are found, there is discussion within the marking team.

Markers compare results after marking different papers
The marking team meets (face to face or electronically) after each has marked a few papers at random to discuss the pros and cons of what they have found in the characteristics of student performances. They debate any differences of emphasis or other variations between markers' perceptions of levels of quality with reference to their marking scheme.

Moderating borderline results

While overall results for a subject are necessarily moderated when all the assessment tasks are completed, it is also helpful to review borderline cases after they have been marked but before they have been returned to students. If marking is standards based, and descriptions of the characteristics of each grade have been developed, it is possible to compare borderline results with these descriptions and make decisions about where, overall, the student's performance best matches the grade description.

Each marker marks the same question on each paper

A variation in marking practices is where each member of a marking team marks one part (or one question) in each of the papers that are submitted, thereby aiming for consistency within each question. A problem with this approach is that the parts are not put together to assess overall student performance across the range of questions.

Double marking

In this method of achieving consistency, each paper is marked individually by two markers who then debate the differences and come to agreement. This is time consuming and costly. In a variation on double marking that is fairly common, two markers each mark the same paper but do not discuss the results of the marking exercise. The official subject assessor can either award the average of the two grades, or choose the higher or lower grade. Biggs (1999a) says that this 'blind' double marking is 'bizarre' because it does not involve debate around each marker's emphases.

Feedback to students

When teachers give feedback to students it is rather like a reply to the assessment task. It is about the strengths and the weaknesses of student work and it should be aligned with all other elements of assessment: the desired learning outcomes, assessment tasks and marking schemes. If feedback is aligned this way, it will help students to see how they are progressing so they can consolidate their strengths and learn about their weaknesses. Giving students feedback is a core responsibility and an integral part of the whole teaching process.

Feedback is particularly crucial for open and distance learners because they have less contact with their teachers than do on-campus students. They are often adult learners who manage their studies around busy lives, or they might be new to higher education and inhibited from making contact with their teachers because they don't want to ask 'stupid' questions. Contacts are legitimated around assessment, including feedback on their performance in assessment tasks. Feedback might provide the trigger for these learners to make contact with their teachers to ask specific questions or to debate points of theory or practice, thus enriching their learning experiences.

The timeliness of feedback is a significant factor in its effectiveness for student learning, as discussed in Chapter 20. It does not matter how much valuable and detailed feedback is provided on an assessment task if it is not returned in time for the student to reflect upon it and incorporate learning into future assessment tasks for the subject. The turnaround time after the receipt of assessment tasks for open and distance learners has traditionally been longer than it is for on-campus students because of the critical time taken to send marked papers by post. However, this problem is removed when students can send and receive their papers online, via e-mail or student intranet systems, and this way of submitting and returning work is increasingly used in higher education.

The pressures of increased workloads that arise from teaching higher numbers of students alongside the need to meet quality assurance imperatives are great, as we have already acknowledged, and we are fully aware that providing detailed student feedback can be very time consuming. But there is nothing worse for a student than investing a great deal of time and effort into an assessment task, only to have it returned with a mark and a bland meaningless comment or no feedback at all, so we would like to look at some ways of providing useful and timely feedback that do not have a huge impact on markers' workloads:

- Develop marking schemes that have provision for showing the strengths and weaknesses of student work in relation to standards and that have spaces for individual feedback. Marking is then combined with feedback.
- Design a statement bank (maybe as an electronic file) with common comments to which you can refer individual students (Brown, Rust and Gibbs, 1994).
- Mark selectively and target misconceptions: for example, there is not much point in marking every spelling, grammatical or stylistic error in an essay. Mark the first page or two and make a general comment about how the student can improve.
- Provide group feedback. Compile a general document that discusses the group's strengths and weaknesses and attach it to each marked assignment.

- E-mail and student intranet forums can be used to give timely individual or group feedback, especially when you notice an issue that needs clarification immediately prior to a submission date.
- Provide model answers or worked solutions to problems as part of feedback. These only have to be developed once, and can be attached to marked work so that students can compare them to their own answers and see how to improve.
- Ask students who receive a high grade for an assessment task if you may copy and distribute their work to others. This can be sent to weaker students with their own marked papers as an exemplar to assist when they prepare future papers.
- Use formative assessment methods such as self-assessment and peer assessment with quizzes and diagnostic activities. Use CML and CAA if you have access to this technology. Such activities can assist students to reflect and to learn about how to approach summative assessment tasks. Insights can improve assessment techniques and avoid the need for lengthy feedback.

Awarding final grades

As we said earlier, marks and percentages are not mystical entities. They need to be viewed in their context, and are purely a means by which student performance is reported, usually over a number of assessment tasks, leading to a final grade. We have looked at different types of assessment systems, such as norm referencing and criterion- or standards-based assessment. The system that is used in your institution will affect how you make the final judgement on awarding grades. Most systems include bands or ranges of marks that constitute grades, although some use a pass/fail system as described earlier.

There is no foolproof way to determine grades with objectivity because, as has been said many times, assessment is complex and subjective in all its forms. We would agree with Biggs (1999a) that holistic assessment has the best chance of providing a realistic representation of student ability. To that end we would promote the concept of grade descriptors that provide standards and characteristics of performance to be achieved at each grade. We would rather make our judgements holistically using grades, bands or ranges than individual marks but we recognize that individual marks and marking schemes are the foundations of grading decisions in many higher education institutions.

Cut-off points

The cut-off points for each grade range can seem arbitrary, but can be used in conjunction with detailed descriptions that indicate the characteristics of student performance at each grade.

We have seen several examples of grade descriptions in Chapter 3 and Chapter 21 (Example 1). In the following example of grade descriptors used for extended tasks in a school of humanities, there are cut-off points in terms of both the percentage ranges for each grade and detailed descriptions of the expectations of performance at each grade level. The requirements of the lower grades are incorporated into those higher in the scale:

- *High distinction* (HD). Originality in synthesis at a high level of consistency through argument; mastery of material; extensive range of sources showing evidence of wide, systematic and creative information retrieval; thought provoking; effective and interesting use of English prose.
- *Distinction* (D). Understands and compares theories, concepts, ideas systematically; evidence of use of a wide range of resources; makes critical comment on the literature; stylish composition; sustained arguments, linking empirical detail with theoretical perspectives.
- *Credit* (C). Concepts, theories used to explain descriptive material; some useful insights; use of a reasonable array of sources; coherent argument that is focused but could be improved.
- *Pass* (P). Readable; descriptive rather than theoretical and analytical; dependent on a limited range of resources; some grasp of concepts and major issues involved; coherent style and composition; reliant on few resources.
- *Fail* (F). Does not meet the minimum requirements for a pass. For example, one or more of the following: irrelevant material included; incomplete; unreadable; little or no understanding of issues or concepts; reliance on few resources; misunderstanding of the topic; superficial; major errors of focus.

Grading at the borders

Decisions that need to be made when student work falls at the borders of grade ranges are made easier when there are grade descriptors, such as those in the example above. A student's final grade can be reviewed in the light of the characteristics of performance identified for each grade, and a decision can be made about the student's complete performance according to which description it best fits.

It is helpful to review borderline cases as they occur, as we suggested earlier, to build up a background to assist when awarding final grades. It may be possible to ask a colleague with relevant expertise to give a second opinion when there are borderline cases.

Record keeping

Keeping records can be a chore, albeit a necessary one. Your institution will have a system for recording final grades that are formalized by bodies such as boards of examiners or assessment committees. Once they are officially approved, records are usually stored electronically in a student administration department. But it is important also to keep your own records because you may be asked to account for how individual assessment tasks were marked, how grading decisions were made or how you managed a student query about a mark or a grade. Records need to be kept for a particular length of time, depending on the rules and legislation that apply in your institution.

The kinds of records you need to keep are:

- All student marks for the range of assessment tasks in the subjects you teach and assess.
- You might consider copying the completed marking schemes for each student before returning them. These record the details of how marks were calculated.
- Notes of relevant interviews with students regarding assessment (face to face, telephone, online or via the post).
- Attendance records or rolls where attendance is a requirement of the subject.
- Applications for extensions of time to complete an assessment task with your notes on whether it was approved.
- Applications for special consideration in relation to assessment, again with notes about whether it was approved.
- A record of the final grades awarded to students.

You could be required to make some of your records available to various authorities in your institution, and anyone who has not kept complete records or has a messy filing system will tell you that it is much more time consuming to try to recreate records than it is to keep them safely and completely in the first place.

Marking and grading at a glance

- A mark does not mean anything out of its context. It needs to be understood within each student's past experiences, and the assessment regime and marking practices used by each institution.
- Grades can be awarded to indicate degrees of success (high distinction, distinction, credit, pass, fail) or on a pass/fail basis.
- Marking practices are reliable when they reflect a student's true performance on an assessment task.
- Everyone is prone to bias of one sort or another but, if you are aware of your particular biases and attempt to overcome them, reliability of marking can and does improve.

- Include self- and peer marking into your summative assessment regime to teach students about how their work is judged.
- The proportion of part-time and casually employed markers to permanent academic staff is increasing in higher education, thus increasing the difficulty of getting together collegially to debate and negotiate to improve the reliability and consistency of marking practices. However, common understandings about marking practices need to be found, and marking teams can find ways to get together electronically, if not face to face.
- Moderation of marking and grading is important to achieve consistency and improve reliability of outcomes when there are multiple markers of a subject.
- Students rely on the feedback that they receive on summative and formative assessment tasks to help focus their efforts in future assessment tasks. This is especially crucial for open and distance learners.
- Awarding final grades is not just a matter of adding the marks. There are complexities when there is a variety of types of assessment tasks and standards-based assessment methods.
- It is important to keep good records of marking and grading processes and outcomes for accountability purposes.

24

Evaluating assessment practices

While Part A considered many of the issues around accountability and quality in higher education, the systematic review of quality is part of our overall commitment to rigour in educational practice. Evaluation is commonly used in higher education as a means to improve accountability for effective practices. Most of you will be familiar with evaluations that help to improve your teaching practices and provide documentation for accountability and promotion procedures.

The methods reviewed in this chapter are specifically addressing the question of assessment but can be implemented to evaluate a whole range of teaching and learning activities in general. The topics that follow provide an overview of the most common approaches to evaluation and ways to ensure continuous improvement of assessment practices.

Evaluation of assessment may happen as part of a subject evaluation or a full course evaluation or simply as a task in itself. In this chapter we will be looking at some of the practical issues of evaluation, the models most commonly used, who the stakeholders in the process are and what to do with the data obtained. We'll start with the most common approaches to evaluation and move through to the broader issues of quality. The topics include:

- using formative or summative evaluation;
- obtaining student feedback;
- seeking input from other stakeholders;
- developing evaluation tools;
- analysing the evaluation data;
- reporting evaluation outcomes;
- using information from evaluative processes to improve assessment practice.

Using formative or summative evaluation

Formative evaluation concerns itself with improvements to processes or outputs that are in development. For example, a formative approach to evaluating assessment design might involve the circulation of our proposed assessment tasks to colleagues or professional peers for their comments and critique before we release them for students' attention. Summative evaluation looks at the effectiveness of assessment tasks once they have been used with students.

When deciding upon the effectiveness, value or validity of an assessment design or its success in achieving the desired outcomes, we are in the best position to carry out our own evaluations for the subjects that we teach and assess. You could, for example:

- request a professional peer review of your proposed assessment tasks;
- approach colleagues at your own institution, within your own department or area of teaching and learning, from academic staff development or perhaps from an evaluation section at your own institution;
- consider a reciprocal arrangement where you evaluate and give feedback to a colleague on his or her assessment design and the colleague provides the same kind of critique for you;
- exchange documentation about the aim of the subject, its learning outcomes and the relationship between the assessment tasks and the outcomes to enable the process of collegial critique;
- review the documentation about any requirements stipulated by professional bodies;
- if relevant, consider requesting the input of these professional bodies in the evaluation of the style and relevance of the assessment regime.

Using a learning quality guide in a formative and a summative way
The staff within an academic development unit have prepared a flexible learning quality guide. This contains descriptive, practical and theoretical information about the sequence of events that need to take place in the design, development, teaching and evaluation of subjects. In addition to this information, a series of checklists is provided in the guide so that staff engaged in the various stages of course development and review might be able to assure themselves that they are adhering to recommended practice strategies.

The guide is to be used in both a formative way, as staff measure their progress against the benchmarks described, and a summative way, in the course of formal review processes.

Apart from formative and summative approaches to evaluation, there are a number of other commonly practised models of evaluation such as objectives-based evaluation, qualitative evaluation, multiple methods evaluation, responsive evaluation and action research. Each of these methods has a body of theory and practice that can be found reported in the literature (Reeves and Hedberg, 2003). Suffice it to say here that you will need to make a decision on your own approach, given the particular details of what you want to know, how you plan to gather and analyse the data and how the information will be used.

So, what do we do when we want to know if the assessment tasks in our courses or subjects are valid, reliable or authentic?

Obtaining student feedback

Obtaining feedback from students is the most common and direct method of finding out how our assessment designs are working and overall what difficulties or disappointments students may have experienced. The implementation of large-scale surveys such as the Course Experience Questionnaire (Ramsden, 1992) provides retrospective feedback to higher education institutions on the student perceptions of their courses. At the individual level, feedback is essential to improvement and to inform any change in teaching practices. Personal use is often made of student feedback where it supports a teacher's case for promotion or eligibility for an award in teaching excellence.

A number of methods for collecting feedback are in most common usage, namely questionnaires, focus groups and interviews.

Questionnaires

The basic questionnaire format can be utilized in three main ways – in class, by post or over the Internet. The questions used may be centrally designed and in keeping with national standards, or they may be more tailored for the purpose of the evaluation. If you decide to develop your own questions, there are some basic principles to consider when designing questionnaires (Davidson and Goldfinch, 1998):

- Provide an explanation of why you are asking these questions.
- Give clear instructions on how to complete the questionnaire.
- Decide whether to use open-ended questions or closed questions, or if a mixture of the two would be best.
- Make sure your questions are written in clear and unambiguous language.
- Be consistent in your style, eg use check boxes or Likert scales (strongly agree/disagree or very important/not important), not a mixture of both.
- Keep the questionnaire as short as possible; put more delicate issues at the end.

- Try to adapt an existing questionnaire that has already been trialled, or make time to pilot your own questions with a small sample (four or five peers or graduates).
- Include a note of thanks at the end.

In class

Student feedback can be quickly obtained anonymously using sheets handed out in class towards the end of the semester. While this has the advantage of working with a captive sample and therefore results in higher response rates, it does have its limitations in terms of assessment. As this process usually takes place prior to the final exam or assignment submission, the feedback often does not provide information about the assessment tasks but can be used to inform future design of the syllabus or teaching and learning activities.

One useful method of checking on student understanding and their satisfaction with the learning process is called the 'two-minute feedback'. This is a system where, at the end of each class, students are given two minutes prior to leaving in which to jot down what they gained from the session, what they hope to gain in the next session and a brief note of any difficulties or dissatisfactions that have emerged. Such ongoing and timely feedback is also not specific to assessment but, if established as a class routine, can yield information about the assessment tasks as they occur.

Post

Historically, mailed questionnaires have suffered from low response rates. When used with on-campus learners, even if supplied with a stamped self-addressed envelope, these surveys require large sample sizes to obtain any significant results. Despite this constraint such questionnaires are still used with distance education students, as in these cases the respondents who answer will often have something of significance to convey or suggest. Responses are not necessarily seen as representative but more in the light of a 'suggestion box', and specific action can be taken in response to ideas put forward.

As this may be the only chance the off-campus students have to comment on our assessment practices, consider carefully what you wish to ask about. The following questions are examples of what you might want to know: Was the flexibility of assessment design of benefit to off-campus learners? Were there any unintended side effects of the assessment design? Was the feedback provided in a timely and instructive manner?

Online/Web

E-mail surveys have the benefit of convenience and speed of delivery. Where you have the e-mail addresses of your sample group, a bulk mailing can readily take place with a reply-by date noted. To ensure that anonymity is preserved, the recipient list must be suppressed in this case. The ease of completing an e-mail questionnaire and its rapid return to the evaluator are two of the main benefits of this method. However, while the data are available electronically, it can sometimes be a little cumbersome to transfer them into other software packages for analysis, eg NVivo™, Excel or SPSS.

The feature of Web surveys that makes them more attractive for respondents to complete is their immediate convenience and the possibility of anonymity being guaranteed. The benefit for evaluators is that data can be delivered in the format desired for analysis, eg spreadsheet or word-processed. No data entry or transcribing is needed.

Use the online format to its benefit by asking questions that can immediately inform your assessment practices, or by allowing students to comment in an ongoing online forum so that problems can be addressed before they become significant stressors to students. For example, were the materials and assessment instructions made available to students on time? Was the feedback clear and thought provoking? If group work was a feature of assessment, how did this work for the students? In the context of group work, did they feel they were able to achieve the learning outcomes?

Phone

Questionnaires can be administered over the telephone and, while this individual approach is more time consuming, it allows for clarification and further probing on the spot. Recording the responses to the structured questions can be kept simple, and supplemented by additional comments made. In this case it is best if the interviewer is not the same person who taught the subject. Students will feel more at liberty to give feedback on the assessment task if they feel protected by a guarantee of anonymity.

Phone interviews can explore students' responses to the assessment tasks. For example, how did students perceive the tasks being asked of them? How appropriate did they feel the assessment tasks were in terms of size, frequency, diversity, alignment with learning outcomes and relationship to the programme objectives as a whole? (Morgan and O'Reilly, 1999)

Focus groups

A focus group is a group of 'involved' people who are called together to answer a semi-structured set of evaluation questions you have prepared. The group might consist of students who have volunteered to participate or who have been invited through your sample selection process (see 'Selecting your sample' below). It is important that there is flexibility in the focus group process for issues to emerge that are of particular importance to the group or the individuals within it.

Since your interest will be around evaluating your assessment tasks, this would form the broad theme that gets the discussion going. Some general principles of running focus groups are (McAteer, 1998):

- Start with a broad theme and keep some of your other questions on hand to prompt the discussion in case it doesn't occur spontaneously.
- Set the group size and composition (a representative sample of 6–12 is best, so for example you might include a student who did well, one who did poorly, a student studying off-campus, one studying on-campus, a younger one, an older one, a female, a male, someone from another culture in your class, one of your markers and a tutor).
- Alternatively you may decide to run a series of focus groups, one for each stakeholder group, and you may decide it is necessary to bring participants back for a second session to explore specific issues in more depth.
- Decide how you will record the sessions – audiotape, notes, video recording, doing it yourself or working with an assistant.
- Decide in advance the level of analysis you are prepared to use, given the available time and resources and keeping in mind the purpose of analysis. For example, will you use systematic content coding, qualitative analysis of emergent themes, notes against predetermined criteria or a combination of methods?
- Incorporate findings with information gained through other data collection methods.

Using findings from a focus group

An experienced lecturer in anatomy and physiology was consistently finding a high failure rate in her subject that was assessed by a mid-semester and a final exam. She told an educational designer she had tried everything, including referring her students to the academic studies unit as well as offering extra tutorials to go over the concepts one more time between lectures. The lecturer and educational designer evaluated the assessment tasks, confirming that exam format was, in principle, an appropriate approach to assessing the subject and in keeping with the learning objectives. It was clear that the subject relied upon a great deal of information being retained and reported in context by the student.

A focus group was convened in an informal setting at the end of the semester, and students were able to report that, no matter what additional help was provided, they were not able to take advantage of the assistance. As first-year undergraduates they felt overwhelmed by the amount of content to be learnt, and feared that time taken for extra tutorials or academic studies assistance would not be worth while or would not focus on their specific areas of difficulty.

On this basis the lecturer decided to arrange for the academic studies staff to be available in the faculty by appointment throughout semester. She spread the assessment across four tests as well as including the weekly laboratory work as an assessable component of the overall grade. The next group of results from students was markedly improved, and further online self-assessment quizzes are planned for additional assistance.

Interviews

There are a few different approaches to gathering information using interviews and each provides a way of building up a picture that has partially been obtained through other methods such as questionnaires and focus groups. The three methods we'll look at here are the structured, semi-structured and unstructured interviews. Each of these methods can be used to support formative evaluation or summative evaluation:

- *Structured interviews.* Structured interviews are based on a set of questions and while this ensures a consistent range of topics is covered by all respondents there is a likelihood that useful feedback will be lost if it does not fit with the established interview questions.
- *Semi-structured interviews.* The semi-structured interview includes enough specified questions to keep the interview focused but also includes follow-up questions so that respondents can add any relevant experiences and comments from their own perspective. Interviews flow best when questions are mainly open ended.
- *Unstructured interviews.* The unstructured interview can begin with one main focus question (see 'Focus groups' above), but can take a much more responsive pathway since the interviewer pursues topics as they emerge in discussion with respondents.

Interviews can take place in person (face to face), over the telephone, by e-mail or synchronous chat, or may be self-recorded on audiotape or videotape in accordance with a prepared set of broad questions or topics (Lockwood, 1991):

- *Face-to-face.* Face-to-face interviews can be recorded on tape and later transcribed, or notes may be taken during the interview process. Each of these documents arising from interviews will need to be checked by the interviewees, primarily for errors but also for clarification and attention to detail. You may also be happy for interviewees to provide additional information at this stage.
- *Telephone.* Telephone interviews may be more cost effective than interviews conducted in person if the sample is widely distributed and the cost of travel to each location is prohibitive. This method still allows for a responsive exchange and can also be recorded for later transcription or summary notes.
- *Online.* Online real-time interviews can be conducted using chat software if this is available to the whole sample, or as a supplementary method where

costs may dictate the necessity to avoid both travel and extensive long-distance phone calls. Some clear protocols need to be established at the start. For example, you might request that replies be kept to one paragraph at a time, or alternatively you might only want to ask one focus question and then hand over to the respondent for his or her extended input.

E-mail can also be used but, because of the lag time for two-way responses, this more closely resembles the questionnaire style of survey rather than the interview style.

- *Self-recorded audiotape.* In cases where on-the-spot reflections and descriptions are required, participants can be asked to record their own stories on audiotape. A schedule of questions or topic prompts might also be provided to focus all participants on the same set of core issues.

(Lockwood, 1991)

With each method of interview it can also be helpful to keep a log of events, noting any details that occurred at the time or that failed to occur. These notes of the procedure itself can provide additional background information for your analysis. From all the methods of interview, qualitative data are generated and you will need to undertake an analysis of text in some way. Organizing the responses according to the questions asked, developing profiles of respondents or emerging themes and so forth are helpful prior to commencing the full analysis. A number of books are available to help with practical ideas on how to handle qualitative data. These are invaluable sources of advice, as are any conversations you might be able to have with colleagues about their successful approaches and their mistakes.

It is difficult, if not impossible, to find out all about assessment in one round of interviews. It is therefore important to focus your evaluations and decide in advance the specific areas you wish to explore through interviews, eg the assessment design, practical or technical issues, the integrity of assessment as demonstrated through a clear relationship to the learning objectives, the effectiveness of feedback systems or the timeliness of information provided. All evaluative information gained via interview in regards to the assessment tasks can be integrated with other sources of information such as the questionnaires and focus groups in order to gain a fuller picture of what is working and the areas for improvement.

Observation

In some cases information can be obtained about assessment processes and tasks by arranging to observe them as they occur. Students may be observed carrying out tasks in a range of contexts such as clinical, computer-based or workplace-based environments. In terms of gathering evaluation data, it is not the students' performance on tasks that is the concern but the functionality of the clinical or workplace environment, the software or the arrangements with teaching associates. In off-campus contexts where students are required to learn and demonstrate competent performance of real-life techniques and procedures, arrangements frequently involve teaching associates who have been approved by the educational institution to carry out certain forms of student assessment.

To conduct a useful observation, first decide:

- Who will you be observing, eg students, staff, all stakeholders and their interactions?
- What will be your key areas of interest, eg the learning situation, the assessment event, student collaborations, issues arising from previous interviews?
- Will you be an active or passive observer?

In planning your observations, it is also helpful to design a pro forma that can remind you of the main concerns you are looking for. It needs to be an easy-to-follow document that includes checklists where your notes and comments can be inserted at a glance, as you will not have much time for note writing when there is a lot going on as you watch.

On the day, it is important to explain to students why the observer is there, that the focus of the observer's interest is not the students' performance on the assessment task as that is the role of the teaching associate, and that the observations recorded will not impact upon the students' grade (Calverley, 1998).

An observation evaluation study

To answer the question 'How do nursing students organize a skills-based assessment on the ward?', an evaluation researcher visited a sample of hospitals in the region. He was able to see for himself the wide range of variation between students' circumstances. One student in a small remote hospital had the opportunity to perform the clinical assessments on one day a month when the specialist visited to conduct patient rounds. At this small hospital the evaluator also found that the equipment and resources being used for student assessment were well worn from much use and did not function as well as the newer equipment in other hospitals.

It was also through personal visits that the evaluator was truly able to see the daily constraints on part-time students who were expected to concentrate on their normal duties when at work, rather than carrying out simulated procedures for assessment purposes. This evaluation study was able to suggest some recommendations for continuing professional development for nurses that included exposure to modern equipment and allocated time for skills training outside of the students' working hours but within the working hours of the clinical teaching associate.

Reflective logs

In conjunction with other evaluation methods, the use of reflective logs can provide useful information about the practicality and effectiveness of assessment tasks. Logs kept by both students and teaching staff can be used for this purpose. Logs differ from journals in that they are not narrative in style, but simply attend to core areas of interest.

Ways of utilizing reflective logs include: focusing on one specific assessment task and details of its completion; and as an ongoing record of experience with specific emphasis on the preparation for and completion of assessment tasks and exams.

Logs may be structured with a number of headings and check boxes to help record details relevant to the evaluation question. Consider how the log will be circulated to stakeholders and how they will return it upon completion. Reports arising from logbook information contain frequencies of critical incidents or similar experiences and the accumulated reflective evaluations.

Using reflective logs

An undergraduate politics subject was being taught on-campus and off-campus at the same time. Since the on-campus group was much smaller than the off-campus group, the decision was made to open up online discussions and require a level of participation that was to be assessed.

At the same time it was decided that a small group of honours students needed a forum for sharing their ideas on their politics project. They were invited to make presentations to the online undergraduate forum during two weeks in the early part of semester. While this provided a forum for honours students to reflect upon their project structure and direction, the discussions that took place around the honours projects were also focused on the assessment topic for the undergraduates and as such formed the basis for an early component of the undergraduates' assessment.

Reflective logs were issued to record features of this two-week event and were returned by students as appendices to their written assignment. The honours students also returned the logs, as they understood the interest in reviewing the effectiveness of such an unusual assessment task.

On the basis of this combined log information, the assessable event was run again with the same level of structure but over two occasions – one early and one later in semester. Logs continue to be a tool for gathering information about this assessment task.

Seeking input from other stakeholders

Students themselves are not the only source of information about the value of our assessment tasks. Several stakeholders may be involved in the question of quality practices in assessment, and the primary concern with evaluation is to consider who the stakeholders are who might contribute their perspectives to the evaluation study, and to whom we will report the outcomes of this study.

Teachers

Teachers need to know what students have gained through the assessment process and how effectively assessment designs have led students to achieve the relevant learning outcomes. Teachers may want specific information about an innovative form of assessment or to reflect upon the circumstances surrounding an assessment event.

Students and their peers

The students are the next biggest stakeholder group in terms of quality of assessment. It is in their immediate interests to be presented with assessment tasks that directly pertain to the objectives of the subject and dovetail with any professional or vocational expectations in the workplace. It is also important for students that their overall experience of assessment makes sense. This implies that we need to know the relationship of our assessment tasks to those of prerequisite or co-requisite subjects.

Students can be asked their own perceptions of achievement, for example:

- Did they meet their own learning goals through the assessment tasks?
- How useful were the assessment tasks for them?
- Do they have any further comments about the assessment process as they experienced it?
- If students were involved in evaluating peer review and assessment processes, they may also have some ideas about how this worked and whether it might have been more successfully facilitated.
- If computer-mediated methods of assessment were used such as online quizzes or reference to archives of discussions, what feedback can students give us about how this worked to support their learning?

The institution

Programme evaluation and subject evaluation processes are commonly standardized across institutions so that data may be analysed for trends and aberrations. Regular programme reviews need to consider the processes of assessment as they are embedded within the broader curriculum (see Chapter 20).

> Do you know what the current assessment policy is in your institution? When you find the assessment policy, you can see how your assessment designs and the outcomes of your students measure up against the stated policies.

Professional associations

Professional associations are also interested in the outcomes of our evaluations especially when curriculum changes are expected to keep pace with changes in professional practice. We may be required to submit information showing how we are complying with the changes in content being taught, how students are being assessed and how they are performing in terms of the revised criteria. Evaluations often explore how relevant assessment tasks are to the requirements of the profession.

Government and funding bodies

Governments and private funding bodies will wish to access evaluation data when considering if money has been well spent in certain key areas. It may well be, for example, that external invigilated examinations for off-campus students are the focus of a large external investigation and all institutions that conduct such assessment events will be asked to convey their information to fill in the overall picture.

Developing evaluation tools

The discussion in this chapter so far has covered the main priorities to take into account when designing your evaluation study. In brief, when evaluating your assessment practices you must first decide:

- Whose interest will the evaluation serve?
- What will your evaluation do?
- What are the scale, scope and time-frame?
- Who will conduct the evaluation?
- When should it be conducted?
- What method will you use?

Upon resolving the key questions in this list, no matter what design you have conceived of for your evaluation study, it will be important to find or develop some tools and systems for use in gathering the data. Let's look at two of the most commonly used tools, ie Likert scales and checklists, as well as two of the main issues to resolve, ie selecting a sample and assuring anonymity.

Using Likert scales

A commonly used method of structuring questions is to pose a statement that requires a response on a five-point scale, known as a Likert scale. For example, the respondent might be given a collection of statements including the statement 'The marking of assessment items by staff is fair.' Throughout the survey they are asked to circle one of the numbers that correspond to the notion of frequency – none of the time, some of the time, half of the time, most of the time, all of the time.

Data collected in this way are ordinal and cannot be used in averaging or summing the total responses. To find out more about applying statistical methods of analysis to these data, refer to a text on statistical methods or consult within your institution for practical advice when undertaking such analyses.

Using checklists

Checklists provide a simple and easy-to-use method of gathering basic data. Decide if you prefer to ask 'yes/no' questions or 'Tick the box' questions. As with questionnaires in general, make sure your questions or prompt statements are clear. Even more useful is to relate the questions to specific elements of your interest, eg objectives, group work, exams, workplace assessments and so forth.

Your decision when using checklists will involve the degree of detail you may need usefully to evaluate your assessment process. Relying solely on a checklist may not provide you with enough information to solve emerging problems. To improve the response rate for checklists try to make an explicit link to the improvement of future versions of the assessment tasks. Providing a summary of feedback of results of the checklist and any subsequent actions you may have taken to students also reinforces this.

Selecting your sample

There are a number of options when choosing the participant sample for your evaluation. Consider again the stakeholders for your study and decide the best way to get the information you need (Harvey (ed), 1998):

● Will you let the sample self-select? That is, will you be able to make judge-ments on the outcomes of the evaluation if your sample is made up purely of volunteers?
● Will you purposefully select the sample? That is, will you be selecting from the whole group those individuals or sub-sets that you think represent a cross-section of the group?
● Will you survey the whole group by handing out your evaluation survey when everyone is present and collecting all responses on the spot?

In each case you will need to be mindful of the benefits and limitations of the particular approach you choose and be sure your choice supports the purpose of your evaluation.

Assuring anonymity

Students will often provide full and frank feedback on your assessment task when they feel their anonymity is assured. In this way they feel safe from any repercussions should they have strong criticism or complaint. If you want to undertake a study where some follow-up interviews or focus groups are planned, it will be helpful to invite the survey respondents to provide their contact information. In most cases and especially when sensitivities are at stake, it is best that the evaluator is a neutral person and not also the unit assessor.

Analysing the evaluation data

In analysing the data about your assessment, it is often the time constraints that dictate your approach. Presumably the information that has been gathered is needed for revisions to an assessment task or an assessment regime. If you have gathered qualitative data and you wish to transcribe the interviews and discussions, it is suggested you allow between two and four hours for every hour recorded on audiotape and even longer for videotape (McAteer, 1998).

If using quantitative data analysis techniques, the best advice is to spend most of your time designing the evaluation strategy, and the analysis will then be much more efficient and straightforward to carry out. Software packages can be very useful for working with inferential statistics. However, Mogey (1998: 30) lists several key questions to ask yourself before you get into the detailed analysis of statistical data. For example:

- What will a statistical analysis tell you that you couldn't establish in any other way?
- Have you thought about your sample and how it was selected? Is the number of missing responses satisfactory and why are they missing?
- Do your data include outliers or unusual observations? Why? Will they have undue influence on your conclusions?
- Is the size of your sample sufficient to make a full analysis worth while?
- How reliable do you really think your data are?

As a rule, if you are not experienced or confident with qualitative data collection and statistical analysis you would be advised to work with a research statistician at your institution to help with designing your data collection and overall analysis strategy as well as an educational designer to help frame your evaluation questions.

Reporting evaluation outcomes

When reporting your findings it helps to consider the following framework:

- *introduction* describing what was evaluated, and why, the major findings and recommendations, and major constraints of the evaluation study;

- *brief background* to the evaluation, including relevant history of the assessment design, how it has worked in the past and any recent changes, and current student group and staff;
- *description* of the evaluation including the purpose of the evaluation, the evaluation design, methodology, and instruments used and procedures for data collection;
- *results* of the study, including diagrams and quotes;
- *discussion* in terms of the original goals of the study and whether the outcomes can be generalized;
- *conclusions and recommendations* in clear and succinct terms.

Whether or not you complete a formal report of your evaluation findings, you will undoubtedly seek to use the information from evaluative processes to improve your assessment practice.

Using information from evaluative processes to improve assessment practice

It is likely that you regularly consider issues of quality in all aspects of your practice, from the relevance of the syllabus, the effectiveness of your teaching, administration and student support, to the details of how your assessment tasks are working to support learning. The regular use of evaluation strategies is of critical importance for informing the cycle of continuous improvement.

To undertake evaluation so that you can demonstrate existing quality or the process of improvement, ideally you need to begin when you conceive your teaching, learning and assessment designs and return to it when you have just completed your teaching or marking and while the experience is fresh in everyone's minds. Focusing your evaluation of assessment practices works well when incorporated within this broader context.

One of the frustrating issues with evaluation is in the case where casual staff are appointed to teach on a sessional basis. The evaluation comments may or may not apply to their role in the assessment process and they may or may not be there to follow up on the results. Ideally the person following up on the evaluation will be the person who is in the best position to implement changes and bring about improvements based on the outcomes of evaluation.

Before concluding this chapter, ask yourself:

- How do you and your colleagues currently evaluate the assessment tasks and the coherence of the assessment regime in the subjects and programmes in which you teach?
- What kind of information do you receive?
- How do you use this information?

- Examine the documentation for one of the subjects in which you teach: how flexible is the assessment regime?
- Could it be more flexible?
- Are the assessment tasks constructively aligned with curriculum objectives and teaching and learning activities?
- How well does the assessment for this subject contribute to the achievement of the desired graduate outcomes for the whole course?
- How do you ensure validity and reliability of assessment in this subject?
- What would be the best way of confirming or disconfirming your perceptions?

Evaluating assessment practices at a glance

- Understand what you want to know, who you will be asking, what other sources of data you might need to use, how you propose to collect this information and how you might want to analyse or interpret it.
- Use formative evaluation for improving processes and outputs that are in development.
- Use summative evaluation to explore the effectiveness of assessment tasks once they've been given to students.
- Student feedback can come in several forms – questionnaires, focus groups, interviews, pre-test and post-test methods, observation and reflective logs.
- Be clear about the stakeholders who will need to contribute data as well as those for whom the outcomes will be of interest.
- Choose your evaluation tools with due consideration.
- Analyse and report your findings in accordance with your original intentions.
- Treat qualitative and quantitative data with equal respect.
- Use your findings to feed directly into the cycle for continuous improvement.

25

Dealing with plagiarism

In Chapter 9 we discussed in some detail issues relating to academic fraud committed by students in their assessment tasks. This kind of fraud includes cheating on examinations or coursework assignments and it also includes plagiarism, but we are focusing upon plagiarism in this chapter. As we said in Chapter 9, plagiarized work is that which is knowingly copied, bought or stolen and passed off as one's own. The perception that plagiarism by students is increasing is of great concern in higher education because of the high value placed upon the intellectual ownership of academic work. The perception of the increased level of fraud is probably correct, as studies have shown that around two-thirds of students surveyed recently had knowingly plagiarized the work of others in one form or another (Marsden, Carroll and Neill, in press). It also seems that many students unwittingly plagiarize when they are not aware of the academic rules for acknowledging other people's work.

Much of the concern about academic plagiarism in recent years relates to the ease with which students can gain access to the work of others electronically, usually through the Internet and the World Wide Web (Carroll, 2000). If they are familiar with Internet searching, and most are, students can copy and paste material into their academic essays so smoothly that it is difficult to detect without specialized electronic tools.

Although worry about the increasing incidence of cheating and plagiarism appears to be well founded, plagiarism has always been around, although it was more time consuming for students when they had to look in the library for passages to copy (Carroll, 2000; Evans, 2000). Now there are sites on the World Wide Web devoted to giving or selling papers on almost any topic that students require (Evans, 2000). So, is it possible to prevent or avoid plagiarism in assessment practices?

Dealing with plagiarism is a complex matter, and we are warned that there is no one easy solution and that 'a combination of actions and approaches' is more likely to have an effect (Carroll, 2000). With this in mind, we explore a number of strategies from which you can choose to reduce the incidence of student plagiarism in assessment tasks:

- Seek out policies and practices about plagiarism.
- Use strategies to minimize plagiarism.
- Change your assessment regime to make plagiarism more difficult.
- Teach your students to avoid plagiarism.
- Establish ways to detect plagiarism.

Seek out policies and practices about plagiarism

Most teachers are given their institution's policy handbook with an induction kit when they join, but many do not fully understand the policy on plagiarism until they are faced with possible academic fraud by one or more of their students. It is worth while familiarizing yourself with your institution's policies on cheating and plagiarism so that you can approach possible plagiarism cases with confidence.

Use strategies to minimize plagiarism

At the teacher level

Zobel and Hamilton (2002) held workshops with teaching staff to brainstorm ways of minimizing or preventing plagiarism, beginning with the design of the curriculum. One strategy is to require additional, explanatory material including photocopied source materials, with assessment tasks. These authors also argue that assessment tasks submitted electronically can easily be checked by a search engine, and that copies of early drafts, plans and diagrams can be required to be submitted with an assessment task so that, by checking the entire 'portfolio', teachers can authenticate the work. Zobel and Hamilton also suggest limiting group work but setting individualized, summative assessment tasks where the demarcation lines with plagiarism are clearly drawn to students. Additional strategies that we would consider include:

- requiring students to summarize their submitted assignments at the end of their final examination;
- allowing students to set their own assessment tasks to maximize intrinsic motivation;
- providing very clear and specific steps for task completion and requiring students to summarize how they have achieved each step;
- being very clear about expectations in assessment tasks, especially about the degree of collaboration;

- requiring students to use certain academic sources in their assessment tasks, such as journal articles or Internet sites, or interviews with experts, thus customizing the task;
- requiring an annotated bibliography with assessment tasks;
- setting examination questions that cannot be answered by rote learning.

At the faculty level

Of course, implementing strategies to prevent plagiarism by individual teachers cannot work unless teachers share a policy and a set of procedures in support of their efforts, as noted above. The first step is to open up the discussion with colleagues so that there can be a shared understanding of the nature and extent of the problem within the faculty, and preventive measures that can be introduced. If a consistent approach is not adopted, students will soon get to know those teachers in the faculty who are unconcerned about plagiarism and those who will not tolerate it.

Once a consistent approach is negotiated, it is important for a faculty to develop a policy on academic fraud, consistent with institution policy, which covers plagiarism and other forms of cheating and which is clearly articulated to teachers and students. The policy should be clear about the processes for educating students about what is expected of them, the processes undertaken when plagiarism is suspected and the various punishments for the seriousness of the offence or for repeat offences. Each case is different and may require consideration of mitigating circumstances, so staff need to identify an appropriate range of options for preventing and identifying plagiarism. From their empirical study Zobel and Hamilton identified a number of important steps that faculties should initiate if they are properly to support teaching staff in the management and prevention of plagiarism. These include:

- deterring plagiarism by publicizing demonstrated cases within the faculty;
- introducing consistent processes and penalties, with centralized record keeping, and ensuring that all parties are aware of student rights and appeal processes;
- instituting faculty discipline hearings for serious cases;
- providing consistent penalties for various degrees of cheating and plagiarism and also for repeat offences.

In one large faculty over a teaching period, cases of plagiarism had been detected on a scale not known in previous years. The faculty head identified the precise areas of the policy that had been breached and held meetings with the staff to debate the breaches, the policy and a consistent approach to applying penalties.

Change your assessment regime to make plagiarism more difficult

In some subjects, essay topics do not change from year to year and some practical tests are the same from one semester to another, thus making it easy for students either to obtain copies of past essays or to find out what was on the practical tests (Carroll, 2000). If a subject has too many assessment tasks for students to handle, if the level of challenge is too high or if students cannot understand what is required in an assessment task, they may feel pressured into cheating or plagiarizing in order to survive in their programme.

Here are some strategies you can use to make your assessment tasks less prone to cheating and plagiarism:

- Examine the assessment tasks in your subject for the amount and level of assessment, and consider whether it is excessive.
- Link assessment tasks so that each one builds upon the former, preferably with some application to individual student circumstances.
- Individualize topics as far as possible with use of students' own workplaces, lives and values as a source of discussion.
- Use self-directed forms of learning such as learning contracts.
- Use work-based mentors, supervisors or assessors to report on work-based learning projects and performance-based assessments.
- Use video- and audio-based presentations as an alternative to print.
- Undertake oral assessment tasks either in person or by telephone.
- Adapt or change assessment tasks regularly (but without losing the match between intended learning outcomes and assessment tasks).

Teach your students to avoid plagiarism

As we have seen throughout this book, the conventions of academic writing, including citation and acknowledgements, are dependent upon disciplinarity. This can be very confusing for students who change faculties. They might have received high grades for their essays or projects in one faculty and then find they are writing in an inappropriate style when they study in another.

Different genres of writing, too, require different approaches to citation and acknowledgement of sources. For example, an unseen examination, a thesis or a report each require an understanding of the specific rules about writing style. The difference between collaboration and collusion is also a problem for students. You need to clarify the limits of collaboration in group work or individual study groups. Students need guidelines concerning the use they may make of each other's work and how to show the outcomes of collaborative activity. Writing and citation style needs to be explicitly taught.

Students may not understand how to avoid plagiarism even if they have been provided with copies of the overall institution's policy and the faculty guidelines. They might 'nod their head' that they understand but that does not mean that they do (Harris, 2000). Interpretation of the policy and guidelines may be difficult, there could be grey areas about what constitutes plagiarism and lines can be crossed without the intention to defraud.

A teacher wrote several short case studies to illustrate how the policy on academic fraud should be interpreted in practice. Students discussed the case studies, asked questions and raised their own issues. This led to a discussion about appropriate citation, inappropriate use of sources and the meaning of the terms 'direct quote' and 'paraphrase'.

(from Harris, 2000)

A teacher organized a formal debate on the topic: 'Plagiarism is always wrong.' Students had a lively debate around the concept that plagiarism is cheating and lying and neither is ethical or acceptable in other aspects of life. They learnt that cheating shows contempt for others and it is not worth the risk.

(from Harris, 2000)

Harris (2000) finds a very effective discussion topic to be: 'Who is really being cheated when someone plagiarizes?' The discussion focuses on missed learning experiences, missed insights and missed opportunities to learn research skills.

Establish ways to detect plagiarism

Sometimes a faculty or an individual teacher may find that a group of students is plagiarizing, and so the magnitude of the problem for the cohort – and the individual teacher – is quite serious. Unfortunately the process of checking can become onerous, but there are some strategies to help teachers work out whether plagiarism is really taking place. In the United Kingdom, for example, there is an online Plagiarism Detection Service operated by the University of Northumbria that covers over 800 million Web sites and can find original text, if it exists else-where (http://online.northumbria.ac.uk.faculties/art/information_studies/Imri?Jiscpas/site/detect.asp).

Other strategies you can use if you find yourself in this situation include:

- Use a variety of search engines to track down a string or several strings of words. This is surprisingly easy and fast.
- Search for the title of the assignment, because students sometimes do not bother to individualize them.
- Check for different student names on assignments. A few students forget to change the name on their assignment, curious though this is.
- Use a plagiarism detection site, which usually incurs a fee. These sites are easily found on any variety of search engines.

Dealing with plagiarism at a glance

- Don't wait until you have a suspected case of plagiarism before familiarizing yourself with your institution's policies on academic fraud.
- Discuss with your colleagues strategies to minimize plagiarism.
- Put a range of strategies into place at a faculty and an individual level.
- Examine your assessment regime for flaws that might open the way to plagiarism.
- Change assessment tasks regularly.
- Students may not fully understand the institution's policies and guidelines and unintentionally plagiarize the work of others.
- Teach your students about plagiarism, how to interpret faculty writing conventions and what plagiarism really means to all concerned.
- Use electronic means to make detection of plagiarism less onerous.

References

Alexander, S and McKenzie, J (1998) *An Evaluation of Information Technology Projects for University Learning*, Committee for University Teaching and Staff Development, Commonwealth of Australia, Australian Government Publishing Service, Canberra

Altbach, P (2000) Research and training in higher education: the state of the art, in *Higher Education: A worldwide inventory of centers and programs,* ed G Philip, P G Altbach and D Engberg, pp 1–27, Center for the Study of Higher Education, School of Education, Boston College, Boston, MA

American Library Association, Presidential Committee on Information Literacy (1989) *Final Report,* American Library Association, Chicago, IL

American Library Association (1998) [accessed July 2002] *A Progress Report on Information Literacy,* http://www.ala.org/acr/nili/nili.html

American Library Association and Association for Educational Communications and Technology (1998) [accessed February 2003] *Information Power: The nine information literacy standards for student learning,* http://www.ala.org/aasl/ip_nine.html

Angelo, T (1999) [accessed August 2002] Doing assessment as if learning matters most, *AAHE Bulletin,* May, http://aahebulletin.com/public/archive/angelomay99.asp

Angelo, T and Cross, K P (1993) *Classroom Assessment Techniques,* Jossey-Bass, San Francisco, CA

Armer, D (1999) *Teaching of Ethics in Australian Law Schools: Some academic perspectives,* Faculty of Education, Monash University, Victoria, Australia

Ballard, B and Clanchy, J (1991) *Teaching Students from Overseas,* Longman Cheshire, Melbourne

Barnett, R (1997) *Higher Education: A critical business,* Society for Research into Higher Education/Open University Press, Buckingham, UK

Barrie, S, Brew, A and McCulloch, M (1999) [accessed August 2002] *Qualitatively Different Conceptions of Criteria Used to Assess Student Learning,* Paper presented to Australian Association for Research in Education (AARE) conference, Melbourne, http://www.aare.edu.au/99pap/bre99209.htm

Bates, A W T (1995) *Technology, Open Learning and Distance Education*, Routledge, London

Baume, D (2001) [accessed February 2003] *A Briefing on Assessment of Portfolios*, Learning and Teaching Support Network Generic Centre, UK, http://www.ltsn.ac.uk/

Bazerman, C (1981) What written knowledge does, *Philosophy of the Social Sciences*, **2**, pp 361–87

Becher, T (1987) The disciplinary shaping of the profession, in *The Academic Profession*, ed B R Clark, University of California Press, Berkeley, CA

Becher, T (1989) *Academic Tribes and Territories*, Open University Press, Milton Keynes, UK

Becher, T and Trowler, P R (2001) *Academic Tribes and Territories*, 2nd edn, Open University Press, Milton Keynes, UK

Benner, P (1984) *From Novice to Expert*, Addison Wesley, San Diego, CA

Benson, R (1996) *Assessing Open and Distance Learners: A staff handbook*, Centre for Distance Learning, Monash University, Victoria, Australia

Bensur, B J (2002) Frustrated voices of art assessment, *Art Education*, **55** (6), pp 18–23

Biggs, J (1990) Teaching design for learning, *Higher Education Research and Development Society of Australasia Annual Conference Keynote Discussion Paper*, Griffith University, Brisbane

Biggs, J (1999a) *Teaching for Quality Learning at University*, Society for Higher Education Research/Open University Press, Buckingham, UK

Biggs, J (1999b) What the student does: teaching for enhanced learning, *Higher Education Research and Development*, **18** (1), pp 57–75

Biggs, J B and Collis, K F (1982) *Evaluating the Quality of Learning: The SOLO taxonomy*, Academic Press, New York

Black, P and Wiliam, D (1998) *Inside the Black Box: Raising standards through classroom assessment*, Department of Education and Professional Studies, King's College, London

Bloom, B S (1976) *Human Characteristics and School Learning*, McGraw-Hill, New York

Bonk, C (2000) *Advances in Pedagogy: Finding the instructor in post-secondary online learning*, EdMedia, Montreal

Bonk, C J and Dennen, V P (1999) Teaching on the Web: with a little help from my pedagogical friends, *Journal of Computing in Higher Education*, **11** (1), pp 3–28

Boud, D (2000) Sustainable assessment: rethinking assessment for the learning society, *Studies in Continuing Education*, **22** (2), pp 151–67

Boud, D and Feletti, G (eds) (1991) *The Challenge of Problem Based Learning*, Kogan Page, London

Boud, D, Keogh, R and Walker, D (1985) *Reflection: Turning experience into learning*, Kogan Page, London

Bramley-Moore, G and Stewart, D (2000) Information literacy for Southern Cross University, Unpublished report, Southern Cross University Library, Lismore, Australia

Brem, S K and Boyes, A J (2000) [accessed July 2002] Using critical thinking to conduct effective searches of online resources, *Practical Assessment, Research and Evaluation*, **7** (7), http://ericae.net/pare/getvn.asp?v=7&n=7

Bridges, P *et al* (1999) Discipline-related marking behaviour using percentages: a potential cause of inequity in assessment, *Assessment and Evaluation in Higher Education*, **24** (3), pp 285–300

Brockett, R G and Hiemstra, R (1991) *Self-Direction in Adult Learning: Perspectives of theory, research and practice*, Routledge, London

Brown, K (1998) *Education, Culture, and Critical Thinking*, Ashgate, Aldershot, UK

Brown, S, Rust, C and Gibbs, G (1994) *Strategies for Diversifying Assessment in Higher Education*, Oxford Centre for Staff and Learning Development, Oxford Brookes University, Oxford, UK

Burton, G and Dimbleby, R (1990) *Teaching Communication*, Routledge, London and New York

Butler, R (1988) Enhancing and undermining intrinsic motivation: the effects of task-involving and ego-involving evaluation on interest and performance, *British Journal of Educational Psychology*, **58**, pp 1–14

Byrnes, T [accessed July 2002] *Critical Thinking in the Social Sciences*, http://online.valencia.cc.fl.us/tbyrnes/poscritical.htm#SIMPLE

CAA Centre [accessed January 2003] http://www.caacentre.ac.uk

Calverley, G (1998) in *Evaluation Cookbook*, ed J Harvey, Learning Technology Dissemination Initiative, Edinburgh

Candy, P (1991) *Self-Direction for Lifelong Learning*, Jossey-Bass, San Francisco, CA

Candy, P, Crebert, G and O'Leary, J (1994) *Developing Lifelong Learners through Undergraduate Education*, Commissioned Report No 28, Higher Education Council, National Board of Employment, Education and Training, Canberra, Australia

Cannatella, H (2001) Art assessment, *Assessment and Evaluation in Higher Education*, **26** (4), pp 319–26

Carroll, J (2000) [accessed February 2003] Plagiarism: is there a virtual solution?, *Teaching News*, November, http://www.brookes.ac.uk/services/ocsd/2_learntch/plagiarism.html

Carroll, J and Appleton, J (2001) Plagiarism: a good practice guide, Unpublished paper, Oxford Brookes University, Oxford, UK

Chambers, E and Northedge, A (1999) Disciplinary differences and commonalities across the humanities, arts and social sciences, in Improving student learning through the disciplines, *Proceedings of the 7th International Symposium Improving Student Learning*, ed C Rust, pp157–67, Oxford Centre for Staff and Learning Development, Oxford Brookes University, Oxford, UK

Chapman, D (1999) Issues and impacts of using computer-based assessments (CBAs) for formative assessment, in *Computer-Assisted Assessment in Higher Education*, ed S Brown, P Race and J Bull, pp 72–85, Kogan Page, London

Cole, S and Kiss, E (2000) What can we do about student cheating?, *About Campus*, May–June, pp 5–12

Cooper, I *et al* (2002) Teachers' conceptions of memorising in learning science, *Higher Education Research and Development*, **21** (3), November, pp 305–21

Cowan, J (1996) New thoughts on assessment in open learning, *Open Learning*, June, pp 58–60

Culwin, F and Naylor, F (1995) Pragmatic anti-plagiarism, *Proceedings, 3rd All Ireland Conference on the Teaching of Computing*, Dublin

Dahlgren, L (1984) Outcomes of learning, in *The Experience of Learning*, ed F Marton, D Hounsell and N Entwistle, Scottish Academic Press, Edinburgh

Dannels, D P (2002) Communication across the curriculum and in the disciplines: speaking in engineering, *Communication Education*, **51** (3), July, pp 254–68

Dator, J (1994) [accessed March 2003] *How to Conduct a Futures Visioning Workshop*, http://www.soc.hawaii.edu/future/dator/futures/how2.html

Davidson, K and Goldfinch, J (1998) in *Evaluation Cookbook*, ed J Harvey, Learning Technology Dissemination Initiative, Edinburgh

Dowsing, R D (1999) The computer-assisted assessment of practical IT skills, in *Computer-Assisted Assessment in Higher Education*, ed S Brown, P Race and J Bull, Kogan Page, London

Drew, S, Thorpe, L and Bannister, P (2002) Key skills computerised assessments: guiding principles, *Assessment and Evaluation in Higher Education*, **27** (2), pp 175–86

Eisner, E (1991) *The Enlightened Eye: Qualitative inquiry and the enhancement of educational practice*, Macmillan, Indianapolis, IN

Elliott, D J (1995) *Music Matters: A new philosophy of music education*, Oxford University Press, New York and Oxford

Entwistle, N and Ramsden, P (1983) *Understanding Student Learning*, Croom Helm, Beckenham, UK

Entwistle, N and Tait, H (1995) Approaches to studying, *New Directions for Teaching and Learning*, **64**, Winter, ed N Hativa and M Marincovic, Jossey-Bass, San Francisco, CA

Evans, J (2000) [accessed February 2003] The new plagiarism in higher education, *Interactions*, **4** (2), Summer, http://www.warwick.acukETS/interactions/vol4no2/evans.html

Evans, T (1994) *Understanding Learners in Open and Distance Education*, Kogan Page, London

Fain, M and Bates, P (2001) Cheating 101: paper mills and you, *Teaching Effectiveness Seminar*, rev 26 March 2001, Coastal Carolina University, SC, http://www.coastal.edu.library/papermil.htm

Fairhead, W (1990) Drama and co-operative learning, in *Perspectives on Small Group Learning*, ed M Brubacher, R Payne and K Rickett, Rubicon Publishing, Ontario

Fisher, K (1998) *Politics and Decision Making: Study guide*, Southern Cross University, Lismore, Australia

Gerholm, T (1990) On tacit knowledge in academia, *European Journal of Education*, **25** (3)

Gibbs, G (1995) *Assessing Student Centred Courses*, Oxford Centre for Staff and Learning Development, Oxford Brookes University, Oxford, UK

Gygar, T and Cassimatis, A (1997) *Mooting Manual*, Butterworths, Sydney

Habeshaw, S, Gibbs, G and Habeshaw, T (1993) *53 Interesting Ways to Assess your Students*, Cromwell Press, Melksham, UK

Hanrahan, S J and Isaacs, G (2001) Assessing self- and peer-assessment: the students' views, *Higher Education Research and Development*, **20** (1), pp 53–70

Harris, R (2000) [accessed February 2003] *Anti-Plagiarism Strategies for Research Papers*, March 2000, Vanguard University of Southern California, http://sccu.edu/Faculty/R_Harris/antiplag.htm

Harvey, J (ed) (1998) *Evaluation Cookbook*, Learning Technology Dissemination Initiative, Edinburgh

Hativa, N and Marincovic, M (1995) Disciplinary differences in teaching and learning: implications for practice, *New Directions for Teaching and Learning*, **64**, Winter

Heaslip, P (1996) [accessed May 2002] *Critical Thinking: To think like a nurse*, http://www.cariboo.bc.ca/psd/nursing/faculty/heaslip.nrsct.htm

Heift, T *et al* (2000) An interactive course-support system for Greek, *Proceedings of EdMedia 2000 World Conference on Educational Multimedia, Hypermedia and Telecommunications*, ed J Bourdeau and R Heller, pp 394–99, AACE, Montreal

Hughes, C and Magin, D (1996) Demonstrating knowledge and understanding, in *Assessing Learning in Universities*, ed P Nightingale *et al*, University of New South Wales Press, Sydney

James, P (2000) A blueprint for skills assessment in higher education, *Assessment and Evaluation in Higher Education*, **25** (4), pp 353–67

James, R, McInnis, C and Devlin, M (2002) *Assessing Learning in Australian Universities*, Centre for the Study of Higher Education, Melbourne University, Melbourne and Australian Universities Teaching Committee, Canberra

Jenkins, A (1994) Conveying your message by poster, in *The Complete Student Handbook*, ed D Saunders, Blackwell, Oxford, UK

Johnson, D W and Johnson, R T (1994) Encouraging thinking through constructive controversy, in *Enhancing Thinking through Cooperative Learning*, ed N Davison and T Worsham, Teachers' College Press, Columbia University, New York

Johnstone, R, Patterson, J and Rubenstein, K (1998) *Improving Criteria and Feedback in Student Assessment in Law*, Cavendish, Sydney

Kolb, D A (1981) Learning styles and disciplinary difference, in *The Modern American College*, ed A Chickering, Jossey-Bass, San Francisco, CA

Krendl, K (1998) [accessed March 2003] personal communication in regard to T204: Living in the information age, Indiana University, IN, http://www.icn.org/courses/syllabi/infoagesyll.html

Langtry, B (2000) Ends and means in university policy decisions, in *Why Universities Matter*, ed T Coady, pp 85–98, Allen & Unwin, Sydney

Lave, J and Wenger, E (1991) *Situated Learning: Legitimate peripheral participation*, Cambridge University Press, New York

Lisman, C D (1996) *The Curricular Integration of Ethics*, Praeger, Westport, CT

Lockwood, F (1991) *Data Collection in Distance Education: The use of self-recorded audiotape*, Open University study guide H801, Open University, Milton Keynes, UK

Lockwood, F (1992) *Activities in Self-Instructional Texts*, Kogan Page, London

Lockwood, F (1995) Students' perception of and response to formative and summative material, in *Open and Distance Learning Today*, ed F Lockwood, Routledge, London

Lombardo, T (nd) [accessed March 2003] *General Model for Futures Education*, http://futures.rio.maricopa.edu/workshop.html

Lovie-Kitchen, J (1991) Problem-based learning in optometry, in *The Challenge of Problem Based Learning*, ed D Boud and G Feletti, Kogan Page, London

Marland, P *et al* (1990) Distance learners' interactions with text while studying, *Distance Education*, **11** (1), pp 71–91

Marsden, H, Carroll, M and Neill, J T (in press) Who cheats at university? The contribution of demographic, situational and psychological factors to dishonest academic behaviours, *Australian Journal of Psychology*

Marton, F, Hounsell, D and Entwistle, N (eds) (1984) *The Experience of Learning*, Scottish Academic Press, Edinburgh

Marton, F and Säljö, R (1976) On qualitative differences in learning: outcome and process, *British Journal of Educational Psychology*, **46**, pp 4–11

Marton, F and Säljö, R (1984) Approaches to learning, in *The Experience of Learning*, ed F Marton, D Hounsell and N Entwistle, Scottish Academic Press, Edinburgh

Math Forum [accessed July 2002] *Re: Knowledge and understanding*, http://math-forum.org/discussions/

McAteer, E (1998) in *Evaluation Cookbook*, ed J Harvey, Learning Technology Dissemination Initiative, Edinburgh

McCroskey, L, McCroskey, J C and Richmond, V P (2002) The scholarship of teaching and learning: contributions from the discipline of communication, *Communication Education*, **51** (4), October, pp 383–91

McLaughlan, R *et al* (2001) Academic and institutional issues related to the planning and implementation of a multi-disciplinary roleplay-simulation involving collaboration across institutions, in *Meetings at the Crossroads: Proceedings of 18th Annual Conference of the Australasian Society for Computers in Learning in Tertiary Education (ASCILITE)*, ed G Kennedy *et al*, pp 407–15, Biomedical Multimedia Unit, University of Melbourne, Melbourne; also see newsletter article [accessed March 2003] http://www.ascilite.org.au/newsletter/2.02/index.html

Mezirow, J (1981) A critical theory of adult learning and education, *Adult Education*, **32** (1), Fall, pp 3–24

Miller, C and Parlett, M (1974) *Up to the Mark: A study of the examination game*, Society for Research in Higher Education, Guildford, UK

Miller, C and Parlett, M (1976) Cue consciousness, in *The Process of Schooling: A sociological reader*, ed M Hammersley and P Woods, Routledge & Kegan Paul/Open University Press, London and Henley, UK

Mogey, N (1998) in *Evaluation Cookbook*, ed J Harvey, Learning Technology Dissemination Initiative, Edinburgh

Moore, B (ed) (1993) *Australian Pocket Oxford Dictionary of Current English*, 8th edn, Oxford University Press, Melbourne

Morgan, A (1993) *Improving Your Students' Learning: Reflections on the experience of study*, Kogan Page, London

Morgan, C, Dingsdag, D and Saenger, H (1998) Learning strategies for distance learners: do they help?, *Distance Education*, **19** (1)

Morgan, C and O'Reilly, M (1999) *Assessing Open and Distance Learners*, Kogan Page, London

Morgan, C and Smit, A (2001) Mentoring in open and distance learning, in *Innovation in Open and Distance Learning*, ed F Lockwood and A Gooley, Kogan Page, London

Neumann, R (2001) Disciplinary differences and university teaching, *Studies in Higher Education*, **26** (2), June, pp 135–46

Neumann, R, Parry, S and Becher, T (2002) Teaching and learning in their disciplinary contexts: a conceptual analysis, *Studies in Higher Education*, **27** (4), pp 405–17

Newble, D and Cannon, R (1995) *A Handbook for Teachers in Universities and Colleges*, Kogan Page, London

Nightingale, P et al (1996) *Assessing Learning in Universities*, University of New South Wales Press, Sydney

Nightingale, P (1996a) 'Communicating' in Nightingale, P *et al, Assessing Learning in Universities*, University of New South Wales Press, Sydney

Nightingale, P (1996b) 'Accessing and Managing Information' in Nightingale, P *et al, Assessing Learning in Universities*, University of New South Wales Press, Sydney

Noah, H and Eckstein, M (2001) *Fraud and Education: The worm in the apple*, Rowman & Littlefield, Sydney

NTEIU v University of Wollongong, FCA 1069 (8 August 2001) by Justice J Branson; the Full Court appeal of the decision is *University of Wollongong v National Tertiary Education Industry Union*, FCA 360 (2002), New South Wales

Nulty, D (1997) The constructs of examiners in higher education: what do academic standards mean?, Unpublished PhD thesis, University of Queensland, St Lucia, Australia

Oliver, R (2001) It seemed like a good idea at the time, in *Online Learning and Teaching with Technology*, ed E Murphy, R Walker and G Webb, pp 81–87, Kogan Page, London

Ommundsen, P (1999) [accessed May 2002] *Critical Thinking in Biology: Case problems*, http://www.saltspring.com/capewest/ct.htm

O'Reilly, M and Newton, D (2002) Interaction online: above and beyond the requirements of assessment, *Australian Journal of Educational Technology*, **18** (1), pp 57–70

Orrell, J (1996) Assessment of student learning: a problematised approach, Paper presented at the Higher Education Research Development Society of Australasia, Flinders University, South Australia

Painvin, C *et al* (1979) The triple jump exercise: a structured measure of problem-solving and self-directed learning, *Proceedings of the 18th Conference of Research in Medical Education*, pp 73–77, Washington, DC

Palloff, R M and Pratt, K (1999) *Building Learning Communities in Cyberspace*, Jossey-Bass, San Francisco, CA

Parry, S (1998) Disciplinary discourse in doctoral theses, *Higher Education*, **36**, pp 273–99

Parry, S and Dunn, L (2000) Benchmarking as a meaning approach to learning in online settings, *Studies in Continuing Education*, **22** (2), pp 219–34

Patel, A, Russell, D and Kinshuk (1999) Assessment in a cognitive apprenticeship-based learning environment: potential and pitfalls, in *Computer-Assisted Assessment in Higher Education*, ed S Brown, P Race and J Bull, Kogan Page, London

Paul, R (1993) *Critical Thinking: What every person needs to survive in a rapidly changing world*, Foundation for Critical Thinking, Santa Rosa, CA

Pincas, A (1997) Instructional design for group-based learning by computer conferencing, in *Implementing Flexible Learning*, ed B M Bell and A Trott, pp 183–90, Kogan Page, London

Postle, G *et al* (1999) Flexible delivery and inclusivity: pedagogical and logistical perspectives, 8th EAN Annual Convention, 7–10 July, Malta

Pritchett, N (1999) Effective question design, in *Computer-Assisted Assessment in Higher Education*, ed S Brown, P Race and J Bull, Kogan Page, London

Ramsden, P (1984) The context of learning, in *The Experience of Learning*, ed F Marton, D Hounsell and N Entwistle, Scottish Academic Press, Edinburgh

Ramsden, P (1992) *Learning to Teach in Higher Education*, Routledge, London and New York

Reeves, T and Hedberg, J (2003) [accessed February 2003] *Interactive Learning Systems Evaluation*, http://it.coe.uga.edu/ treeves/evalbook/eilsbook.html

Roche, J (2003) personal communication in regard to CSC00228: Database systems 1, Southern Cross University, Lismore, Australia

Rowntree, D (1987) *Assessing Students: How shall we know them?*, rev edn, Kogan Page, London

Ryan, G (1996) Solving problems and developing plans, in *Assessing Learning in Universities*, ed P Nightingale *et al*, Professional Development Centre, University of New South Wales Press, Sydney

Ryan, J (2000) *A Guide to Teaching International Students*, Oxford Centre for Staff and Learning Development, Oxford, UK

Sawyer, T (2002) [accessed 28 March 2003] *Percussion Techniques and Materials*, Westgate University, Toronto, http://www.westga.edu/ musicdpt/courses/ Sp02/MUSC3603.PercTech&Mat.Sp02.pdf

Schön, D A (1987) *Educating the Reflective Practitioner*, Jossey-Bass, San Francisco, CA

Schön, D A (1995) *The Reflective Practitioner: How professionals think in action*, 2nd edn, Ashgate, Aldershot, UK

Shuell, T J (1986) Cognitive conceptions of learning, *Review of Educational Research*, **56**, pp 411–36

Sly, L (1999) Practice tests as formative assessment improve student performance on computer-managed learning assessments, *Assessment and Evaluation in Higher Education*, **24** (3), pp 339–43

Smart, J C and Etherington, C A (1995) Disciplinary and institutional differences in undergraduate education goals, in Disciplinary differences in teaching and learning: implications for practice, *New Directions for Teaching and Learning*, **64**, Winter, ed N Hativa and M Marincovic, Jossey-Bass, San Francisco, CA

Smit, G N and van der Molen, H T (1996) Simulations for the assessment of counselling skills, *Assessment and Evaluation in Higher Education*, **21** (4), pp 335–45

Snape, J and Watt, G (1997) *The Cavendish Guide to Mooting*, Cavendish, London

Society of College, National and University Libraries (SCONUL) [accessed January 2003] *Information Skills in Higher Education: A SCONUL position paper*, http://www.sconul.ac.uk

Southern Cross University Learning Assistance Web site [accessed 28 March 2003] http://study.scu.edu.au/la/index.html

Steven, C and Hesketh, I (1999) Increasing learner responsibility and support with the aid of adaptive formative assessment using QM designer software, in *Computer-Assisted Assessment in Higher Education*, ed S Brown, P Race and J Bull, pp 103–12, Kogan Page, London

Student Assessment and Classification Working Group (SACWG) (P Bridges *et al*) (1999) Discipline-related marking behaviour using percentages: a potential cause of inequity in assessment, *Assessment and Evaluation in Higher Education*, **24** (3)

Taylor, J (2001) Fifth generation distance education, Keynote address at International Conference on Distance Education (ICDE), Düsseldorf, Germany

Teaching and Learning Unit (1998) *Guide to Student Assessment*, Southern Cross University, Lismore, Australia

Toohey, S (1996) Managing and developing oneself, in *Assessing Learning in Universities*, ed P Nightingale *et al*, University of New South Wales Press, Sydney

Toohey, S and Magin, D (1996) Performing procedures and demonstrating techniques, in *Assessing Learning in Universities*, ed P Nightingale *et al*, University of New South Wales Press, Sydney

Trevitt, A C F *et al* (1997) The role of student assessment: to gauge students' performance, to enhance learning and professional skills, or to inform program evolution?, Chapter 3 in *Learner Assessment and Program Evolution in Problem-Based Learning: A monograph*, ed G Ryan, pp 33–50, Australian Problem Based Learning Network, University of Newcastle, Newcastle, Australia

University of North Carolina Center for Teaching & Learning (1992) [accessed 16th June, 2003] *The Guided Discussion: For your consideration*, http://ctl.unc.edu/fyc12.html

Usher, J R, Simmonds, D G and Earl, S E (1991) Industrial enhancement through problem-based learning, in *The Challenge of Problem Based Learning*, ed D Boud and G Feletti, Kogan Page, London

van Veuren, P (1995) [accessed May 2002] *Does It Make Sense to Teach History through Thinking Skills?*, http://www.chss.montclair.edu/inquiry/spr95/veuren.html

Washington State University Critical Thinking Project [accessed July 2002] *Critical Thinking Rubric*, http://wsuctproject.wsu.edu/ctri.htm

Westra, M, Geoheagan, A and Flores, L (1997) [accessed 28 March 2003] *Critical Thinking across the Curriculum Project*, Longview Psychology Department, Missouri, http://www.kcmetro.cc.mo.us/longview/ctac/psylink.htm

Woodcock, L (2003) personal communication to authors, Southern Cross University, Australia

Xueqin (2002) Chinese academics consider a 'culture of copying', *Chronicle of Higher Education*, **48**

Yeoman, E (1996) Sam's café: a case study of computer conferencing as a medium for collective journal writing, *Canadian Journal of Educational Communication*, **24** (3), cited in K Bach, How do I evaluate networked learning?, in M Haughey and T Anderson, *Networked Learning: The pedagogy of the Internet*, pp 129–45, Cheleliere/McGraw-Hill, Montreal and Toronto

Zobel, J and Hamilton, M (2002) Managing student plagiarism in large academic departments, *Australian Universities Review*, **45** (2), pp 23–45

Index